Global Capitalism, Culture, and Ethics

Richard A. Spinello

Routledge
Taylor & Francis Group
NEW YORK AND LONDON

First published 2014
by Routledge
711 Third Avenue, New York, NY 10017

and by Routledge
2 Park Square, Milton Park, Abingdon, Oxon OX14 4RN

Routledge is an imprint of the Taylor & Francis Group, an informa business

© 2014 Taylor & Francis

The right of Richard A. Spinello to be identified as author of this work has been asserted by him in accordance with sections 77 and 78 of the Copyright, Designs and Patents Act 1988.

All rights reserved. No part of this book may be reprinted or reproduced or utilized in any form or by any electronic, mechanical, or other means, now known or hereafter invented, including photocopying and recording, or in any information storage or retrieval system, without permission in writing from the publishers.

Trademark notice: Product or corporate names may be trademarks or registered trademarks, and are used only for identification and explanation without intent to infringe.

Library of Congress Cataloging in Publication Data
Spinello, Richard A.
　Global capitalism, culture, and ethics / Richard A. Spinello.
　　pages cm
　Includes bibliographical references and index.
　1. Economic policy—Moral and ethical aspects.　2. Business ethics.
　3. International business enterprises—Moral and ethical aspects.
　4. Social responsibility of business.　I. Title.
　HD87.S7295 2014
　174'.4—dc23　　　　　　　　　　　　　　　　2013040827

ISBN: 978-0-415-84394-2
ISBN: 978-0-415-84396-6
ISBN: 978-0-203-75505-1

Typeset in Adobe Caslon
by RefineCatch Limited, Bungay, Suffolk

Dedication

In memory of Carl J. Frappaolo, 1956–2013

Contents

Preface		ix
Acknowledgments		xiv

Part I Theoretical Perspectives

1	A Brief History of Global Capitalism	3
2	Free Markets and Government Regulation	28
3	Cultural Diversity and Cultural Relativism	55
4	Law, Ethics, and Corporate Social Responsibility	78

Part II Doing Business in a Global Environment: Industry Analyses and Case Studies

5	Multinational Corporations and Internet Freedoms: Cisco, Yahoo, and Google In China	115
6	Patents, Patients, and Medicine: Big Pharma and Developing Countries	148
7	Corporate Environmental Responsibility and the Petroleum Industry	179
8	Political Activism and Disinvestment	207
9	Responsible Sourcing and Offshoring	241

PART III CONCLUSIONS
  10 EPILOGUE   271

FURTHER READING   276

INDEX   281

Preface

This book's primary aim is to deepen the reader's knowledge about the complex moral dimensions of globalization. There has been surprising neglect of the ethical realities of globalization despite their prominence as globalization intensifies. Yet there is a nagging concern that, while globalization promotes economic growth it continues to threaten economic security and basic human rights. The core idea of this book is that the multinational corporation, which drives the process of globalization, is an international moral agent that must be guided not just by the laws of host countries, but by the moral imperative to uphold and protect universal human rights. The book's defense of a moderate but authoritative universalism is predicated on the equality of persons as the foundation of human rights and justice. At the same time, multinationals must be sensitive to the legitimate demands of local culture.

A secondary objective of this text is to provide a modest defense of globalization. Countries committed to free trade and market liberalization tend to grow faster, and economic growth is one factor that inevitably leads to a decline in the poverty level. A rise in the quantity of economic activity is not a panacea for global poverty, but the impressive growth in economies such as China, India, and Brazil has certainly helped to diminish the level of social deprivation in these countries.

This book has a definite point of view about ethics, but it is not dogmatic. At the center of the debates about globalization are some striking philosophical controversies that will be objectively and impartially presented: universalism versus ethical pluralism, the connection between law and morality, the logic and adequate specification of natural human rights, and so forth. We will seek to bring philosophy's ample resources to bear on these theoretical problems, while always recognizing the practical implications of these issues.

This analysis of globalization will not be confined to a treatment of the moral obligations of multinational corporations, but also reviews the history of globalization, the virtues and deficiencies of capitalism, the interrelationship between states and markets, and the beneficial and detrimental effects of globalization on social welfare. It should be obvious that, because of its inter-disciplinary nature, this is not a conventional book. Themes from economics, history, philosophy, and law are woven together so that the reader can appreciate the phenomenon of globalization from multiple perspectives.

Globalization is one of the most significant trends in human history, as the world moves from a state of fragmentation to one of deep-seated interdependencies. It is essential, therefore, to appreciate the historical evolution of globalization to grasp the dynamics of this movement and perhaps discern its future. This historical overview unveils the weaknesses of global capitalism along with the frequent failure of multinationals to moderate their quest for revenues and profits. After this cursory treatment of globalization's non-linear history, we briefly present the case, going back to Adam Smith, that trade within and across borders is critical to economic growth and that growth is critical to the reduction of poverty. The capitalist system is ideally structured to promote such growth, but capitalism comes in several different versions. We consider the nature of entrepreneurial capitalism, and why some economists regard it as the system ideally suited for the maximization of aggregate social welfare.

The moral logic of capitalism, predicated on free choice and voluntary exchange, is challenged when market failures lead to impaired choice, environmental degradation, or "slavish" working conditions. Regulations are necessary to fix such failures but they sometimes go unenforced or foster a "compliance mentality." Laws must be supplemented, therefore, by proactive ethical self-regulation that emphasizes individual and corporate responsibility. However, in striving to be morally responsible even conscientious multinationals must confront the challenge of cultural diversity and the tensions between local cultural identity and universal human identity. We claim that the latter is the ground for a set of fundamental, universal human rights that can direct moral choices no matter where multinationals compete. These rights are justified as the conditions of human flourishing and a successful personal life. In this context, we also consider the challenge of ethical pluralism and the sources of law's moral authority. Finally, what, if anything, do corporations owe to the public good beyond complying with the law and acting within the bounds of moral probity? Is it enough to uphold and protect human rights or should a corporation use its resources to correct human rights abuses and to focus on social justice issues?

With these foundational questions addressed, the book proceeds to apply this rights-based moral framework to specific situations. We review first the problems companies have had in dealing with the Orwellian censorship and surveillance regimes in authoritative countries like China. As Yahoo, Microsoft, and Google expanded their operations into this market, they were forced to support various censorship laws and other online restrictions. Should these Internet intermediaries abide by local law and help the host country discipline its citizens by censoring the Web? Or should they attempt to follow a higher ethical standard that acknowledges the universal right to free speech?

The next chapter looks critically at Big Pharma and the importance of industrial patents for innovation. Generous standards of patentability are particularly welcome in the pharmaceutical industry, where research investment is so high. Patents, however, are limited monopolies that lead to high prices and lower output. Lower output means that life-preserving drugs will be inaccessible to some of the people who need them. Do pharmaceutical companies have some responsibility to deal with the distributional inequities that arise from these high drug prices? Why was Big Pharma so recalcitrant about waiving their intellectual property rights during the African AIDS crisis? This chapter also focuses on the World Trade Organization's TRIPS policy. By normalizing intellectual property regimes through international agreements like TRIPS, Western countries export a set of binding intellectual property rules that may or may not benefit developing nations.

Chapter Seven scrutinizes environmental issues and corporate responsibilities. It highlights several environmental debacles in developing countries, such as Texaco's pillaging of the Ecuadorean Amazon and the environmental degradation that has occurred in Nigeria's Niger delta, at the hands of companies such as Royal Dutch Shell. To some extent, these problems have arisen because oil companies have been prone to exploit dysfunctional governments with weak institutional structures. How can this controversial industry optimally deal with externalities and support the goal of sustainable energy sources, especially when there is no assistance or direction from the host country's government?

The book then moves on to the topic of political activism and disinvestment. We demonstrate the dangers of excessive political activism, especially when aimed at regime change. Despite their power and financial resources, however, multinationals have not been successful in manipulating political events in developing countries. The discussion sets the stage for the treatment of disinvestment. Are there countries where human rights abuses are so pervasive that business should not invest? What are the exact conditions in such countries that warrant disinvestment? A condition-of-doing-business principle is proposed and defended.

The final chapter does not deal with ethical problems arising from foreign direct investment, but focuses on companies that source their goods from contractors abroad. One of the biggest ongoing scandals in the history of globalization is the chronically poor working conditions in most low-wage countries. Years after the Nike and Wal-Mart scandals first surfaced in the 1990s, we learn about terrible working conditions in Bangladesh, where a series of deadly fires and a building collapse have catapulted this issue back into the news. But what is the scope of a corporation's responsibility to the workers of its contractors' suppliers in these low-wage countries, and how far up the supply chain does that responsibility extend? Issues reviewed in this context include the criteria for determining a decent work environment, the definition of a fair wage, and the problem of child labor.

All of these topics are quite controversial and we try to present both sides of each issue whenever possible. There is copious material here for thinking about and debating the social valences of moral situations and the intricate ethical aspects of globalization. Many of those aspects revolve around the issue of cultural identity. In general terms, the biggest test for the multinational is resolving the tension between respect for cultural diversity and local sovereignty and the protection of universal human rights. How multinationals deal with this tension is decisive for a world that is growing more ambivalent and wary about globalization's future.

Acknowledgments

I wish to thank the Carroll School of Management at Boston College for its ongoing support for my scholarship. My special gratitude extends to the Chairperson of the Management and Organization Department, Judy Gordon, and to Dean Andy Boynton for creating such an hospitable environment conducive to this sort of research. I am grateful to the CSOM students I have taught in globalization courses over the years for their perceptive questions and comments, which have helped me to refine several of the arguments in this book. I am indebted to my colleague, Professor Sarah Cabral, for her helpful insights on some of the issues covered in Chapter Five. Special thanks to Michael Smith for assisting me in handling some of the logistics of manuscript preparation. My deep gratitude goes to the editors at Routledge, especially to Sharon Golan for her confidence in this project. I also wish to thank my wife, Susan, for her patience and encouragement.

Finally, the book is dedicated to the memory of Carl "Frapp" Frappaolo, a close friend and colleague for many years. In some respects, this book is about virtuous entrepreneurship, and Carl was the epitome of the virtuous entrepreneur. Carl belonged to that special breed of "midnight programmers," working long hours to write computer programs that became the foundation of an exciting new company called the Delphi Group. He was a true pioneer in the field of information technology, but always found a way to bring a sense of humanity, humor, and exuberance to the arid world of databases and knowledge management that occupied so much of his time. Carl lived on the edge of technological innovation and died moving forward. Those of us who were privileged to be his friends, think of him often and miss him deeply.

Richard A. Spinello
Dedham, Massachusetts
September 2013

PART I
THEORETICAL PERSPECTIVES

1
A Brief History of Global Capitalism

Introduction

The period immediately after World War II was one of unremitting gloom for many people in war-ravaged Europe. The grim statistics only dimly reflected the human reality of the war's devastation. It was an especially trying time for the citizens of Germany, who wondered how German culture could be revived and how their once powerful economy could ever be restored. Like all institutions, German businesses were in a shocking state of disarray after incessant waves of Allied bombing. Manufacturing plants in the Ruhr valley, and in industrial cities such as Hamburg and Mannheim, had been prime targets of the United Kingdom's bombing offensive. Aside from the daunting challenges of re-building factories and supply chains, some companies had to cope with allegations of collusion with Hitler's brutal regime. As Hitler had consolidated power, it had become increasingly difficult and perilous for businesses to avoid full co-operation with the Nazi government. All foreign and domestic businesses had to comply with the policy of *Gleichschaltung*, or total coordination with the state.[1]

The post-war era was particularly challenging for Krupp, the legendary German munitions manufacturer, which was accused of having used slave labor during the war, including POWs and civilians from occupied countries such as France. These abuses, along with the many other war crimes of the Nazi regime, demanded justice and fair retribution. After the war the Nuremberg trials were convened to punish Hitler's collaborators and to help exorcize the ghost of the Third Reich. Alfred Krupp and the company's directors were indicted "as the focus, the symbol, and the beneficiary of the most sinister forces engaged in menacing the peace of Europe." Krupp's lawyers protested that the company had no choice—it had to fill Nazi orders for weapons or face dire consequences, and the labor shortage forced the company to rely on foreign laborers. But the Nuremberg judges were not persuaded by this reasoning. Krupp and the directors were convicted of using slave labor and "the plunder of occupied Europe."[2]

The Krupp enterprise, which has been vilified by many business historians and journalists for its role in World War II, traces its roots to a small steel-mill built in the city of Essen in 1810.[3] The iconic German company quickly moved into a diverse range of products that took advantage of the industrial age and its insatiable demand for steel to construct buildings, ships, and railroads. Krupp soon became a major manufacturer of steel rollers, ship shafts, and railway tires. Many of Krupp's cast-steel products were vital inputs for the transportation innovations that drove economic development and globalization from the mid- to late nineteenth century.[4] But Krupp also specialized in building the tools of war, including rifle barrels and artillery pieces used by the Prussian military. After it perfected these technologies, Krupp became the pre-eminent arms manufacturer in all of Europe.

From its earliest days, the Krupp family was firmly committed to a strategy of globalization. As we will see, the history of globalization mirrors to some extent what transpired at Krupp from the 1850s until after World War I. Krupp was not satisfied with relying on its domestic market. The company realized that it needed to penetrate the dominant English market to preserve its competitive advantage in steel and related industries. Fortunately, Krupp's superior technology gave it a big advantage in the United Kingdom. As word of its quality products spread, the company exported its cast-steel products and weaponry throughout Western Europe and Russia. Krupp also invested abroad, purchasing Spanish mines for raw material and a Dutch shipping company as part of its expanding distribution network.

Krupp's global ambitions and steady growth were interrupted in the early twentieth century, however, when a wary German government imposed restrictions on the sale of weaponry to its potential foes. Those restrictions were intensified during World War I, which unleashed the forces of de-globalization throughout the global economy.

During the war the company's overseas markets were lost, thanks to the Allied blockade. After the war, Krupp was forced to renounce arms manufacturing, at least temporarily. The company found itself on the brink of bankruptcy in the mid-1920s, thanks to inflation, overcapacity, and severe labor problems. But the Krupp enterprise was revived, and by 1930 it was back in the arms business. However, formidable challenges remained. The worldwide depression of the 1930s contributed to Krupp's stagnant export business. With the exception of Russia, export orders still languished from most of its major customers. By 1933, Krupp returned to profitability, though not as a result of demand for military products.

As World War II approached, the company began to rebound more strongly as it made weapons for the Nazi war machine. Its *Germaniwert* shipyard filled orders for submarines and destroyers, while its main plants made howitzers and other artillery pieces. Krupp's profits surged in the late 1930s, though they fell off somewhat during the early war years. After Hitler's ignominious defeat there was another reversal of fortune and prolonged turmoil. The victorious British disassembled major Krupp factories and sequestered its coalmines, while the Russians sequestered its *Grusonwerk* factory in Magdeburg.

In subsequent decades, however, Krupp recovered yet again, thanks to a new "ethos of globalization" that became the focal point of the company's global corporate strategy. The resilient Krupp enterprise acquired major operations in Italy and Mexico and refined its skills in manufacturing specialty steels.[5] Eventually Krupp merged with Thyssen to become ThyssenKrupp, a trust company, partially owned by a foundation. It remains a major worldwide player in steel mass production and in capital goods, such as elevators and industrial equipment.

The Krupp story dramatically illustrates the twisty path of global capitalism, which has been massively disrupted at times by economic nationalism and international conflicts. Like Krupp, globalization's fate seems closely tied to politics, as it treads a course marked by sharp discontinuities and an uncertain future. We turn now to an examination of economic globalization's past so we can better understand the present and perhaps discern its future trajectory. During this discussion we also concisely treat the economic advantages of trade and foreign investment that were perceived so clearly by savvy and resourceful enterprises such as Krupp.

Globalization Before World War I

In order to properly understand the dynamic of global capitalism it is essential to appreciate its origins and its history. This condensed historical analysis provides a broad context for the remainder of the book and it allows us to appreciate the paramount role of the multinational corporation in the globalization process.[6] Some naively think that globalization is a purely contemporary phenomenon that has only recently sprung forth with the help of modern communication and transportation technologies. But this is definitely not the case. Globalization, broadly defined as the "process of increasing integration in world civilization," has a long and tangled history.[7] Since our focus is on economic aspects of globalization, perhaps a more useful definition is the following: "the integration of economic activities across borders, through markets."[8] Thanks to liberal economic policies, the world economy was once closely integrated and seemed to be advancing towards even greater economic integration and global cooperation. Progress was cut short, however, in 1914 and in the turbulent interwar years.

The history of globalization, therefore, is not marked by some sort of relentless upward spiral. The nineteenth century German philosopher Georg W.F. Hegel conceived history as a teleological force, always moving forward toward the final end of absolute freedom. For Hegel, the history of the world, despite whatever appears on the surface, reflects a deeper reality and "presents us with a rational process."[9] However, the history of globalization has been distinctly nonlinear, a sometimes arbitrary and irrational process. There is no immanent dynamic, no sense that polities, following the arc of history toward its final end, necessarily aspire to construct a fully integrated global economy, supported by the proper social systems and multilateral regulations. The history of globalization is much more chaotic, with ebbs and flows, advances and sometimes stunning reversals. Accordingly, there is no guarantee that the current era of openness and liberal trade policies will come to an abrupt end someday, to be followed by a period of disintegration and isolationism. Such an unwelcome turn of events might come to pass if people rebel against the persistence of world poverty or if slower domestic growth in major economies leads to irrational trade wars and fractionalization instead of greater cooperation.

Business historians divide this messy history of global capitalism into four discrete periods. The first period extends from the mid-nineteenth century or so until 1914, the outbreak of World War I. Although many people think that the current era has exhibited unsurpassed economic integration and growth, the years between 1870 and 1914 represent "the most impressive episode of international economic integration which the world has seen to date . . . [thanks to] the largest decline ever in intercontinental barriers to trade and factor mobility."[10]

The undisputed center of the world economy during this phase of globalization was Europe. During these years there was relative peace and order in Europe. After the defeat of Napoleon in 1815, there were no major wars that engulfed European nations. Peace and political concord created the conditions for a high level of economic integration, which occurred through trade, foreign direct investment (FDI), short-term capital flows, and the movement of workers across national boundaries. FDI is an especially important dimension of globalization. Multinationals and corporations engage in FDI through acquiring an existing firm in a foreign country, or by making a greenfield investment involving construction of a new operation. Although FDI is used as a basic measure for quantifying the direct investment in a country by a foreign firm, it does not capture cross-border flows of ideas or skilled know-how. Nor does it quantify the impact of direct technology transfers and positive spillover effects.[11]

As economies expanded in European countries such as the United Kingdom and Germany, there was a significant increase in international trade. That expansion of trade was enabled by the adoption of liberal economic policies in most European countries. They shunned high tariffs or restrictive quotas and welcomed the advantages of trading with their neighbors. In 1846, for example, Britain's Corn Law was repealed, bringing free trade to England in place of mercantilism. Thanks to liberalization, international trade grew about 16 percent a year between 1830 and 1870, but decreased somewhat after that period.

One of the chief elements in the evolution of a globalized economy is the abolition of political barriers to trade. However, the integration of the first global economy was driven primarily by technological developments in transportation and communications rather than by policy changes.[12] The spread of intercontinental railroads and the increasing use of steamships made it easier to move large quantities of goods efficiently and inexpensively. Improvements in communications were also a critical factor in the integration of world markets. Thanks to the telegraph, electronic communications between Europe and the United States were made possible for the first time when a trans atlantic cable connection was completed in 1866. The telephone, invented in 1876, was another key technology that connected together disparate parts of the world. The level of global connectivity pales by today's standards, but these primitive technologies were fundamental for the evolution of international commerce. The lower countries can drive transportation and communication costs, the greater the level of economic integration they can achieve.

During this period, Europe, led by German companies such as Krupp and Siemens, along with British companies like Lever Brothers, was the export leader in manufacturing goods while it was a net importer of primary products.[13] Exports flowed freely to other European countries, North America, and the colonies of the United Kingdom. Trade has been aptly described as an "engine of growth," and economists like David Ricardo and Adam Smith have developed viable theories demonstrating that countries improve their social welfare when they trade across borders. Smith was convinced that specialization at what a country does best followed up by trade is the key to sustainable economic growth:

> What is prudence in the conduct of every family can scarce be folly in that of a great kingdom. If a foreign country can supply us with a commodity cheaper than we ourselves can make it, better buy it of them with some part of the produce of our own industry, employed in a way in which we have some advantage.[14]

Echoing Smith, Ricardo argued that countries should specialize in what they are *relatively* most efficient in producing. When a country is open to trade for other goods where it does not have such a comparative advantage, its domestic factors of production get the highest returns. In addition, there are static advantages such as economies of scale in production and procurement that can be exploited when trade expands markets. Finally there are dynamic advantages since trade encourages competition and productivity growth.[15]

After 1880, however, protectionism surfaced in Europe, partly inspired by a surge in nationalistic sentiment. The United States also adopted protectionist policies such as the McKinley Act of 1890 which placed tariffs on many manufacturing goods and occasioned a steep rise in prices. This legislation was followed by the Wilson tariff (1894) which went into effect during the worst industrial depression in the United States since the 1870s. Nonetheless, the overall momentum of globalization was not deterred by these policies.

During this same pre-1914 period there was a dramatic increase in capital flows between countries. A high degree of capital market integration typified this first global economy. There were several reasons for this. Adoption of the gold standard minimized foreign exchange risk, since exchange rates were fixed and expressed in terms of gold; a country's domestic money supply was also tied to its gold stock. Hence that standard forced governments to adopt conservative fiscal and monetary policies. The absence of military conflict and political strife also created a climate highly favorable for lending and investment. Political stability and fiscal prudence made it easier for banks and other institutions to lend money to companies in other countries. For the United Kingdom, for example, there are reliable estimates that 32 percent of its net national wealth was held overseas.[16] Some economists contend that the integration of global capital markets actually reached its pinnacle in 1913 and has not yet been surpassed even in the twenty-first century.[17]

FDI also increased substantially during the pre-war years. There was a high level of multinational manufacturing but also foreign investment in agricultural and raw materials. Buoyed by success in its domestic market, companies such as Bayer and Siemens in Germany or Lever Brothers in the UK, built manufacturing plants around the world. Bayer became one of the chief foreign manufacturers in the United States. Siemens, which pioneered electricity and telegraph technology, quickly extended its reach into Britain and Russia. Lever

Brothers had 33 foreign factories, in countries ranging from Canada and the United States to South Africa and Australia. By 1914, Nestle, the famous Swiss corporation, produced its condensed milk and baby formula in Norway, Spain, Canada, and the United States. The growth in FDI was facilitated by the rapid adoption of international property law, but Europe's colonialism also helped to reduce the risks of foreign investment in developing countries. The UK controlled a sprawling empire with over 400 million inhabitants, into which British corporations felt secure in extending their operations.[18] In 1914 the United Kingdom accounted for 50 percent of the world's stock of FDI.

While the United States was not yet a prominent player in the global economy, it still accounted for about ten percent of the world's FDI. Some of its major corporations like Singer Sewing, founded in 1854, benefited enormously from overseas investment. The Singer sewing machine, first designed and built in the U.S., became one of the world's first global products. Confronted with high freight costs for its heavy cast-iron sewing machines and their stands, Singer opened its first overseas plant in Glasgow. Singer's technology, combined with Scotland's low wages, provided Singer with a potent formula for success. Singer was also quite proficient in marketing and selling its expensive machines. Its installment plan system was an important innovation that allowed the company to sell its equipment to the many eager households that could not afford its $100 price tag. With some modifications that system was successfully introduced in Europe. When the European markets became fairly saturated, Singer pushed into Russia and found a vigorous demand for its products. In the face of high Russian tariffs in the 1890s Singer built a plant in Podolsk, a city located 26 miles south of Moscow. Thanks to its coherent globalization strategy, Singer achieved astonishing results: global sales of 2.5 million sewing machines by 1913.[19]

By 1914, with a world war on the horizon, FDI reached $14.5 billion—or approximately one third of total world foreign investment. A large percentage of this was European FDI. This investment, along with a steady annual volume of exports, had accelerated Europe's economic growth. European GDP, which was 47 percent of world GDP by 1914, grew at a compound annual growth rate of 1.32 percent between 1870 through 1913.[20] Growth in world trade seemed indispensable for a reliable and steady economic growth. But as peace and prosperity gave way to a protracted war and political discord, the trend toward greater economic integration abruptly lost its momentum.

Globalization Constrained and Reversed

Beyond any doubt, an integrated global economy was firmly in place by 1913. The world, thriving with global trade, was hopeful and optimistic about its future. Industrialization had led countries like the UK and Germany out of stagnant economic growth. Some believed that the interdependencies created by globalization would insulate Europe from self-destructive conflict and the terrible economic consequences of war. Dependency on international trade and foreign investment made European countries more vulnerable for sustained interruptions in their supply of food and other materials.[21] The business community certainly did not want war but there seemed no way for countries to avert this impending calamity.

When World War I began in August 1914, with the assassination of Archduke Ferdinand, blame was rightly cast on Serbia for harboring the terrorist group that carried out the assassination. But more thoughtful individuals like the philosopher, Max Scheler, lamented the "common guilt" of Europe for creating the sort of decadent cultural milieu that made the war possible.[22] Initially, hopes were high that war would swiftly come to an end with minimal casualties, but that was not to be. This international conflict, which divided Europe, dragged on for four long years. Predictably, it led to massive reductions in trade and a sharp curtailment in foreign investment. As a result, the first global economy was fatally disrupted.

During the height of this chaotic world war there was another severe political shock that also contributed to economic turmoil and disintegration. The Russian Revolution, sewn in the intellectual soil of Marxism, commenced in 1917 when Nicholas II, the Czar of Russia, abdicated his throne. The revolution eventually triggered a large-scale sequestration or expropriation of foreign property.[23] The new Russian government nationalized the banking system and confiscated all private enterprises. American companies like Singer, Kodak, and Otis Elevator lost all of their substantial assets. Singer, for example, had to relinquish investments of plants and equipment in Russia worth $84 million. With these dramatic actions, Leninist Russia became relatively isolated from the global economy. There was some trade with other countries but no FDI, which was banned until the collapse of the Soviet Union in 1989.[24]

World War I predictably led to a wave of expropriations. After the entry of the United States into the war in April 1917, on the side of the allies, the German government began to move against U.S. businesses in Germany. It conducted several punitive actions, such as the nullification of all American-owned patents and copyrights. By 1918, Germany had sequestered 159 American businesses and properties. Steinway & Sons, for example, lost its $1.6 million investment in its German plant in Hamburg. In retaliation, the United States executed its Trading with the Enemy Act, cutting off economic relations with Germany.[25] When the war ended, Germany's foreign investments were at high risk of expropriation. Siemens lost both its foreign factories and its patents, and Merck's U.S. operations were expropriated by the American government.

After the war, the United Kingdom suffered a serious recession that lasted many years. Europe's share of the global economy began its steady decline. During the post-war years there was a strong push for protectionism, especially in Europe and America. In America, the dreadful Smoot-Hawley legislation was passed in 1930, putting major restraints on American trade. Tariffs were also substantially higher throughout Europe. As a result, the total volume of exports declined steadily, with European exports in 1929 well below the level of 1913.[26]

Nonetheless, some American enterprises aggressively sought to expand their operations during the 1920s. New international companies emerged,, such as Aramco International partnership, B.F. Goodrich, and Crown Cork International. General Electric and International Telephone and Telegraph (ITT) also expanded mightily into foreign countries. Attitudes to U.S. investment, however, were mixed and often ambivalent. There was antagonism toward some companies such as the giant oil operation, Jersey Standard. Spain had nationalized its petroleum industry in the 1920s and the threat of further nationalizations seemed possible. The United Kingdom was worried that its worldwide economic power was now being eclipsed by this heavy U.S. foreign investment. In 1922, for the first time, the value of U.S. investment in Canada overtook the value of U.K. investment there.[27]

Just as the world economy was recovering in the post-war period, there came the stock market crash in the United States in 1929. This event, precipitated by a speculative fever that had gripped the whole U.S. economy, ushered in a deep economic depression that adversely affected the entire world economy. That crash led to contradiction and panic, and ultimately a "contagion of fear," with over 4 million Americans unemployed by the spring of 1930.[28] America's economic woes contributed to the depression in Britain and weighed down the whole world economy. These events rapidly depressed trade volumes throughout Europe.

At the same time, developing countries began to resist any foreign control over their natural resources. Hence, companies in the extractive industries such as petroleum found themselves in perilous conditions. Standard Oil discovered oil in Bolivia in the 1920s but a military junta seized all of their properties in 1933. In Mexico, oil production was on the rise during this same period. But in a devastating blow to the oil industry, the country nationalized all foreign oil companies in 1938, citing Article 27 of the Mexican Constitution. The pretext for this sequestration was a dispute over wages and the provision of generous social benefits. The properties of Royal Dutch Shell, along with Standard Oil of New Jersey and Sinclair & Standard Oil of California, were all nationalized by the Mexican government. The United States Ambassador to Mexico described the country's action as a "bolt from the blue" but, to the chagrin of U.S. oil companies, the American government refused to take action.[29]

Despite this series of exogenous shocks to the global economic system, things were not completely bleak during the interwar years. Aside from the increase in U.S. activity prior to 1929, there were innovations such as the internal combustion engine and new applications of electricity, which led to more productive use of resources in America and Europe. The countries of Eastern Europe made valiant efforts to modernize their economies with mixed success.[30]

The final shock, of course, was World War II, which began in September 1939 when Hitler's troops crossed over the Polish border. France and Great Britain had promised to stand by Poland, so Europe was once again thrust into a terrible conflagration. Hitler's belligerence had already led to an exodus of foreign capital from Europe. The heavy resources demanded by the war effort put European economies under immense strain. The war impacted international trade policies immediately as trade between the two military blocs ceased completely. This conflict created major complications for U.S. companies operating in occupied countries like France and Belgium. Many ceased operations there, while others curtailed them significantly. Combatants also shifted resources to war materials production, placing a further stress on consumption. In beleaguered Britain, U.S. subsidiaries and affiliated companies converted their factories to make munitions for the war effort. The trade controls put in place when the war began were only gradually dismantled during the post-war era.[31]

Origins of the Second Global Economy

Two world wars, sweeping communist revolutions in Russia and China, a wave of protectionism and expropriation, and even a prolonged worldwide depression—all of these forces dealt a harmful blow to global capitalism until the early 1950s. At this point, thanks to rebuilding efforts after the war that yielded robust economic growth, globalization begins a gradual process of renewal, liberalization displaces protectionist policies in some countries, and foreign trade slowly expands.

Many developing countries, however, vigorously resisted this new trend toward greater economic integration and persisted in their closed economies. Countries in Africa and in other parts of the world, which had recently been granted independence, had tenuous national identities and were anxious to assert their economic and political independence from their former colonial powers.[32] India, for example, imposed many restrictions on foreign investment after it won independence from the United Kingdom in 1947. Often this wariness of foreign investment was accompanied by explicit or latent sympathy with socialist ideologies. During Indira Ghandi's leadership from 1966 to 1984, India nationalized mines, banks, and insurance companies, and imposed limits on urban incomes and property. Laws like the Foreign Exchange Restriction Order (FERO) diluted foreign investment in Indian companies. The result of India's government controls and relative isolationism, however, was stagnant economic growth, as per capita income rose a meager 0.3 percent annually between 1965 and 1975.[33] Things began to change dramatically for India only when it pursued a growth-oriented strategy based on a more open economy.

Similarly, in the Middle East there was a potent bias against liberal economic policies. Countries like Turkey did not welcome FDI and did not open their markets to trade and imports. Instead, Turkey pursued a strategy of import substitution and planned economic development. It was only thanks to local entrepreneurs, like Vehbi Koc, that Turkey was able to take advantage of new technologies, through licensing and joint ventures, and thereby modernize itself to some extent.

The situation was much different in the United States, however, where major corporations like IBM, General Electric, Pepsi, and Ford were making substantial investments in foreign countries. By the early 1970s Pepsi produced its soft drinks in 512 plants located in 114 countries. In that same time frame, 62 of the Fortune 100 American firms had production facilities in at least six nations. And outgoing U.S. FDI rose from $11 billion in 1950 to $100 billion in 1972. At this point America, followed by Europe and Japan, was driving the globalization of production.[34]

American investment in developing countries such as Latin America remained quite modest, however, thanks to the challenging political climate and economic conditions in those countries. Poverty and crime, currency fluctuations, and political instability created big risks even for adventurous American firms. Some countries severely restricted investment because they feared it might impede indigenous economic development, leaving its economy exploited and too dependent on multinationals. But there were limited entrepreneurial opportunities in certain Latin American countries like Brazil and Argentina. Both countries implemented laws virtually requiring local production for certain manufacturing goods (such as automobiles), and that proved successful in inducing U.S. firms to commit to building large factories.[35]

These investment conditions in South and Central America sometimes created exigent circumstances for investors. As a result, the expansion of American investment overseas had a dark side. This period of corporate history stands out because of the unwarranted political activism of several corporations, which were concerned about the spread of communism in a risky world environment. Companies confronted by a hostile regulatory environment and anti-capitalist ideologies sometimes take unorthodox steps to protect their investments. United Fruit Corporation (later Chiquita Banana) was the largest private company operating in Guatemala and accounted for 75 percent of its banana exports. In the 1950s the banana enterprise found itself embroiled in controversy as it lobbied to overthrow the Arbenz regime in Guatemala. Jacobo Arbenz was determined to do something about unequal land distribution and so he embarked on an ambitious land reform program. As part of that program, he sought to appropriate some of United Fruit's unused plantations in exchange for its fair market value. But the company disputed the market value of that land and regarded the socialist government's policy as brazen expropriation of its legally owned properties. Consequently, to protect its interests, United Fruit openly supported the overthrow of the Arbenz regime, lobbying the United States State Department, and anyone in Washington who would listen, that a military coup was necessary.

In Chile in the 1970s ITT played a similar role in the overthrow of the socialist Allende government. ITT, a massive international conglomerate, was worried that Allende would soon expropriate its operations in Chile. Accordingly, ITT devised a plan to spread "economic chaos" in Chile through the cut-off of credit and aid, and the support for insurgents against the Allende regime. As in Guatemala, so in Chile, the United States pursued devious policies oriented to regime change in order to stop the infiltration of communism into Latin America and to protect corporate interests. According to critics, the ITT and UFC cases demonstrate how major corporations had amassed such excessive power that they could actually shape U.S. foreign policy toward the countries where they operated.[36] Due to this unfortunate legacy, it is easy to understand why multinationals have been stigmatized in the past as agents of imperialism.

In general, most multinationals focused their attention on growing their businesses and not on politics or regime change. With domestic markets saturated, they looked for ways to sustain growth by expanding abroad. Like the United States, Japan was particularly aggressive as many of its companies expanded through inexpensive capital available through its insulated financial markets. Japan's targeting of certain strategic industries led to the rise of companies like Hitachi and Fujitsu, who challenged IBM on the world stage. Japan, the United States and Europe were now the leaders in foreign investment.

By the late 1970s the seeds were being sewn for the rise of a new and more inclusive global economy. The transformation of the Chinese economy was slowly getting underway, thanks to the visionary leadership of Deng Xiaoping. The "household responsibility system," which spontaneously emerged in rural China in the 1970s, allowed farmers to sell their goods at free-market prices. This policy resulted in a major increase in food production. There were special economic zones in cities like Shenzen where free market principles were introduced. Today that city of ten million people is one of the most profitable and productive manufacturing centers in the world. This gradual withdrawal of the government from the economy set the stage for economic reforms that have sustained China's extraordinary economic growth in recent decades.[37] Market forces had already transformed the economies of Hong Kong, Singapore and Japan; China was slowly preparing to follow in their footsteps.

At the same time, when the Polish Pope, John Paul II, visited his homeland in the spring of 1979, he contested the moral legitimacy of the Soviet empire. With his bold pronouncements, the Pope helped to set in motion a chain of events that would lead to the collapse of the powerful Soviet Union. In a series of 39 sermons, attended by millions of Poles, he challenged entrenched Marxist doctrine centered on materialist philosophy and the absolute power of the state. As journalist Christian Caryl points out, "Never before had a Communist party in the Soviet bloc endured such a direct public challenge to its ideological and informational hegemony."[38] As a result of the Pope's visit, and many other factors, communism in Eastern Europe began to rapidly unravel, no longer able to suppress the people's longing for truth and freedom. Unable and unwilling to stop the events in Poland, Russia stood idly by as it watched this rebellious Polish spirit spread to other countries in the Soviet bloc.

Thanks in part to visionaries like Deng Xiaoping and Pope John Paul II, the stage was now set for a major transformation of the world's geopolitical structure which would reverberate throughout the global economy.

Rebuilding and Expanding Global Capitalism

Economic historians mark the beginning of the full rebirth of global capitalism in this pivotal year, 1979. Western Europe, Japan, and North America initially came to dominate this revived borderless global economy, but that dynamic would change in the twenty-first century as emerging economies began to play a more active and substantial role. Globalization in this new century no longer implies that corporations in developed countries invest in emerging economies.

The drivers of this new and prolonged era of globalization are familiar enough. They begin with the emergence of new communications and digital technologies that have reshaped the world economy. Networked computer systems created a vast web of digital information, which provided a global platform for collaboration and online commerce that transcended national boundaries. The Internet, the "network of networks," has emerged as a particularly important connectivity tool. The Web, invented in 1989 by Tim Berners Lee, also enhanced connectivity, making possible an unprecedented level of information egalitarianism that opened the way for the further commercialization of cyberspace. From an economic point of view, the revolutionary impact of these technologies was their ability to reduce the transaction costs that once blocked the seamless delivery or exchange of goods and services.[39]

The collapse of communism in Russia and Eastern Europe created vast new markets for trade and investment. No longer was there an Iron Curtain dividing East and West Germany. In Europe the events of 1989, another pivotal year in world history, culminated in the fall of the Berlin Wall. This set in motion the forces that would allow for the European Union and its expansion from 15 to 25 countries. Similarly, China's economic transformation, through its endorsement of free market principles, has also been a major factor in globalization's expansion. Casting off Marxist socialism, China began implementing free market policies in the 1980s and joined the World Trade Organization (WTO) in 2001. China's low wages and its tax structure became a major impetus behind the sudden rise of offshoring, as companies moved their factories abroad to dramatically lower their own cost structure.

There has also been a sharp decline in protectionism. To some extent, falling tariffs reflected the growth in regional trade groups such as the European Union, NAFTA (U.S., Canada, Mexico) or Latin America's Mercosur. NAFTA led to explosive growth of U.S. investment in Mexico during the 1990s. However there are always pockets of protectionism as countries seek to protect infant industries or use tariffs and quotas to advance certain policy agendas. The European Union still imposes tariffs and quotas on bananas coming from South and Central America in order to favor bananas from its former colonies in the Caribbean and Africa.

In an abrupt reversal, most developing countries no longer opposed or restricted international firms. Instead, there was a renewed eagerness to attract FDI, which was seen as a partial solution to poverty and other social ills. Foreign companies are often induced to invest abroad by inexpensive labor and cheap natural resources. From the 1990s there has been a worldwide trend to re-locate labor-intensive industries abroad, in countries (like China) where there is an abundance of cheap labor. FDI enables companies to locate different stages of the value chain in different, strategic locations: "marketing where consumers are close at hand, research and development where workers are smart, assembly where they are cheap."[40]

What sets this second wave of globalization apart from the first wave, that ended in 1914, is the high level of FDI originating from emerging markets. The British tea firm, Tetley, was purchased by India's Tata Group in 2000. Budweiser, America's most popular beer company, was purchased in 2008 by a Belgian–Brazilian conglomerate. In 2010 Volvo was purchased by Chinese carmaker Zhejang Geely. And several years earlier, Lenovo, the Chinese computer company, purchased IBM's personal computer business for $1.75 billion. *The Economist* has labeled companies like Lenovo, or India's Tata Group, the "new champions," catering to the huge consumer markets now opening up in China and India.[41] Thus, unlike the first wave of globalization, the second one is considerably more inclusive; and bi-directional, with FDI flowing to and from emerging economies.

This broader participation deepens interdependencies but should also go a long way to alleviating poverty in those countries that participate in this revived global economy. In India millions of people have escaped the shackles of poverty as they precariously moved up into the country's burgeoning middle class. Consider the continent of Africa. Over the ten years 2002–12 real income per person increased by 30 percent because of the country's booming economy. International firms are attracted by Africa's vast natural resources such as oil and copper. FDI has increased from $15 billion in 2002 to $46 billion in 2012. Poverty and unemployment is still widespread but the continent's economy will continue its upward trajectory so long as it embraces democratic reforms and remains committed to building new infrastructure.[42]

This intensification of globalization, beginning around 1979, was accompanied by some notable political and ethical disputes that caught less vigilant companies off guard. An endless string of corruption scandals has embroiled reputable organizations, such as Siemens, Monsanto, and Avon, in acute bribery controversies. In addition, there is a long list of other moral calamities: Union Carbide's chemical spill in Bhopal, the reluctance of many multinationals to depart Apartheid South Africa, the callousness of outsourcers like Nike, the complicity of Yahoo in human rights violations in China, Philip Morris International's manipulation of lax overseas regulations to sell cigarettes without adequate warning labels,[43] Nestle's dubious tactics in promoting infant formulae in developing countries, the environmental irresponsibility of oil companies like Texaco in Ecuador and Royal Dutch Shell in Nigeria. More recently, a devastating series of deadly fires, followed by a factory collapse in Bangladesh that killed over 1,100 people, have underscored the unsafe working conditions for workers making products for Western retailers like Wal-Mart and Benetton. All of these moral crises symbolized the inherent problems and social costs associated with globalization and foreign investment. Corporate misdeeds and apparent indifference to the bleak working conditions of their low-cost suppliers have stoked fears that global corporations have come to represent an ominous new form of imperial domination. Adolph Berle's remark that multinational corporations "can be thought of only in somewhat the same way we have heretofore thought of nations" would certainly strike a responsive chord with the opponents of globalization.[44]

At the same time, there has been increased attention, in the media and academia, to corporate social responsibility. As the process of globalization intensified, activist groups known as non-governmental organizations (NGOs) also proliferated. These self-governing, non-profit, private organizations represent a "global third sector … pursuing public purposes outside the formal apparatus of the state."[45] NGOs focused on globalization issues keep a close eye on corporate performance especially in vulnerable emerging economies. Spar refers to this as the "spotlight effect" which causes strategic decisions to be constricted not by governments but by these determined private organizations with their own social agenda.[46] New technologies such as social networking have also enabled the rapid mobilization of large groups for political influence. These phenomena were distinctly absent during the first era of global capitalism where a company's overseas operations and misdeeds were far less transparent and concealed from the eyes of its home country. As a result, multinationals can no longer segregate their foreign operations, but must face the reality that whatever they do, even in the most exotic locations, will be subject to some measure of global scrutiny.

In this new era globalization is moving forward and there seems little that can stop its momentum, unless there is a sustained deterioration of economic conditions or an escalation of regressive forces, such as a wave of nationalistic sentiment that reshapes the landscape for future investment. FDI has recovered, after several years of persistent declines following the 2008 global financial crisis: in 2012 it exceeded $1 trillion, with the United States, Germany and France as the top three investing countries.[47] This era of globalization is also broader in scope, encompassing far more countries than it did in the nineteenth century. The balance of power is shifting to countries like Brazil and China, which have become economic powerhouses. In many respects, the BRIC countries (Brazil, Russia, India, China) are beginning to dominate the second wave of globalization in the way European countries so thoroughly dominated the first wave.

Although most economists, political leaders, and managers believe that further economic integration has the force of inevitability, there are others who stridently oppose this integration and liberal capitalism in general. But what is the alternative? Some critics and committed anti-globalizers propose a return to more fragmented markets and localization, where every country is self-reliant and each national economy is as self-sufficient as possible. These isolated economies would erect major barriers to foreign investment and trade, although trade would continue to exist as a "final resort."[48] However, self-sufficiency and economic isolationism have failed to produce prosperity anywhere in the world, and pursuit of such policies usually leaves an economy in tatters.[49] Cuba and North Korea come closest to this ideal of self-sufficiency but what country would want to emulate their abysmal economic performance?

Conclusions

The history of global capitalism is not a straight, ascending line but a jagged one with upward spurts and sharp reversals. Therefore it is not easy to fathom its future direction. After the devastation of World War II, few would have predicted that a new era of economic globalization was on the horizon. Yet liberal reforms, and a brisk retreat from socialist models in key countries, quickly created new opportunities for trade and investment. So what are the lessons of this non-teleological history of global capitalism? Some are fairly obvious. First we can specify the primary motivations behind FDI. Companies like Singer or Nestle believed they could leverage their competencies abroad and outperform foreign competitors thanks to their superior resources. Since they often faced protectionist measures like tariffs, or logistical problems like high shipping costs, they opted for direct investment rather than trade. Moreover, the transaction costs associated with using foreign agents were too high, and this led these companies to set up their own manufacturing and marketing operations abroad. The same factors undoubtedly motivate foreign investment in the twenty-first century.[50]

Second, an abundance of evidence affirms the correlation between rapid expansion of trade, coupled with FDI, and steady economic growth. This correlation between GDP and economic integration was evident in the first era of globalization, that ended in 1913, and is more evident today. According to economists, the East Asian miracle was based to some extent on an outward orientation to trade and foreign investment. The impressive rise in exports from these countries is a direct result of integration into the global economy.[51] Furthermore, such economic growth is crucial for overcoming poverty and reducing global inequality. It stands to reason that more growth will create jobs and open up opportunities for the poor. The economic histories of China and India appear to confirm this thesis. Once these countries repudiated a socialist economic model and allowed their citizens to create wealth, with the indispensable help of foreign investment and technology transfers, poverty sharply declined. Also, in countries like South Korea and Taiwan evidence shows that strong economic growth, propelled by global trade, has "pulled up" the poor into productive employment and out of the depths of poverty.[52] On the other hand, there are no examples of countries that have increased income and standards of living through isolationism. As economists Lindert and Williamson have observed, "There are no anti-global victories to report for the postwar era."[53] Economic growth may not be a sufficient condition for alleviating poverty but it is arguably a necessary condition.

There are some deeper lessons of history, such as the constraints globalization imposes on a country's sovereignty by linking its fate so closely to that of other economies. There is also an intimate interconnection between states and markets, even in a borderless world. Contrary to some circles of popular opinion, globalization has not marginalized politics. The interdependency between politics and economics becomes apparent in the complicated relationship between the state and foreign investment. The state essentially needs to embrace globalization and foreign investment or it will fall behind and be deprived of technology transfers and the opening of export markets. At the same time, the economic fate of multinationals depends upon a stable political environment, along with their ability to contend with political and ethical risks in their host countries.[54]

This interdependence of politics and economics poses formidable challenges for the multinational enterprise. Multinationals must adapt to many diverse environments and overcome political and cultural distance. They must find a way to respect local culture and indigenous societies, while always being alert to transcultural values that transcend both culture and geography. These corporations must balance respect for the sovereignty of their host country with fidelity to ethical ideals and to international standards of decency that no government or international moral agent has a right to cast aside. How multinationals handle the moral tensions inherent in this relationship with foreign governments is intrinsically important but also vital for the future credibility of globalization.

Unfortunately, the multinational corporation, modernism's response to an open economy and a broad social landscape, has not demonstrated sufficient moral sensitivity. Why is this so? Part of the problem is that ideological individualism, a fundamental tenet of modernism and liberalism, still shapes corporate identity. This ideology expresses itself in corporate self-determination and strategic rationality that knows few boundaries in the pursuit of its goals.[55] A positive side of postmodernism's sweeping critique has been the unveiling of individualism's crippling liabilities. Individualism, often oblivious to the needs and interests of others, accounts for the moral disorientation that taints the history of global capitalism. A far superior ideology is solidarity, which encourages co-responsibility for what happens beyond the corporate hierarchy, cooperation for the sake of the common good and an ordered liberty. Solidarity implies that the corporation must assume greater responsibility for the welfare of its primary stakeholders, including its employees, the local community, and even the laborers of their suppliers, who sometimes work slavishly in sweatshops like those to be found in Bangladesh. In future chapters we will demonstrate how this vision of solidarity is actualized first and foremost by respect for universal human rights, provided that those rights themselves are reasonably limited by each other and by other demands of the common good.

Notes

1 William Shirer, *The Rise and Fall of the Third Reich: A History of Nazi Germany* (New York: Simon & Schuster, 1960), 196–202.
2 Quoted in Harold James, *Krupp: A History of the Legendary German Firm* (Princeton, NJ: Princeton University Press, 2012), 2.
3 See, for example, William Manchester, *The Arms of Krupp: 1587–1968* (Boston, MA: Little, Brown, 1968). The Krupp family was also the subject

of an unflattering film by Luchino Visconti called "The Damned" (1969). A biography of Alfred Krupp by Thomas Mann's son provides two conflicting views of the company's leader during the war: "One is that he cooperated in as much as he needed to hesitatingly and under pressure, and occasionally resisting. The other is that he and his company cooperated willingly and with pleasure, much more intensively than they needed to." See Tilman Lahme, *Golo Mann: Biographie* (Frankfurt: Fischer, 2009), 390. See also, James, *Krupp: A History*, 172–73.
4 James, *Krupp: A History*, 43.
5 James, *Krupp: A History*, 275.
6 A *multinational* is a firm that controls operations or income generating assets in more than one country. This book also considers *international* corporations that are global in scope because they source, sell, or engage in other activities across national boundaries although the firm or organization remains physically in only one location. The term "transnational" is sometimes used as a synonym for multinational. See R. Vernon and L. Wells, *Manager in the International Economy*, 5th ed. (Englewood Cliffs, NJ: Prentice-Hall, 1986).
7 B. Kogut, "Globalization," in M. Warner (ed.) *Concise International Encyclopedia of Business and Management* (London: Thomson Business Press, 1997), 99.
8 Martin Wolf, *Why Globalization Works* (New Haven, CN: Yale University Press, 2004), 14. Scholars like Peter Berger have analyzed cultural globalization, which is not the axis of discussion in this book. According to Berger, "Globalization is, *au fond*, a continuation...of the perduring challenge of modernization. On the cultural level this has been the great challenge of pluralism: the breakdown of taken-for-granted traditions and the opening up of multiple options for beliefs, values, and lifestyles." See Peter Berger, "Introduction," to *Many Globalizations: Cultural Diversity in the Contemporary World* eds. Peter Berger and Samuel Huntington (Oxford: Oxford University Press, 2002), 16.
9 Georg W.F. Hegel, *Phänomenologie des Geistes*, ed. Johannes Hoffmeister (Hamburg: Meiner, 1940), 34.
10 Kevin O'Rourke, "Europe and the Causes of Globalization, 1790 to 2000," in *Europe and Globalization* ed. H. Kierzkowski (Basingstoke: Palgrave Macmillan, 2002), 65.
11 Geoffrey Jones, *Multinationals and Global Capitalism* (Oxford: Oxford University Press, 2005), 5–15. I am indebted to Jones' insightful treatment of the history of globalization in several key chapters of his book.
12 Jagdish Bhagwati, *In Defense of Globalization* (Oxford: Oxford University Press, 2004), 11.
13 Stephen Broadberry and Kevin O'Rourke, *The Cambridge Economic History of Modern Europe* (Cambridge: Cambridge University Press, 2010), 6–9.
14 Adam Smith, *An Inquiry into the Nature and Causes of the Wealth of Nations* (Oxford: Oxford University Press, 1976), 457.

15 Wolf, *Why Globalization Works*, 80–2. See also Bhagwati, *In Defense of Globalization*, 61.
16 Broadberry and O'Rourke, *Cambridge Economic History of Modern Europe*, 10.
17 See Maurice Obstfeld and Alan Taylor, "Globalization and Capital Markets," in *Globalization in Historical Perspective* ed. M. Bordo and A.M. Taylor (Chicago, IL: University of Chicago Press, 2002), 66–85.
18 Geoffrey Jones, "Multinationals and the First Global Economy Before 1914," (Boston, MA: Harvard Business School Publications, 2004).
19 Don Bissell, *The First Conglomerate: 145 Years of the Singer Sewing Machine Company* (Brunswick, ME: Audenreed Press, 1999). See also Geoffrey Jones and David Kiron, "Globalizing Consumer Durables: Singer Sewing Machine before 1914," (Boston, MA: Harvard Business School Publications, 2008).
20 Angus Maddison, *The World Economy: A Millennial Perspective* (Paris: development Center of the Organization for Economic Cooperation and Development, 2001), 3.
21 See Norman Angell, *The Great Illusion: A Study of the Relation of the Military Power in Nations to their Economic and Social Advantage* (New York: Garland, 1972). See also Broadberry and O'Rourke, *Cambridge Economic History of Modern Europe*, 137.
22 Max Scheler, "Vom kulturellen Wiederaufbau Europas," in *Vom Ewigen im Menschen* (Bern: Francke Verlag, 1954), 405. See John Crosby's commentary in *Personalist Papers* (Washington, D.C.: Catholic University of America Press, 2004), 174–93.
23 Expropriation is defined as "an act whereby government takes into ownership, by compulsion if necessary, private property for a public use." See M.L. Williams, "The Extent and Significance of the Nationalism of Foreign-owned Assets in Developing Countries," *Oxford Economic Papers* 27 (1975): 261.
24 Geoffrey Jones, "Expropriation in International Business," (Boston, MA: Harvard Business School Publications, 2003), 2.
25 Mira Wilkins, *The Maturing of Multinational Enterprise: American Business Abroad from 1914 to 1970* (Cambridge, MA: Harvard University Press, 1974), 23–6.
26 Angus Maddison, *World Economy in the Twentieth Century* (Paris: OECD, 1989), 98.
27 Wilkins, *Maturing of Multinational Enterprise*, 152–5.
28 Arthur Schlesinger, *The Age of Roosevelt: The Crisis of the Old Order* (New York: Sentry, 1957), 166.
29 Wilkins, *Maturing of Multinational Enterprise*, 228–9.
30 Broadberry and O'Rourke, *Cambridge Economic History of Modern Europe*, 206.
31 Shale Horowitz, "Restarting Globalization after World War II," *Comparative Political Studies* 37 (2) (2004): 127–51.
32 See Daniel Litvin, *Empires of Profit* (New York: Texere, 2003), 147–8.
33 Jagdish Bhagwati and Arvind Panagariya, *Why Growth Matters* (New York: Perseus Books, 2013), 8.

34 Robert Heilbroner, *The Making of Economic Society*, 5th ed. (Englewood Cliffs, NJ: Prentice-Hall, 1975), 223–5.
35 Wilkins, *Maturing of Multinational Enterprise*, 350–5.
36 Richard Barnet and Ronald Muller, *Global Reach: The Power of Multinational Corporations* (New York: Simon and Schuster, 1974), 81–6.
37 Ronald Coase and Ning Wang, *How China Became Capitalist* (New York: Palgrave Macmillan, 2013), 122.
38 Christian Caryl, *Strange Rebels* (New York: Basic Books, 2013), 237.
39 Julie Cohen, *Configuring the Networked Self* (New Haven, CN: Yale University Press, 2012), 12–13.
40 "Globalization with a Third-World Face," *The Economist*, April 9, 2005, 66.
41 "A Bigger World: A Special Report on Globalization," *The Economist*, September 20, 2008, 3–6.
42 "Emerging Africa: A Hopeful Continent," *The Economist*, March 2, 2013, 4–9.
43 For more details see "When Health and Trade Policies Don't Jibe," *National Journal*, April 18, 1988.
44 Quoted in Heilbroner, *The Making of Economic Society*, 226.
45 Lester Salamon, "The Rise of the Nonprofit Sector," *Foreign Affairs* 73 (1994): 109.
46 Deborah Spar, "The Spotlight Effect and the Bottom Line," *Foreign Affairs* 77 (1998): 7–12.
47 Organization for Economic and Community Development (OECD) Fact Book, 2012; available at: http://www.oced-ilibrary.org/sites/factbook-2012-en (accessed March 6, 2014)
48 See John Cavenaugh and Jerry Mander, *Alternatives to Economic Globalization: A Better World is Possible* (San Francisco, CA: Berrett-Koehler, 2002).
49 For a more extensive argument see Wolf, *Why Globalization Works*, 199–202.
50 See Jones, *Multinationals and Global Capitalism*, 10–15.
51 Bhagwati and Panagariya, *Why Growth Matters*, xiv–xv. The authors stress that openness to trade is only an "enabling mechanism;" gains from trade will be nullified if other domestic policies are not oriented to take advantage of trading opportunities.
52 Bhagwati and Panagariya, *Why Growth Matters*, 24–5. For data on Taiwan, see Arvind Panagariya, "Trade Openness and Growth Miracles: A Fresh Look at Taiwan," in *Ashgate Research Companion to International Trade Policy*, ed. Ken Heyden and Stephen Woolcock (London: Ashgate Publishing Limited, 2011).
53 Peter Lindert and John Williamson, "Does Globalization Make the World More Unequal?" Paper delivered at Conference on Globalization in Historical Perspective, National Bureau of Economic Research, Santa Barbara, CA, May 3, 2001.
54 "Economics Focus: Too Many Countries," *The Economist*, July 17, 2004, 75. See also, "Beyond Economics," *The Economist*, February 12, 2011, 75.
55 See Albert Borgmann, *Crossing the Postmodern Divide* (Chicago, IL: University of Chicago Press, 1992), 55–62.

2
FREE MARKETS AND GOVERNMENT REGULATION

The multinational enterprise has been the central figure in the evolution and expansion of global capitalism. Throughout history, multinational corporations have helped states to exploit their economic resources and become more competitive within the global economy. These corporations have greatly enhanced social welfare by introducing products and services throughout the world, creating jobs and transferring technologies. But, as we observed in the previous chapter, foreign investment by multinationals is no longer a purely Western phenomenon. Corporations like India's Tata Group, China's Geely, and Saudi Basic Industries have also invested heavily abroad through acquisitions. This sort of investment has provoked protectionist fears over potential job losses and the relinquishment of local control.

However, there is also a more profound apprehension: that the ascendancy of these "new champions" will lead to the advancement of state-led capitalism instead of the more liberal form of entrepreneurial capitalism. The reason for this worry is that many of these "third world multinationals" are owned, in whole or in part, by undemocratic states like China where political interference is high and socialist tendencies still linger. Hence the threat of the state's gradual encroachment into global markets, in ways that will stifle private initiative and impede entrepreneurial innovation.

This chapter will concentrate on these issues, by reviewing the different various forms of capitalism and delineating some of the more conspicuous problems with state-guided capitalism. We also address a more fundamental question: what sets capitalism and free market enterprise itself apart from a purely socialist economic system? The latter question is important for several reasons. Since liberal capitalism is so closely linked with globalization, we cannot understand the forces and benefits of globalization without an adequate understanding of capitalism. Recall that a secondary aim of this book is to offer a modest justification of global capitalism, despite its well-documented deficiencies. But any efforts to justify globalization, or defend it from its ubiquitous critics, cannot succeed apart from some consideration of the ideal of liberal capitalism. In addition, it certainly seems that our primary task would be incomplete if we develop an account of a multinational corporation's social responsibility, while ignoring the capitalist context within which a multinational's policies and actions occur. Corporate social responsibility should be seen in the light of the moral logic of capitalism, which is sorely tested when there are deviations from the ideal of fair market conditions and efficiencies.

Liberal capitalism is predicated on extensive private property rights, along with open and free markets. However, even governments that respect and promote free markets need to intervene sometimes: when there are market failures, such as hidden transaction costs. The nature and scope of that intervention is an important topic for the study of global capitalism. Should government interventions be confined to the correction of these market failures or should government adopt a more expansive role by correcting inequitable market distributions? And how will a deeper commitment to social justice affect the parameters of economic liberty? In some developing countries, a weak matrix of government institutions is unwilling or unable to effectively address market failures such as externalities. This regulatory vacuum puts an extra burden on multinationals to be ethically proactive rather than wait for the government to create value by correcting the market failure. Multinationals have not been sufficiently attuned to this problem. They must learn to take greater responsibility for the social disorder and moral chaos sometimes precipitated by their actions, even if the host country's ruling class is inattentive to these matters.

In corporate affairs, the assertion of moral authority through ethical self-regulation is far preferable to the "visible hand" of government regulation, because it simultaneously sustains free and open markets and promotes fairness. We can also find the basis for a reasonable corporate commitment to fairness and the public interest within the liberal tradition itself. As we ponder in this chapter the role of the multinational within the framework of classical liberalism, we begin with some reflections on capitalism's primary attributes.

Free Markets and Private Property Rights

Defenders of liberal capitalism have cogently argued that economic liberty is a necessary condition for personal freedom. To enjoy personal freedom in its fullness an individual must be free to choose his or her own occupation, free to start a new business whatever the risks, and free to make investments. People clearly value the right to make these sorts of economic choices. And, as Gaus points out, "there has never been a political order characterized by deep respect for personal freedom that was not based on a market order with widespread private ownership of the means of production."[1] Economic liberty, therefore, is heavily dependent on strong private property rights, the lynchpin of liberal capitalism. While the right to property is not absolute, it is a vitally significant right that deserves vigorous protection by the state. Communism on the other hand, categorically rejects extensive property rights. As Karl Marx emphatically declared, "Communism is the positive abolition of private property."[2]

Thus, the ideal of capitalism is characterized by "maximally extensive feasible property rights" (Gaus, 2010 (see endnote 4)). How are these expansive property rights most accurately defined? A property right or right of ownership is actually a bundle of rights, usually separated out in mature legal systems. That bundle of rights includes (but is not limited to) the right to possess (through exclusive physical control or the right to exclude others from use), the right to use, the right to manage, the right to income, the right to alienate (to sell or otherwise dispose of the property), and the right to security (that is, immunity from expropriation). In summary, property rights are best understood as full proprietary rights over tangible or intangible things. Like most rights, property rights can be reasonably restricted and limited by the state for the sake of the common good.[3]

Capitalist systems recognize a broad scope of rights for each individual property owner. But the capitalist system also extends, as far as reasonably possible, the scope or range of things that can be privately owned. Unlike communism, so-called capital goods—the goods of production—can be owned by private companies or individuals. Natural resources can also be owned. In a purely laissez-faire market economy, without any government regulation, there would be no restrictions on the sort of things people could own. However, a mature and responsible government will prohibit ownership of some things, such as people, and hence it will declare slavery to be illegal. But in general the capitalist ideal seeks to maximize the rights of ownership along with the range of objects that can be owned.[4]

Several philosophers have offered thoughtful justifications of the liberal property rights at the heart of capitalism. John Locke's prominent and nuanced theory of property is presented in *Two Treatises of Government*. This influential book, which enthusiastically defends the proposition of "natural rights," is an elaborate attack on monarchical forms of government and the divine right of kings. In Chapter Five of the *Second Treatise* Locke brought property rights directly to the center of political philosophy, as he sought to demonstrate that these rights were not dependent on the arbitrary claims of the monarchy. A property right was the corollary of the right to self-preservation: "if everyone has the natural right to preserve himself, he necessarily has the right to everything that is necessary for his self-preservation."[5] A property right is based on self-ownership, that is, ownership of one's body and the labor it produces. Once the labor is "annexed" to common resources, the laborer justly appropriates the end result. Therefore, Locke insisted that property was not a convention of the state, but a God-given, natural right that precedes civil society. It is reasonable to assume, writes Locke, that God "who bid Mankind increase and multiply should . . . give them all a Right to make use of the food and Rayment, and other Conveniences of life, the Materials whereof he had so plentifully provided for them."[6]

For Locke, the state exists to protect that natural right along with other natural rights such as life and liberty. As he explains, "The great and chief end, therefore, of Men's uniting into Commonwealths, and putting themselves under Government, is the Preservation of their Property."[7] Locke, who convincingly discarded the divine right of kings as the principle of sovereignty, argued for a limited government that respects the needs and rights of citizens to pursue their own objectives. Since the individual in the state of nature agrees to be governed as a means of protecting his or her rights, "the power of the society or legislature constituted by them can never be supposed to extend farther" than what is necessary for the preservation of those rights.[8]

We can infer from Locke's original political analysis that the right to property, which is recognized but not bestowed by the state, is essential for our human flourishing, because it is so closely linked to a person's capacity to apply his or her intellect to material and intellectual objects, to set plans and goals, and to be good stewards of possessions. In general, property contributes to our capacity for self-determination, to put our distinctive mark on the realm of nature. Property rights ensure security of possession and thereby support entrepreneurial freedom and independence, the right to start and operate a business as one sees fit without state interference or the risk of confiscation. Collective ownership, on the other hand, is unworkable and usually turns into ownership by an elite, privileged political class. While collective ownership breeds dependence on the state, private property rights give people autonomy and independence: a necessary stimulus for creativity.[9]

Thus, property rights disperse power and give people an opportunity to properly exercise their autonomy and invest things with a personal meaning. Hegel emphasizes this logical connection between property rights and freedom throughout his political philosophy. One of the most important institutions that constitute the ethical life (*Sittlichkeit*) of a people is property. Hegel explains that a person must be able to control and shape objects in his or her environment over time, otherwise the world will remain an alien place. The human subject requires "the right of putting his will into any and every being and making it his property."[10] The person cannot be free without this ability to overcome the opposition between self and world by projecting his or her personality onto external objects. Property rights, which safeguard secure possession and stability of ownership, are necessary to protect this freedom and to inspire the extension of someone's will and personality into the external world. Hegel agreed with his predecessor, Immanuel Kant, that freedom of choice requires freedom of action and freedom of action requires the right to possess.[11]

Hegel would disagree with Locke's views on the minimal role of the state, but Locke's paradigm has prevailed within the liberal tradition.

Despite Locke's minimalism, there is a firm acknowledgment of law's necessity. Laws give people space to pursue their objectives, preserve strong but limited property rights, and help settle disputes over rights. As Hayek explained, "law, liberty, and property are an inseparable trinity."[12]

In addition to broad property rights that enable economic liberty, capitalism also depends on free and open markets. The presumption is that free or voluntary exchange of the goods in the marketplace by property holders yields the most efficient economic outcome. Individuals and companies "reassign" their property rights when goods are exchanged. These markets will also set wages and prices. The forces of supply and demand determine the market clearing price and the efficient quantity. The entrepreneur must face the discipline of the market and satisfy the consumer's needs at the appropriate price if he or she is to remain in business and make a reasonable profit. In this "commercial society," there is a formal equality as jobs are open to all based on talent and ability.

As Adam Smith has explained, under certain conditions these free markets allocate resources efficiently, producing the right outcome that maximizes social welfare by allowing society to get the most out of its scarce resources. Under the right conditions society is guided to this optimal result by an "invisible hand" that directs uncoordinated individuals to supply the right amount of goods that are demanded by consumers at the appropriate price. According to Smith,

> The natural effort of every individual to better his own condition, when suffered to exert himself with freedom and security, is so powerful a principle that it is alone ... capable of carrying on the society to wealth and prosperity. ... Every individual endeavors as much as he can to direct ... industry so that its produce may be of the greatest value, ... neither intend[ing] to promote the public interest, nor know[ing] how much he is promoting it. He intends only his own gain, and he is, in this, as in many other cases, led by an *invisible hand* to promote an end that was no part of his intention. By pursuing his own interest he frequently promotes that of society more effectually than when he really intends to promote it.[13]

Competition fueled by self-interest rather than a central plan brings about the most effective coordination of individual efforts. Socialist governments often feel ill at ease over the chaotic and disorderly free market and its apparent lack of coordination. As a consequence, they seek to nudge it in one direction or another, though sometimes this intervention is counterproductive. But Smith, who agreed with Locke in the need for governmental restraint, believed that economic liberty supported by property rights along with free markets created their own social order, one which was not imposed by the state but resulted *spontaneously* from the cooperation and competition of ordinary people.[14]

The alternative to free markets and broad property ownership is constrained property rights and central planning where the omniscient and omnipotent state owns and controls virtually all means of production and sets all wages and prices. Communism, defined as the "abolition of private property," eliminates the market and subjects the entire economy to the management of "associated producers" controlled by the state.[15] These producers represent "socialized man" who is finally free and no longer at the mercy of "the blind forces of Nature."[16] The planners in these economies attempt to organize all of society as if it were one large factory. In communist handbooks we find comments like the following:

> We must know in advance how much labor to assign to the various branches of industry; what products are required and how much of it is necessary to produce; how and where machines must be provided. These and similar details must be thought out beforehand, with approximate accuracy at least; and the work must be guided in accordance with these calculations.[17]

As Friedrich Hayek has been at pains to insist, however, the central planner suffers from a "fatal conceit," a sort of "synoptic delusion," believing that he or she can somehow know and evaluate all the relevant information necessary to operate and control an efficient economy. But policymakers can never have such perfect knowledge about the behavior of people and must always deal with the unintended consequences of their policies. Moreover, Hayek explains that economic planning has broad and possibly inhumane consequences: "Economic control is not merely control of a sector or human life which can be separated from the rest; it is the control of the means for all our ends."[18]

In Hayek's view, what is far superior to central planning is decentralized planning, by many individual persons and disparate communities. Capitalism creates economic opportunity since it encourages competition, innovation, and efficiency through market rewards. It rewards the entrepreneur for creating value and for efficiently serving the wants and needs of others. Socialist systems, however, not only provide few incentives for innovation that benefit individuals, but also fosters dependence on the state and on the schemes of its planners.

Within the thought of Locke, Smith and Hayek, one finds the rudimentary ideas of liberal capitalism, which is committed to a "thick" conception of economic liberty, supported by strong and expansive property rights, and to formal equality or equality of opportunity within the marketplace.[19] Economic liberty implies liberty of labor ("the liberty to employ one's body and time in productive activity one has chosen or accepted") and liberty of transacting (the freedom to manage one's own economic affairs).[20] The classical liberal tradition also accepts the efficacy of free markets and a limited role for the state, which must provide social services, education, and a social safety net. In China, this vision of economic liberty, coupled with strong property rights, has displaced economic socialism, which had so thoroughly depleted the Chinese economy.

Critics of classical liberalism and capitalism claim that liberal property rights and free markets are incompatible with the ideal of social justice, which supposes that the state has an obligation to intrude upon laissez-faire economic arrangements to ensure a more equitable distribution of society's goods. The unrestricted ownership of productive or capital goods and modestly regulated markets produce sizable inequities of wealth and power, to the great disadvantage of vast numbers of people. According to philosophers who advocate this perspective, sometimes referred to as "high liberalism," social justice demands that excessive wealth must be redistributed if real justice is to be achieved.

In his seminal book on justice, written in 1971, John Rawls argued that a well-ordered and just society will provide equal liberties for its citizens and will permit social and economic inequalities only to the extent that they benefit the least advantaged. Preferable to an equal distribution of wealth and income is the toleration of certain inequalities if they improve the condition of those who have the least. But Rawls believed that a necessary condition of justice as fairness was that "property and wealth must be kept widely distributed."[21] This redistribution is necessary even if it means the attenuation of economic liberty. As Tomasi points out, the tradition of high liberalism or social democracy reflected in the work of Rawls affirms a thin conception of economic liberty, a more "substantive conception of equality" that requires goods to be distributed in ways that benefit the least advantaged, and a broader role for the state in regulating the market.[22]

Another criticism of liberal capitalism is that free markets and thick property rights breed corporate malfeasance, which is often advanced by a fixation on the goal of long-term profit maximization. The principles of economic liberty and individual property rights appear to help foster an ideology of individualism that is often reflected in corporate interactions in the marketplace. In their rent-seeking activities, too many corporations in the past have ignored the most primary moral principle: "one should not do harm to any other human being."[23] While some corporations have consistently acted conscientiously, others have willingly produced unsafe products, engaged in fraudulent marketing campaigns, mistreated workers, and encroached upon privacy rights. For a number of years too many corporations were also derelict in their duty to avoid degrading the natural environment.

A thorough treatment of this thoughtful critique of liberal capitalism is obviously well beyond the scope of this book. But let it suffice to say that there is certainly some merit to these familiar objections, particularly about the excesses found in corporate behavior. As we saw in the previous chapter, some companies go too far in their pursuit of property and end up exploiting workers or harming consumers. However, the myopic moral vision of individualized and unrestricted property rights, to be exercised without concern for others, is not faithful to the intellectual roots of liberalism, which is disposed toward some measure of distributive equity. John Locke, for example, contended that property rights must be limited by what he called a "charity proviso," which recognizes that the poor sometimes have a claim on the assets of valid property holders. Thus, a commitment to property rights and economic liberty does not preclude a concern for social justice issues. Implicit in Locke's analysis is the need for corporations and other property holders to accept charity as an ethical duty, an intrinsic constraint on their property rights. As we will discuss in Chapter Seven, when property rights like patents interfere with the need for life-preserving medicine, pharmaceutical companies must moderate those rights for the sake of the common good.

Moreover, it is far from obvious that a more socialistic economic system, or excessive regulation that grants government undue powers, will suddenly eliminate corruption, greed, and bias from marketplace interactions. Most forms of social democracy, committed to distributive equity, favor constraints on private economic freedom in order to open the door for government's expanded role in the market place. On the other hand, a strong case can be made that there is no reason to reject the whole economic system of liberal capitalism, especially when competitive systems based on central planning have performed so poorly. While there may be room for marginal increases in government intervention in liberal capitalism, the best resolution to corporate malfeasance is ethical self-regulation. Corporations themselves should seek to curb these excesses with a proper focus on the moral duties consistent with their mission. Ethical self-regulation will keep markets unfettered by excessive regulations that often displace private initiative and it will ensure that market participants will be treated with the fairness and respect which they deserve.

This ideology of excessive individualism that still plagues the corporate mentality can be overcome by a careful rethinking of the role of the corporation in society. The purpose of the corporation cannot be narrowly conceived in terms of long-term profits or the maximization of shareholder wealth. Nor should corporate purpose be represented as the maximization of stakeholder equity, especially if that equity is measured primarily in financial or economic terms. Rather, corporate purpose must be regarded in terms of the common good of the business as a community of persons. These persons cooperate in specific activities as they work together toward certain objectives for which the company was organized. A private, profit-making corporation is an "association" that exists for ongoing cooperation and economic motivation.[24] It invests in assets for the purpose of creating value. In the paradigm case of a manufacturing firm, value is created through the deployment of labor resources to shape raw materials (delivered from its suppliers) into a finished product that is then distributed through the appropriate channels to its customers. The company's common good, therefore, is efficient economic cooperation that maximizes added value and fairness to all cooperating participants (investors, managers, workers, etc.), who should benefit in such a way that what they receive is proportionate to their contribution.[25]

Along these lines, two apologists for modern capitalism, John Mackey and Raj Sisodia, argue that the capitalist system has been misunderstood and therefore it has been falsely maligned by its critics. To some extent, this is the fault of far too many corporations, which view their purpose too narrowly as long-term profit maximization. These companies must raise their consciousness level and recognize a higher purpose which addresses the contribution they intend to make to society. That purpose can usually be uncovered by contemplating the reason the company was founded in the first place. Every organization should consider how its value-added activities contribute to social welfare. Southwest Airlines, for example, exists to give people the freedom to fly. Genzyme, the Cambridge biotech firm, believes that its mission is to serve the needs of the patient. This higher purpose, which underscores the contribution firms make to society even as they make profits doing so, reflects the virtuous nature of free-enterprise capitalism which is necessary for democracy and prosperity. According to the authors,

> This is what we know to be true: business is good because it creates value, it is ethical because it is based on voluntary exchange, it is noble because it can elevate our existence, and it is heroic because it lifts people out of poverty and creates prosperity. Free-enterprise capitalism is one of the most powerful ideas we humans have ever had.[26]

Capitalism must become "conscious" of its heroic or noble nature. This happens when corporations clarify their original purpose for coming into being (beyond long-term profits), and consider the valid needs of their stakeholders. The value of Mackey and Sisodia's somewhat idealistic analysis is that it underscores how the market-driven corporation exists primarily to provide a service to society and to fill the needs of its customers.

Good Versus Bad Capitalism

Now that we comprehend the tradition of liberal capitalism and what sets it apart from the economic system of communism, we can review the different forms of capitalism. In *Good Capitalism, Bad Capitalism*, Baumol and his co-authors argue that globalization enhances economic growth, and economic growth goes hand in hand with the reduction of poverty. As we noted in the previous chapter, it is quite difficult to find examples of countries where poverty has waned without a significant increase in the quantity of economic activity. Although there are various drivers of economic growth, one key driver is innovation and technological progress, but what economic conditions are conducive for innovation? The short answer is capitalism, but what type of capitalism?[27]

The authors explain that there is no uniform definition of capitalism and no one form of economic organization in economies laying claim to the capitalist pedigree. Rather, they contend that there are several types of capitalism which are qualitatively different. Some forms of capitalism approximate socialistic systems while others are more firmly committed to broad property rights and the free market. Accordingly, they present four fundamental archetypes of capitalism: state-guided capitalism; oligarchic capitalism; big firm capitalism; and entrepreneurial capitalism. While these models are quite distinct, they have in common the recognition of private property rights, including the right to own capital goods and the means of production. Also, in all these versions of capitalism, a preponderance of productive assets is usually controlled by the private sector. However, in their view, there is only one sure path to sustainable economic growth.[28]

In state-guided capitalism, governments rather than markets take the lead in deciding which industries deserve an influx of capital investment because of their potential for growth or strategic significance for the national economy. Policymakers in these governments seek to choose and support the winners as they determine which firms should thrive and grow. Sometimes the state exercises direct control by owning a preponderance of shares in the targeted companies. The state need not own a majority stake in these proclaimed winners; it can also support them by means of tax breaks, subsidies, government contracts, and other mechanisms. Examples of state-guided capitalism include many of the countries in South East Asia and Latin America; and, of course, China. In China, four state-owned banks dominate the financial system. As the economic history of these countries has shown, state capitalism can sometimes be quite successful and enduring. Companies in state capitalist systems typically achieve success, not through innovation and true entrepreneurship, but by importing foreign technology and combining it with their own low-cost labor. The primary problem with this system is the naïve belief that the state's benevolent guidance can go on indefinitely. Moreover, governments do not have a good track record in picking winners and losers. When countries approach the "technological frontier," where there are no market leaders to follow and imitate, they tend to stumble and to make major investment mistakes. Finally, once a state has committed its resources and reputation to a particular project, it can be difficult to "pull the plug."[29]

In oligarchic capitalism government policies are oriented toward the promotion of the vested interests of a small segment of the population, such as the family and cohorts of the ruling autocratic dictator. The goals of economic growth and the welfare of workers and consumers are secondary to the goal of wealth aggrandizement for the privileged few. What oligarchic economies have in common is extreme inequality in the distribution of wealth, which is usually found only in the hands of the political elite. These economies are plagued by cronyism, pervasive corruption, and intolerance of internal dissent. Moreover, within these economies there tends to be considerable "informal activity," such as construction without permits and informal systems of property rights.[30] Some African countries, such as Nigeria or Libya, which suffer from the "resource curse" of superabundant oil, clearly resemble oligarchic capitalism. These regimes use oil or diamonds to enrich themselves rather than benefit their impoverished citizens. At the same time, the sale of these natural resources raises the value of the currency and makes the country's other goods too expensive on world markets. Hence the notion that abundant natural resources can be a curse rather than a blessing for a national economy. In summary, economies that fall under oligarchic capitalism are not driven by the quest for economic growth but by the impulse to increase and preserve wealth for the privileged few who make up the ruling class.[31]

Big firm capitalism is dominated by large corporations, whose ownership is typically dispersed among institutional investors which represent millions of small shareholders. They are run by professionally trained managers who act as trustees of the corporate institution.[32] This sort of oligopolistic capitalism is found predominantly in Western Europe, the United States, and Japan. Entrepreneurs in big firm economies are typically situated at the margins of these large corporations. These "big firms" are usually found in oligopolistic industries that can support only a few sellers due to capital requirements and steep economies of scale. Often these companies survive by harvesting established brands, which become profitable cash cows. They thrive by keeping costs low and usually concentrate only on incremental innovations. While this form of capitalism is beset with problems, such as the lack of innovation and industry-wide competition, it is not without merit. There is a certain logic to an oligopolistic industry or even a monopoly structure if network effects are in play. Big firms like General Electric, Wal-Mart, and Intel have become masters of efficiency by stressing productivity gains. They achieve certain economies of scale and scope that keep costs down and prices low. Big firms are needed to efficiently produce the innovations discovered by entrepreneurs by developing manufacturing processes and distribution networks so those products can be made and sold efficiently. On occasion big firms (like Apple, Inc.) can act like entrepreneurs, but they tend to eschew major innovation and to resist transformative changes.[33]

Finally, entrepreneurial capitalism is a system in which many small firms consistently innovate and take the initial steps necessary to commercialize their innovations. Radical rather than incremental innovations occur within this capitalist framework, where the risks and expense of innovating can lead to high economic rents. These innovations would not exist without entrepreneurs who perceive an opportunity to sell a bold new product or service that often changes an entire industry. The entrepreneur is the "contrarian" value creator who sees "extraordinary" economic value where others see only dead ends and blind alleys.[34] Sometimes these substantive innovations become platforms for complementary products and thriving ecosystems.

Microprocessors, operating systems, and browsers are examples of platforms. Platform leaders like Microsoft and Intel seek to drive innovation in their respective industries.[35] With rare exceptions, entrepreneurs are found in capitalist economies (instead of communist ones) where the innovators' rewards are ample. Capitalist systems adequately protect intellectual property (through patents and copyrights) so that the innovator can be ensured of that reward. Without suitable intellectual property protection, companies and individuals cannot appropriate the value of their creations.

The United States, claim the authors, is "a unique blend of entrepreneurial and big firm capitalism."[36] Entrepreneurs prosper in this dynamic environment, where change and innovation quite often disrupt entrenched industries and established technologies. Steve Jobs, Bill Gates, and Andy Grove were pioneering innovators who made the revolutionary personal computer a reality. The platforms they engineered, such as operating systems and microprocessors, led to countless other innovations. The PC industry grew exponentially in the 1980s and 1990s and displaced the giants of the mini-computer and mainframe computer industries, such as IBM, Honeywell, and Digital Equipment Corp. (DEC). Economies cannot survive without entrepreneurs, whose radical innovations fuel new waves of economic growth. But big firms are still necessary to efficiently produce and market the innovations conceived by these entrepreneurs. Unlike state capitalism, the U.S. system epitomizes liberal capitalism with its commitment to property rights (including liberal intellectual property rights) and minimal state involvement.

This unique blend of entrepreneurial and big firm capitalism is a prime example of "good capitalism" because it promotes both innovation and efficiency. Innovation in turn promotes economic growth and growth inevitably leads to lower poverty levels. Governments do not pick the winners or direct the economy, but create the conditions such as reasonably thick property rights that allow entrepreneurs to thrive. They remove barriers to entry and make it easier for entrepreneurs to form companies and they offer mechanisms such as nuanced intellectual property rights that protect innovative technologies and inventions from free riders. Government may also have a role to play in funding research and development, but private corporations rather than government bureaucrats must be the ones to guide innovations through the thicket of commercialization.

"Bad capitalism," on the other hand, is state-guided or oligarchic capitalism. Oligarchic capitalism has no redeeming features and has spelled disaster for many countries in Africa. Oligarchic capitalism marginalizes the goal of economic growth and is not committed to globalization. But what about state capitalism, which is markedly different from liberal capitalism? Are Baumol and his co-authors correct in their assessment that this is also a bad form of capitalism? Is it salutary for the global economy that the invisible hand is being replaced by the visible hand of state capitalism? Since this form of state capitalism is becoming more predominant in the global economic system, it needs more critical scrutiny.

Elements of state-guided capitalism have surfaced in the past, especially in the rise of Japan in the 1950s and 1960s, and in Singapore in the 1980s. Singapore's version of state capitalism was crafted by Lee Kuan Yew, who planned an information technology infrastructure and an economic environment that proved to be attractive to foreign investors. But state capitalism now plays a much larger role in the global economy. The Chinese state, for example, is the primary shareholder in the country's 150 biggest corporations. It directs money to favored industries and works closely with Chinese companies that have invested abroad. India's economy has also been a model of paternalistic guidance by the state. The current versions of state capitalism are far superior to their predecessors. States like China are more powerful than countries like Singapore and they have at their disposal more sophisticated capitalist tools, which they do not hesitate to deploy. These states usually keep state-owned firms in the hands of professionally trained managers rather than turning them over to cronies and state bureaucrats.[37]

State capitalist systems often boast of "national champions," corporations in strategic industries that enjoy the favor and unyielding support of the government. South Korea and Brazil, for example, were both successful in directing their respective economies through import substitution policies. The South Korean government invested capital to develop an automobile industry as it championed companies like Daewoo and Hyundai. South Korean policies called for importing technology and then exporting aggressively so that their plants could reach the proper scale. As a result, South Korea became a major new entrant in the highly competitive global automotive industry.

State capitalism has been successful in building infrastructure and in producing national champions, like Lenovo, that compete effectively in global markets. However, there is evidence that guidance and direction by the state is not the optimal path to economic growth. A World Bank report documents the failure of South Korea's championing of chemical industries and Singapore's failure to exclude labor-intensive industries from its economy by boosting wages. The report concludes that "attempts to guide resource allocation with non-market mechanisms have generally failed to improve economic performance."[38]

The fundamental problem with state capitalism is that politicians have far more power in this system than they do under liberal capitalism where government involvement is constrained. In Russia, for example, it's not uncommon for government cabinet members to be at the head of large corporations. The government's lack of independence suggests problems: how can it regulate companies it also runs? Gazprom, Russia's state-owned natural gas producer, must serve two masters: as a corporation with outside investors it strives to maximize profit, but because it is owned by the state, the company also pursues political objectives. Gazprom has been used as a foreign policy instrument by Russian leaders, who have ordered it to cut off gas supplies to countries (for example, to Georgia) when there is a political dispute.[39] Citizens may also begin to feel powerless in the face of a highly centralized political bureaucracy. Moreover, the operation of a market which is closely linked to the bureaucratic state has a stifling effect on people and favors an "atomist and instrumentalist stance to the world."[40]

Finally, there is mounting evidence that many state-owned companies are far less innovative than private companies. Governments may be "good at providing the seedcorn for innovation ... but they are bad at turning that seedcorn into bread."[41] Notable failures include Malaysia's ill-advised investment in biotechnology (BioValley) and Russia's high-tech park known as Skolkovo. Several high-profile and large-scale projects in China, such as a $91 billion industrial project in Caofeidian, have also failed because they are redundant and simply create overcapacity in steel, concrete and other industries.[42] Furthermore, there is evidence that state-owned companies are less productive and efficient than private firms. A study showed that between 2001 and 2009 the average real return on equity for state owned firms was −1.47%.[43] State-controlled Russian companies like Gazprom, Unified Energy Systems, and Aeroflot, have fewer incentives to relentlessly increase productivity and drive down costs than big private firms like General Electric and Wal-Mart. Despite low taxes and preferential access to gas fields, Russia's Gazprom has a high cost structure because of this lack of market discipline.

At this juncture in globalization's history state capitalism seems to be advancing, to the detriment of entrepreneurial capitalism. Through major corporate acquisitions by companies operating within state capitalist systems, the role of the state in the global economy is expanding. For some economists, this is cause for grave concern because it concentrates far too much power in the hands of the authoritative state, which has more control over private industry. Politicians can dictate strategies to big companies and even impose restrictions on entire industries. This expansive role of these states in the market also creates an unlevel playing field, where well-managed private firms lose out to less well-run competitors which have the benefit of subsidized capital.[44] It may be too much to assert that state capitalism necessarily amounts to "bad capitalism," but this form of capitalism surely has severe limitations, such as the failure to promote indigenous innovation. Those limitations are not conducive to economic growth, which is so heavily dependent on sustainable entrepreneurial success.

Pure socialism has been vanquished but state capitalism, despite its faults, seems to have a bright future. As *The Economist* points out, the "defining battle" of the twenty-first century will not be between capitalism and socialism but between these different versions of capitalism.[45]

Market Failures

All forms of capitalism depend on a voluntary exchange system known as the free market. A fundamental principle of liberal capitalism is that the free market economy maximizes aggregate social welfare and thereby contributes to the common good. However, markets sometimes fail to function properly. Market failure does not suggest a complete collapse, or some sort of radical malfunction, but simply implies that the market is producing less than optimal results. A market failure is a deviation from the ideal of economic efficiency. That ideal supposes many buyers and sellers (no monopolies), no entry barriers, no differentiated goods or services, clearly assigned property rights, perfect information, and no switching costs. Since markets function properly and efficiently only under these conditions of perfect competition, which are hard to satisfy in the real world, market failures are commonplace.[46]

There are four types of common market failure: monopoly or insufficient competition, public goods, externalities, and imperfect information. In the absence of competition, monopolists or single sellers under-produce and charge higher prices and reap monopoly rents; without the push of competition there are few incentives for efficiency or innovation. For example, in the oligopolistic pharmaceutical industry strong patents and other entry barriers preclude competitors from introducing competitive products that drive drug prices down to the range of the marginal cost of production. At the same time, demand is diminished by these high prices, so these companies produce less than the optimal amount.

Negative externalities constitute side effects of production that impose costs involuntarily on others who are powerless to affect the decisions about that production.[47] Markets ignore externalities such as pollution, which leads to the underpricing and overproduction of goods. If a cement company's manufacturing processes heavily pollute the local environment that manufacturer imposes a cost on others (for example, damage to their health) that is not reflected in the price of the cement nor in the amount of cement to be supplied. If the manufacturer had to cover these externalized costs, the price of cement would go up and the amount consumed would be reduced. However, this cement-maker has no incentive to internalize these costs and therefore is not likely to do so unless coerced by regulatory constraints.

Informational problems are another source of market failure. Efficient markets rely on available information, so when there are information asymmetries one party (the seller) is in a position to exploit the other party (the buyer). In these situations the seller is better informed than the potential buyers about the quality of goods he is attempting to sell. Buyers will then be forced to expend resources to confirm the quality of these goods. Sellers will also be tempted to invest resources to convince a skeptical public about the quality of their merchandise. Since these activities do not create value, they amount to an inefficient allocation of resources from the market's perspective.[48]

Finally, some goods such as "public goods" cannot be adequately supplied by independent markets. These public goods exhibit two chief qualities. First, their consumption is non-rivalrous. This means that, unlike private goods (such as a cake), one person's consumption of a public good (a cake recipe) does not reduce what is available for others. These goods are also non-excludable, which means that it is difficult to exclude or keep out those who haven't paid. Markets reward producers for the private goods they produce but not for the public goods they preserve. Since public goods, including information-based goods, are vulnerable to free riders, they tend to be under-produced in unregulated markets that lack some sort of protection, such as patents and copyrights.

In an imperfect world these markets' failures and inefficiencies are inevitable. But how should we address these failures? One possibility is to turn to the market itself for relief. We can be patient and wait for the "invisible hand" of the market to unleash its self-correcting mechanisms. Free market enthusiasts, and even some libertarians, argue that in due time the markets will correct their own failures and thereby will bring about the most efficient use of economic resources in the long run. In other cases, they argue, the failures cause no demonstrable harm, and therefore do not require an outside fix. In general, market-based solutions are advantageous since they are voluntary and usually more efficient than solutions imposed by government. This viewpoint is consistent with classic liberalism, which sees only a limited role for the state.

However, while the market can bring about some progress in eliminating certain imperfections and correcting externalities, it is generally recognized that government intervention will be necessary at times to fix these failures. The warrant for government intervention in situations of market failure should be twofold: the failure must be serious and harmful; there is a high probability that government intervention will be welfare-enhancing: its benefits will exceed the cost of intervention. Sometimes it can be exceedingly difficult to assess the level and scope of consumer harm and predict the effects of government intervention. Consider the case of Microsoft. The U.S. government's antitrust case against the giant software company at the turn of the century was momentous. Microsoft was accused of maintaining its monopoly through anti-competitive means and leveraging its monopoly power to achieve control of the browser market. But it was far from evident that consumers were being harmed by Microsoft's behavior, so it might have been preferable to let the markets correct Microsoft's dominance.[49] This correction began to unfold several years after the trial concluded in 2001 thanks to the meteoric rise of companies like Google. Also, intervention can be ineffective if regulated firms "capture" their regulators or the weak incentives for efficiency within the public sector produce ineffectual results that do not adequately address the failure in question.[50]

Of course, high liberalism envisions a much larger role for government than fixing these four market failures (along with providing necessary social services and a safety net). It is more concerned with distributional equity and the material well-being of citizens, rather than economic liberty. Social democrats, therefore, would be apt to regard market failures in broader terms as a deviation from a social ideal, as well as the ideal of economic efficiency. For example, some goods are important for human flourishing and so they are classified as socially important goods. The government provides some of these goods (such as education), but markets have been expected to provide other goods, such as health care and life-preserving pharmaceutical products. However, while markets can provide such goods they may not produce them in adequate quantities or distribute them in a way that is socially optimal. Thus, it could be argued that when people who need health care or life-preserving drugs cannot get access because the market prices are so high, there is a market failure of sorts that demands decisive government intervention.[51]

When intervention is warranted, policymakers have many tools at their disposal as ways of resolving market failures. Price regulations, along with restrictions on anti-competitive acquisitions, can curb monopoly power. Taxes and other mechanisms can be used to force companies to internalize the costs of negative externalities. Requirements to disclose a product's ingredients or its side effects can limit information asymmetries, and a system of limited intellectual property rights, that take the form of copyrights and patents, can protect innovators from free riders.

In most of the environments where multinationals operate they will be forced to abide by laws that restrict any opportunistic behavior that would allow them to exploit these potentially harmful failures, such as externalities or information asymmetries. However, where governments are dysfunctional and apathetic, such failures may abound, with the result that many consumers and communities are unjustly victimized. Given the great harm to the public caused by some of these failures, multinationals must be especially proactive to ensure that the effects of these failures are mitigated. For example, when there is such a policy vacuum a multinational must take the steps necessary to correct and compensate for negative externalities. This includes environmental disasters such as oil spills. American citizens could depend on their government to ensure compensation for the damage caused by the great BP oil spill in the Gulf, but the people of the Niger Delta could not count on the Nigerian government to be as responsive when Royal Dutch Shell spilled so much oil in their region. Thus, in the absence of effective government institutions, companies must pay careful attention to the social and environmental consequences of their actions. These firms cannot be passive about market failures but must expediently fill the gap left by impotent governments and implement welfare-enhancing solutions when they cause or contribute to a market failure.

But even when governments are not dysfunctional or completely indifferent, multinationals should still strive for ethical self-regulation rather than allow excessive rules and regulations to become a substitute for their own discretion and self-control. Corporations committed to this ideal of moral responsibility can help preserve economic liberty in the private sector but also ensure that harm is minimized by dealing proactively with hidden costs, informational asymmetries, and other market failures. For example, if corporations doing business in cyberspace had realized the need to limit their property claims over collected digital information in favor of reasonable privacy rights, the expensive regulatory regime protecting those rights might have been avoided.

Conclusions

We have presented the traditional arguments that liberal capitalism, which has historically been linked with globalization, is superior to pure socialist collectivism or Communism, which rely on a command system of central planning rather than free and open markets. Capitalism respects extensive property rights and modestly regulated markets, while communism seeks to do away with the market and severely limits property rights. As philosopher Charles Taylor observes, however, economic history in the previous century has demonstrated that "market mechanisms in some form are indispensable to an industrial society, certainly for its economic efficiency and probably also for its freedom."[52]

The problem with liberal capitalism is that it tolerates an arbitrary distribution of goods and a lack of equality. It also promotes an ideology of individualism, a strategic rationality focused almost exclusively on the deployment of corporate assets to achieve its economic objectives. But there is a disposition within classical liberalism to preserve economic liberty and property rights without neglecting distributional equity. In the spirit of Locke's charity proviso, multinationals should assert property rights, but in a way that takes account of the relevant needs of the destitute where they do business. Corporate self-moderation and a "community-centered rationality" are more effective than reactive regulations and they can lessen the need for costly government intervention in the marketplace that sometimes constrains economic liberty.[53]

Although capitalism does preserve economic liberty, not all forms of capitalism are created equal. This is the thesis of some economists, who claim that we must differentiate between good and bad forms of capitalism. The former includes entrepreneurial capitalism and "big-firm" capitalism, while the latter includes state-guided and oligarchic capitalism. The United States is a unique blend of entrepreneurial and big-firm capitalism. Both are necessary to ensure that there is radical innovation and that those innovations can be produced efficiently. The synthesis of big-firm and entrepreneurial capitalism is "good capitalism," because it is focused on innovation, the key to economic growth, which in turn is a chief contributing factor in the reduction of poverty. While state-guided capitalism, which explicitly directs resources to favored industries or national champions, has its faults it continues to advance in China, Russia, and throughout Southeast Asia. There is evidence that state-owned firms are less innovative and less productive and hence not so likely to spur faster economic growth and higher living standards. Also the growth of state capitalism implies an increasing encroachment of the state on the global economy, and that worries some economists because it concentrates too much power in the hands of government bureaucrats. Empirical evidence has also shown that state-owned firms are less innovative and productive than their private counterparts.

Finally, even within so-called good capitalism that is oriented to radical innovation and efficiency, markets will fail sometimes and government intervention will be necessary. But not all government intervention will necessarily increase aggregate welfare, so government must resist the temptation to overregulate the market. Even on purely economic grounds it is difficult to fix the correct boundary between the state and the market.[54] Determining that boundary is far more difficult if social ideals and values are involved. In general, a presumption in favor of markets whenever possible seems sensible in order to avoid starting down the well-trodden road to serfdom.

Notes

1 Gerald Gaus, "Coercion, Ownership, and the Redistributive State: Justificatory Liberalism's Classical Tilt," *Social Philosophy & Policy* 27 (2010): 252.
2 Karl Marx, *Economic and Philosophical Manuscripts of 1844* in Marx/Engels Collected Works trans. T. Bottomore vol. 4 (London: Lawrence and Wisehart, Ltd., 1959), 293.
3 Lawrence Becker, *Property Rights: Philosophic Foundations* (London: Routledge & Kegan Paul, 1977), 18–22. For a full specification of ownership rights see A.M. Honore, "Ownership," in *Oxford Essays in Jurisprudence* ed. A.G. Guest (Oxford: Clarendon Press, 1961), 107–47.

4 Gerald Gaus, "The Idea and Ideal of Capitalism," in *The Oxford Handbook of Business Ethics* ed. George Brenkert and Tom Beauchamp (Oxford: Oxford University Press, 2010), 73–99.
5 Leo Strauss, *Natural Right and History* (Chicago: University of Chicago Press, 1950), 233. Strauss goes on to explain that food and other basic goods are necessary for our "comfortable self-preservation," but this natural right to appropriate such things as our property "must be limited if it is not to be incompatible with the peace and preservation of mankind," 236.
6 John Locke, *Two Treatises of Government* ed. Peter Laslett (Cambridge: Cambridge University Press, 1988), §41 (original work published 1698).
7 Locke, *Two Treatises of Government*, 124.
8 Locke, *Two Treatises of Government*, 98.
9 Rev. Robert Sirico, *Defending the Free Market* (Washington, D.C.: Regnery, 2012), 28–36.
10 Georg W.F. Hegel, *Philosophy of Right* trans. T. Knox (London: Oxford University Press, 1952), § 39.
11 Robert Merges, *Justifying Intellectual Property* (Cambridge, MA: Harvard University Press, 2011), 72. See Merges' thoughtful account of Kant's views on property, 68–101.
12 Friedrich Hayek, *Law, Legislation and Liberty: Rules and Order* (Chicago, University of Chicago Press, 1973), 107. Quoted in John Tomasi, *Free Market Fairness* (Princeton, NJ: Princeton University Press, 2012), 19.
13 Adam Smith, *An Inquiry into the Nature and Causes of the Wealth of Nations*, (New York: Penguin, 1973), 162.
14 Tomasi, *Free Market Fairness*, 6.
15 Marx, *Economic and Philosophical Manuscripts*, 132.
16 Karl Marx, *Capital* (New York: International Publishers, 1967), vol. III, 820.
17 Quoted in Michael Ellman, *Socialist Planning* (Cambridge: Cambridge University Press, 1979), 9.
18 Friedrich A. Hayek, *The Road to Serfdom* ed. Bruce Caldwell (Chicago, IL: University of Chicago Press, 2007), 127.
19 Tomasi, *Free Market Fairness*, 22–6.
20 James Nickel, "Economic Liberties," in *The Idea of Political Liberalism: Essays on Rawls*, ed. Victoria Davison and Clark Wolf (Lanham, MD: Rowman and Littlefield, 2000), 155–67.
21 John Rawls, *A Theory of Justice* (Cambridge, MA: Harvard University Press, 1971), 225.
22 Tomasi, *Free Market Fairness*, 51.
23 St. Thomas Aquinas, *Summa Theologiae*, I–II, q. 100, a. 3c.
24 John Roberts, *The Modern Firm* (Oxford: Oxford University Press, 2004), 74–5.
25 Germain Grisez, *Difficult Moral Questions* (Quincy, Il: Franciscan Herald Press, 1997), 456–8.

26 John Mackey and Raj Sisodia, *Conscious Capitalism* (Boston, MA: Harvard Business Review Press, 2013), 21.
27 William Baumol, Robert Litan, and Carl Schramm, *Good Capitalism, Bad Capitalism, and the Economics of Growth and Prosperity* (New Haven, CN: Yale University Press, 2007), 21–5. For empirical evidence supporting a positive correlation between economic growth and poverty reduction, see David Dollar and Art Kraay, "Growth is Good for the Poor," *Journal of Economic Growth* 1 (2002): 195–225.
28 Baumol *et al.*, *Good Capitalism, Bad Capitalism*, 60–1.
29 Baumol *et al.*, *Good Capitalism, Bad Capitalism*, 62–70.
30 See Hernando de Soto, *The Mystery of Capital* (New York: Basic Books, 2000). The problem with these informal property systems, which are rampant in some cities in developing economies (e.g., Cairo, Lima, Manila, Port-au-Prince, Mexico City), is that these assets are "dead capital," which means that it is difficult to use them for collateral for loans to generate more capital. De Soto advocates bringing these rights into the formal legal system to make this capital productive. According to de Soto, "Just as a lake needs a hydroelectric plant to produce usable energy, assets need a formal property system to produce significant surplus value," 48.
31 Baumol *et al.*, *Good Capitalism, Bad Capitalism*, 71–9.
32 See E. Merrick Dodd, "For Whom are Corporate Managers Trustees?," *Harvard Law Review* 45 (1932): 1149–50. According to Dodd the "beneficiaries" of this trust are the stockholders "who have put their capital in the company," but also its employees, customers, and the general public.
33 Alfred Chandler, "The Enduring Logic of Industrial Success," *Harvard Business Review*, March–April (1990): 33–41. See also Baumol *et al.*, *Good Capitalism, Bad Capitalism*, 80–4.
34 Daniel Isenberg, *Worthless, Impossible and Stupid: How Contrarian Entrepreneurs Create and Capture Extraordinary Value* (Cambridge, MA: Harvard Business Review Press, 2013).
35 Annabelle Gawer and Michael Cusumano, *Platform Leadership* (Boston, MA: Harvard Business School Press, 2002), 2–14.
36 Baumol *et al.*, *Good Capitalism, Bad Capitalism*, 90.
37 "The Visible Hand: State Capitalism," *The Economist*, Special Report January 21, 2012, 3–7.
38 World Bank, *The East Asian Miracle: Economic Growth and Public Policy* (New York: Oxford University Press, 1993), 9–10. See also Baumol, *et al.*, *Good Capitalism, Bad Capitalism*, 142–3.
39 "Gazprom: Russia's Wounded Giant," *The Economist*, March 23, 2013, 68–9.
40 Charles Taylor, *The Ethics of Authenticity* (Cambridge, MA: Harvard University Press, 1992), 43.
41 "The Visible Hand: State Capitalism," 14.
42 Dinny McMahon and Bob Davis, "Troubled Megaproject Spotlights China Woes," *The Wall Street Journal*, July 25, 2013, A7.
43 "The Visible Hand: State Capitalism," 14–15.

44 "A Bigger World: A Special Report on Globalization," Special Report, *The Economist*, September 20, 2008, 6.
45 "The Visible Hand: State Capitalism," 18.
46 See Gregory Dees, "Responding to Market Failures," (Boston, MA: Harvard Business School Publications, 1996), 2–4.
47 There are also positive externalities which diffuse benefits beyond the buyer.
48 Roberts, *Modern Firm*, 82. See also the research of Robert Spence, "Job Market Signaling," *Quarterly Journal of Economics* 87 (1973): 355–74.
49 For details of this case see *United States of America v. Microsoft Corporation*, 253 F. 3d 34 D.C. Cir. [2001].
50 "State and Market," *The Economist*, February 17, 1996, 64–5.
51 Dees, "Responding to Market Failures," 3.
52 Taylor, *Ethics of Authenticity*, 110.
53 Kenneth Goodpaster, "The Concept of Corporate Responsibility," in *Just Business: New Introductory Essays in Business Ethics* ed. Tom Regan (New York: Random House, 1984), 319. See also Tomasi, *Free Market Fairness*, 127–42.
54 "State and Market," 65.

3

CULTURAL DIVERSITY AND CULTURAL RELATIVISM

Introduction

In a classic article written for the *New York Times Book Review* called "The Opening of the American Mind," the distinguished American historian, Arthur Schlesinger, makes a compelling case for overthrowing transcultural and universal moral standards. In this essay, which typifies the arguments advanced by thoughtful proponents of relativism, Schlesinger eloquently exposed the perils of moral absolutism. He argues quite forcefully that it can breed intolerance, imperiousness, and an arrogant disregard for other cultures and religions. This uncompromising inflexibility has been the source of endless strife and social discord, particularly when the moral absolutes have their roots in religious beliefs. He praises the American mind, shaped by thinkers like Ralph Waldo Emerson and William James, which is by nature pluralistic and relativistic, and so has little use for the pretensions of absolutism. While moral absolutism is abstract, rigid, and ahistorical, relativism is "concrete, pluralistic, inductive, historical, skeptical, and intimately bound up with deference to experience."[1]

This debate about universalism and pluralism is not new and extends back to the days of Ancient Greece. In ancient Athens the Sophists taught rhetoric and boasted that the study of this art was a great good because it provided the orator with an opportunity to exert power and influence over others. What mattered was the orator's rhetorical skills and not the moral quality of the value judgments he articulated. Rhetoric for the clever Sophists was all about persuasion, never about what was right or wrong, because judgments of this sort were matters of subjective opinion, not matters of truth. While the Sophists relativized morality, Plato and Aristotle were moral realists who saw the precariousness intrinsic to this line of reasoning. They argued vigorously against ethical conventionalism and nihilism, and insisted on the need for general virtues and specific moral absolutes that were necessary for the good life.[2] Their critics claim however, that these brilliant philosophers failed to adequately take into account the cultural and historical conditioning of human reason.

The philosophical thesis of meta-ethical skepticism alluded to in Schlesinger's essay may seem abstract, but actually has great relevance for the policies of multinational corporations as they extend their operations into foreign countries with different cultures. The key axis of concern revolves around respect and appreciation for cultural diversity. How can multinationals transfer their technologies, strategies, and managerial techniques to these different environments without diluting that country's cultural integrity? But by far the most vexing question is whether multinationals should adapt to the local culture or seek to reform that culture when its moral and social norms appear to be deficient. Does a European manager export high safety standards to Thailand if the workers in his plant, and perhaps even the Thai government, resist those standards? There seems to be something wrong with exporting one's home-country standards around the world, but are there some occasions where the host country's norms should not be followed because they undermine the common good? Hovering over this practical consideration that has surfaced for many multinationals is the theoretical issue of cultural moral relativism. Are there absolute and universal values that apply in every cultural context, or are moral values historically and culturally conditioned? Is moral relativism an excusable pretext for corporate self-interest or a legitimate response to cultural diversity?

It seems essential to clarify these demanding questions, even if we cannot completely resolve them. If relativism is really a plausible theory, if there are no objective and cross-cultural values, moral discourse between cultures becomes pointless and futile, an interminable exchange of subjective opinions. More importantly, if morality itself differs by culture and country, it is impossible to defend the validity of global ethical standards for multinationals operating across borders. When moral dilemmas arise, their response can only be to follow the well-known maxim "when in Rome do as the Romans do." But this approach is unsettling and cannot be easily defended when the "Romans" are engaged in acts that abuse basic human rights. Should retailers sourcing apparel and other goods from India accept forced child labor as part of this country's cultural reality? Hence we must explore more deeply the premises and rationale for relativism which, if accepted, would imply that even the most foundational ethical ideals cannot be applied in cross-cultural contexts. But we begin this clarification by looking first at the issue of cultural diversity and how this factors into corporate decisions about morality.

Cultural Diversity and its Challenges

Investing abroad is always a risky affair. Aside from the specter of economic risks, there are political and ethical risks that virtually always accompany foreign direct investment (FDI). In crossing borders, firms encounter alien practices, policies, and cultures, along with a different set of moral norms and laws. One author tersely expresses this experience as "the liability of foreignness."[3] The extent of this liability correlates to the distance between the multinational's home country and the host country where it chooses to make an investment. According to Ghemawat, there are four dimensions of this "distance:" political, geographic, economic, and cultural. Each type of distance can affect businesses in different but dramatic ways.[4]

Political distance is created by an absence of colonial ties between countries along with the absence of a shared monetary and political association. The power dynamics of the Communist government in China is markedly different from democratic governments, and this difference adds complexity for Western firms doing business in China. Political distance is also fostered by policies that create barriers to foreign investment, such as tariffs and trade quotas. Geographic distance is increased by physical remoteness and major climate differences along with weak transportation and communications infrastructure. American and European companies, for example, have not had an easy time of expanding into the desolate and frigid region of Siberia. The International Paper Co., headquartered in Memphis, Tennessee, entered into a joint venture in the Siberian city of Bratsk in order to harvest logs cheaply. Labor costs are low and there are rail connections to China. However, the company must deal with hazardous weather conditions, such as extreme temperatures that plummet to 65 below zero Fahrenheit.[5] Economic differences include disparities in consumer income and also in the quality of a country's infrastructure and human resources. Cultural distance includes dissimilarities in linguistic heritage, religious or philosophical beliefs, ethical standards, and social norms.[6] There is certainly a major cultural difference between the Sinosphere and the Anglosphere. Cultural affinity, on the other hand, "supercharges communication," and fosters trust.[7]

While we focus to some extent on political and policy issues, our main axis of discussion in the latter chapters of this book is on how the multinational corporation can accommodate this cultural distance by handling differences in ethical and social norms with both moral sensitivity and strategic effectiveness. It's imperative, however, that multinationals do not overcome cultural distance at the expense of human rights and the common good.

Culture is defined as what rational people add to nature by their chosen ways of living, thinking, and acting. Cultures differ and that diversity is a great benefit to the global community. People have diverse gifts, resources, and talents that can enrich their authentic human flourishing. When considering the complex interaction between a local culture and a foreign business, two prominent issues need to be addressed. The first involves the impact of multinational operations and technology on that local culture. How will that technology or marketing campaign effect changes or subvert valid cultural norms that have evolved over generations? The second involves the extent to which a multinational enterprise should adopt the ways and norms of that culture. In effect, as we have suggested, corporations must typically make a difficult choice: *either adapt to new cultural and moral standards or initiate some type of cultural and moral reform, even if it threatens a host country's sovereignty.*

Countries are sometimes prone to regard multinationals suspiciously, as a threat to local cultural values. These corporations are large and powerful entities which are disposed to export foreign values, strange technologies, and foreign management techniques. When Toys 'R' Us wanted to start selling its toys in Japan it was described in ominous terms as the "Black Ship of Kawasaki." The toy store's entry into Japan was seen as a vehicle for the imposition of American cultural values through the sale of American toys and artifacts. "Toys are culture," proclaimed one of Japan's disgruntled toy sellers.[8] Toys 'R' Us' use of the discount retailing format was also seen as a threat to the survival of an important cultural tradition: the small "mom and pop," toy store that provided service and convenience to its customers. At a minimum, the giant toy company has an obligation to be sensitive to the cultural issues connected with the toys and other products it sells in its Japanese stores.

The people in many developing countries have often regarded these large vertically integrated behemoths as an alien external force that will inordinately unsettle or corrupt the local culture. Regrettably, this apprehension became a stark reality in parts of Nigeria for the indigenous tribes who had to contend with the petroleum industry invading their lands. There is little doubt, for example, that Royal Dutch Shell drastically disrupted the native culture of the Ogoni people in the Niger Delta with its drilling operations, which polluted the land and lit the sky through gas flaring. It became far more difficult to farm the land and fish the waterways in accordance with tribal customs under these severe conditions. Saudi Arabia offers another example of the threat rapid industrialization poses to local culture. The Trans-Arabian Pipeline constructed by Aramco, a coalition of American oil companies, interfered with many Bedouin traveling routes, while its oil wells disrupted centuries-old migration patterns. Also, the sudden wealth of this country occupied by indigenous cultural groups clearly frayed the country's delicate social fabric.[9] Unfortunately, multinational corporations have usually been obtuse about the social and cultural changes caused by their investments.

Thus, the potential impact of a multinational operation on a local culture and on the ways of indigenous people is a pertinent normative issue, and it must be a key factor in ethical decision-making. Ideally, this can be managed by the host country's government which can control and restrict a multinational corporation's movements so that cultural concerns are duly respected. Government can also make sure that the investment helps out these indigenous people economically. The African country of Botswana is a good example of this sort of management. This country tightly controls multinationals such as

DeBeers in order to minimize the negative impact on its local culture. Botswana also invests diamond revenues in health care, education, and infrastructure so that all people benefit, not just the ruling elite.

Sometimes Western multinationals may not realize that the cumulative effect of their investments and trade is a steady homogenization of diverse cultures. American entertainment, including music and movies, can easily have a negative impact by exporting American values, such as materialism and individualism, that gradually displace the traditional values of local culture. The proliferation of American luxury goods in poor countries can also contribute to the upending of culture. Sophisticated marketing campaigns built around lifestyle advertising often build demand for fashionable products and shape cultural attitudes. Furthermore the democratic Internet can also be the locus of cultural transformation, as it makes more readily available to the youth of the entire world "sex, drugs, and rock and roll." The Internet flattens traditional borders and boundaries, but some worry that it will also flatten out diverse cultures as well. There are no easy answers for dealing with these disparate effects, but information intermediaries like Google need to take these subtle issues into account. In general, the nature and extent of these threats to cultural traditions varies by country. But multinationals must sincerely assess how their products and marketing campaigns may radically alter consumer tastes and thereby begin to undermine cultural integrity.[10]

A second challenge for the multinational along these lines arises from the conflict between local cultural values and ethical norms, and the norms that guide a multinational which are usually cultivated in its home country. Levi Strauss, maker of the famous Levi's jeans, had developed a mission and aspirations statement to govern its home operations, but when it tried to apply its principles in China it faced intractable problems. Sometimes this conflict can be settled by learning to respect local customs, but in other cases there are profound ethical issues at stake that cannot be easily resolved and that make it difficult to follow the host country's standards.

Consider the experience of technology firms operating abroad where they encounter vastly different free speech standards. These companies often find it difficult to preserve their commitment to open communication and free expression in these contexts where they are instructed by local law to censor different content. When companies refuse to censor objectionable content from their sites they can easily risk a confrontation with the host country's government. In India, both Google and Facebook have been taken to court for not blocking content that is forbidden by an austere Indian censorship law (at least by Western standards). That law prohibits blasphemy, ethnic disparagement, and any threats made to the public order. Google, which owns YouTube, ran afoul of Indian law because it failed to remove a video showing someone relating a Hindu story that had been edited to incorporate obscene language. Google regards YouTube as a vehicle for a broad range of free expression and is not inclined to censor it for blasphemous speech. The company is supported by civil libertarians who object that India's Information Technology Act (2008) represents an unjust stifling of free speech. But others argue that India has a right to set its own free speech standards and that Internet companies must follow the local laws and customs of the land.[11]

Who's right in this debate? Is there a universal right to free expression that Google should seek to respect no matter where it does business, or should it adapt and comply with the letter of the Indian law, which reflects a different cultural tradition? And is there a common principle that companies caught up in such dilemmas can follow? In general, multinationals should probably avoid two extremes. In Enderle's terms they should avoid being cast as the "Empire Type," which exports home-country values to any context, usually without any adjustment and concern for negative consequences. It would be a mistake, for example, to assume that people in an Islamic culture would want to adopt liberal, Western views about permissible interactions between men and women. Similarly, multinationals should eschew the "Foreign Country Type," which adjusts its policies to whatever is morally acceptable within a given culture. For this type of company there is nothing to limit the "moral free space" of the host country culture.[12] But is it really possible for companies like Google to stake out an acceptable middle ground between these polarities?

How we address the sensitive matter of adjustment to a country's different cultural and ethical standards turns on the philosophical issue of relativism. Perhaps there is some benefit to the Foreign Country Type. Its pluralistic philosophy at least seems to overcome the trap of ethnocentrism, which insists on subtly coercing other people to conform to our beliefs and values. In addition, companies sometimes face internal and external pressures to behave abroad as if they were confirmed cultural relativists, operating according to prevailing local standards by respecting all of the values, beliefs, and practices of other cultures. But can actions and policies contingent on cultural standards be morally justified if normative relativism is not philosophically tenable? With these questions in mind, we turn to a theoretical treatment of normative relativism and ethical pluralism.

Moral Relativism

Moral relativism has several different permutations, so sometimes it is difficult to know what a person means when he or she uses this term. In its most extreme form, relativism denies that there are any universal basic moral demands and supposes that morality can differ at the level of each individual person. Different people are subject to different moral demands, depending upon many factors, including the customs, practices, belief systems, and values that they accept.[13]

Thus, the theory of individual ethical relativism presumes that the good is not necessarily the same for all persons. Each of us has different beliefs and sentiments about the moral good, although often those beliefs overlap. However, the relativist opines, who are we to question another person's experience or perception about what is good. The individual person is "free" to determine for herself what is good or evil. "Man is the measure of all things," said the ancient philosopher Protagoras, so the good is whatever a person declares it to be. In similar terms, the Romantic writer Johann Herder claimed that each individual is his "own measure" for how to live and how to behave.[14] Accordingly, each moral agent is the standard bearer and the source of his or her own particular moral code. In summary, the thesis of relativism as it is generally understood could be formulated this way: If someone believes that it is right (or wrong) to do A, then it is right (or wrong) for him to do A.[15]

Relativists of this stripe argue, therefore, that morality is purely a matter of personal preference. Morality is reduced to individual, subjective opinion, and what is right for one person may be wrong for someone else. Relativists typically claim empirical support for this viewpoint by citing the plentiful evidence of moral diversity in society—if people cannot agree even on critical moral issues like abortion, euthanasia, and human cloning, how could there possibly be any single moral truth? The frequency of ethical disagreement and conflict about basic moral issues seems to undermine the possibility of objective moral truth to which *all* can give their assent. In a universe where man is the measure of all things the best one can hope for is to make agreements with others to arrive at some social conventions to which the majority can assent, at least provisionally.

Much of the recent momentum for ethical relativism emanates from postmodern philosophy. Postmodernism is notoriously difficult to define, but Lyotard characterizes this movement as an "incredulity toward metanarratives."[16] Postmodernists like Lyotard and Derrida rebuke the grand narrative, that is, any attempt to find a totalizing or systematic explanation of reality. There is no room in their philosophy for some universal set of norms or standards of belief and practice that goes beyond anyone's individual, idiosyncratic narrative. Even more moderate versions of postmodernism are committed to these principles. They are suspicious of the motives behind universal theories and skeptical that an overarching moral theory articulating the requirements of justice for all humanity could ever be validated. As Zygmunt Bauman writes, "the foolproof—universal and unshakably founded—ethical code will never be found . . . and ethics that is [*sic*] universal and 'objectively founded' is a practical impossibility."[17]

The postmodern tradition, therefore, has given ethical relativism new voice and vogue and lent support to an ideology of radical pluralism. There is actually a two-pronged attack on traditional morality that is inspired by this philosophy. First, there is an attack on the metaphysical assumptions of moral philosophy, such as the existence of common humanity as the ground of universal human rights. According to the postmodern paradigm, there is no fixed or common human nature to serve as the foundation of any universal morality, such as one based on natural rights. Nor are there essential truths about human flourishing and rationality to provide a theoretical support for such a morality. Philosophers like Rorty contend that there is no theoretical grounding for human rights because there is no theoretical foundation for any system of beliefs or values.[18] Second, this philosophy fosters an abiding skepticism about the possibility of an objective moral system that expresses the basic requirements of justice for all humanity. That skepticism has implanted itself in modern culture where it is expressed as a non-judgmental stance on the whole spectrum of moral issues. Hence a foundationalist and universal ethic, a system that tries to explain right and wrong in terms of the natural law, or some other unifying principle such as natural rights, is considered suspect and invalid.

The bottom line is that people have a plurality of preferences and desires, and those preferences constitute the only reasonable basis of morality. According to the relativist, the simple truth is that our moral beliefs do not provide evidence of any independent realm of values and moral obligations.[19] Those who favor relativism claim that objectivism has a tragic flaw because it is too dogmatic and has failed to give enough attention to the "politics of difference" and the potential for defining one's own moral and social identity.[20] Multiculturalism, therefore, which inspires a more pluralistic approach to morality, is preferable to the moral certitudes of a shallow objectivism which asserts that there is a single set of moral truths for all men and women.

Thus, the relativist claims that any form of moral absolutism or universalism is false and unproveable. Indeed, all the empirical evidence points to the contrary. There is no ideal moral code or moral law that applies to everyone. There are no moral demands that everyone has a sufficient reason to follow, regardless of their customs and cultural experiences.[21] As a result, there is no normative foundation for society's laws, because law is only a social fact of power and practice.[22] We are left with the reduction of morality to our immediate desires, personal preferences, and subjective opinions. As Mackie concludes, there is nothing that is in truth either good or bad; rather, "'good' and 'evil' are words which express only the relation of things to the speaker's desires."[23]

Cultural Relativism

The most popular form of relativism, however, is somewhat less extreme. It is known as cultural ethical relativism. The normative cultural relativist argues that morality is more than an individual's subjective opinion. There are some durable social values that go beyond individual preference, but they are relative to a given culture. Different cultures have different moral norms or standards, and a person's moral obligation is to conform to the norms of his or her culture. What's right, therefore, is always measured in terms of social custom and cultural tradition. Far more people are sympathetic to this view of morality than the more radical view of individual relativism. As Rachels explains, "This line of thought has probably persuaded more people to be skeptical about ethics than any single thing."[24]

There are two levels or versions of cultural relativism. The first level is descriptive cultural relativism, which states that moral values and practices differ in a significant way from one culture or social group to another. These differences generate deep-seated moral disputes that cannot be rationally resolved.[25] Descriptive relativism is not a philosophical thesis but an anthropological one, because it is based on making scientific generalizations about a certain culture. Some anthropologists, like Ruth Benedict, are convinced of this thesis: "Morality differs in every society, and is a convenient term for socially approved habits."[26] Similarly, Herskovits asserts that cultural relativism is the logical consequence of recognizing the "enculturative conditioning in shaping thought and behavior."[27] How significant and deep are these differences? This is an empirical question about which there has been much debate and disagreement. The strong version of descriptive relativism argues that these differences are fundamental. Weaker versions claim that while there are clearly moral differences on the surface, there is some underlying agreement on core moral beliefs (such as the sanctity of life). What all versions of descriptive cultural relativism have in common is their neutrality regarding the moral principles or norms under consideration. It makes no judgments about the suitability or validity of those norms.[28]

Support for the thesis of descriptive relativism is complicated by the heterogeneity that often exists within particular cultures. Regional variations in social customs make it difficult sometimes to determine whether or not there is true cultural consensus for a moral practice. It is not so easy to construct a reliable description of the moral practice of an entire culture, a description that would warrant a valid judgment juxtaposing one culture's moral beliefs with those of other cultures.[29]

Normative cultural relativism goes beyond descriptive cultural relativism. It contends that whatever moral standards happen to prevail in a given culture have their own validity. Moral judgments are relativized not to the individual but to each culture's prevalent ethical standards. If Filipinos believe that euthanasia is always morally wrong, then euthanasia is morally wrong within the Philippines. But if Canadians are convinced that euthanasia is morally acceptable, then it is morally right within Canada. Thus, the same kind of act may be right within one society and wrong in another. Culture, rather than the individual person, is now the measure of all things. As Herskovits explains, moral evaluations "are relative to the cultural background out of which they arise."[30] Beyond cultural consensus, there is no independent or objective criterion to determine what is morally right or wrong. Everything depends on the social context. Although normative cultural relativism does not follow logically from descriptive relativism, it does rely on the latter as intellectual support for its arguments.

In summary, the doctrine of normative cultural ethical relativism asserts that the moral rightness or wrongness of actions varies from one society to another, and that there are no absolute universal moral standards binding on all people at all times; this doctrine also affirms that whether or not it is right for an individual to act in a certain way is contingent on the society to which he or she belongs.[31] There is no transcultural, objective standard of morality, no transcendent set of principles that can be invoked to judge one society's moral norms as superior or preferable to another's. Therefore, there is no basis to judge a culture's beliefs and norms to be inferior in ways that might even present a formidable threat to the global common good.

Ethicists who embrace this philosophy tend to regard moral norms on the same level as custom and social convention. Like customs, moral norms are "prescriptive"—they are cultural action guides that prescribe certain behavior and tell us what to do. The authority of a moral norm is equivalent to the authority of local customs. It logically follows, therefore, that ethical norms and judgments can have only local validity. They are distinct from the propositions of mathematics and natural science, which have universal validity.[32] Just as the customs of Japan are not followed in the United States, the same could be said for the ethical norms of Japan, which are based on Japanese tradition and values and therefore have validity and normative force only within Japan. The repudiation of moral objectivism implies that moral disputes between cultures are fundamentally irreducible and irresolvable.

Another implication of normative cultural relativism is the need for tolerance. The virtue of tolerance sensitizes us to cultural and *moral* differences that deserve our recognition and respect. Just as the visitor to a foreign country must adapt her behavior to take into account that country's customs, so too that visitor must adapt to their ethical norms. It is arrogance to imperiously judge the normative codes of conduct of other cultures and demand that this code be changed to conform to our way of doing things. This is the fatal error of ethnocentrism. Paradoxically, for some relativists, tolerance becomes an objective and transcultural moral standard.

Normative cultural relativism surely has its problems and inconsistencies, as we will see in the next section. But we should never discount the need for an attitude of openness or tolerance when dealing with other cultures, no matter how diverse they may be. Multinationals can also learn a great deal from other cultures. The real challenge is discerning how to respect cultural diversity without tolerating or accommodating injustice.

Evaluating Cultural Relativism

The doctrine of normative cultural relativism continues to be highly esteemed in some intellectual circles, thanks in part to its linkage with multiculturalism and the deconstruction of objectivism. But is this a tenable theory and is it logically warranted? The theory is certainly attractive and seems to be a remedy for the dogmatism of ethnocentrism. Respect for ethical pluralism and diversity, some argue, is the key to social order, cooperation, and world harmony. A lack of sensitivity to cultural concerns can sometimes be embedded in the mentality of the multinational enterprise, so perhaps endorsing this thesis of relativism can promote greater respect for cultural diversity.

However, while normative cultural relativism has not lost its salience or superficial attractiveness, it is difficult to see how it can withstand critical scrutiny. The objections against normative cultural relativism are powerful, and supporters have been able to mount only a thin defense. The principal argument against this thesis is that the relativist has to tolerate any behavior as morally acceptable, so long as it conforms to a cultural consensus and constitutes part of a society's normative code of conduct. But are supporters of this theory really prepared to accept its brutally harsh ramifications? Some cultures, for example, may well believe that a campaign of genocide against some disabled segment of the population, or some ethnic minority, is morally warranted based on the premise that these individuals are sub-human. Unfortunately, this is not just a remote possibility. The progression of history has been correctly referred to by Hegel as a "slaughter bench," where people are continually sacrificed for some elusive "greater good."[33] As we have seen, genocide has been so justified in Nazi Germany and elsewhere. As one author explains, German culture (though certainly not all Germans) saw itself as "liberated from such 'outmoded' concepts as pity and Christianity," and it viewed humanity "sorted into a table of races, with Aryans and Nordics at the top and Jews and Slavs consigned to the status of vermin."[34] The German elite believed that they were caught up in a life and death struggle for racial superiority and so embarked on its campaign to purge the world of the Jewish race.

How could anyone accept such warped reasoning that gave rise to this "new morality" of Nazi Germany? Yet the relativist, whose own culture would assuredly reject such ideas, cannot reasonably object. Otherwise he would be imposing his own culture's moral code on Nazi Germany, which is incompatible with normative cultural relativism. Instead he must tolerate this difference in moral opinion, no matter how repulsive he finds it. The central problem is that there is no universal and transcendent moral truth to which he can appeal in order to demonstrate why another culture's moral beliefs and practices are woefully misguided. The consistent relativist cannot raise his or her voice in disagreement or protest, since modern German culture alone determines right and wrong. If a consensus within this particular culture has determined that genocide and ethnic cleansing are warranted as part of the Darwinian struggle for survival, these practices become morally valid within that culture.

In her reflections on normative cultural relativism, Mary Midgely has called attention to the reprehensible practices of the Samurai warriors in Japan. The highly skilled Samurai had to slice through their victim with a single stroke or he would botch his effort and offend the Emperor. The sword needed to be tested, and these tests were performed on expendable wayfarers to ensure that the sword worked perfectly. This practice was accepted in Japanese culture as part of the martial Samurai heritage, but are we prepared to tolerate the killing of innocent wayfarers in the name of efficiency and honor? Once again, the sincere relativist cannot find any basis to raise an objection. Midgley concludes that the sort of "moral isolationism" prescribed by cultural relativism amounts to erecting isolating barriers between cultures that blocks praise or blame.[35]

These arguments might begin to convert some aspiring relativists, who will draw the line at the taking of innocent life, and concede that there have to be some universal moral standards, even fairly specific standards, however minimal they may be. Otherwise the consistent relativist has to accept all sorts of extreme behavior as morally permissible, including torture, slavery, rape, and so forth. The need to tolerate this behavior in the name of cultural consensus underscores the implausibility and irrationality of normative cultural relativism.

In addition, if morality is no more than dominant social customs or the prevailing cultural preferences, most forms of productive moral dissent become meaningless and incoherent. The only source of normativity is the culture's assertion of what is right and wrong. The conscientious individual has no recourse if he or she disagrees with that assessment. On what grounds can such an individual validly contest the cultural norms ratified in his particular culture if there is no higher morality or some objective, transcultural standard to which he can appeal? Without higher moral principles it's not possible for those within a society to constructively criticize and assess its moral code. When Martin Luther King Jr. fought so valiantly against discriminatory practices that had become part of American law and woven into its cultural fabric, he appealed to a higher, universal law, the natural law which proclaims that all men and women are equal in their dignity and deserve the same treatment. But this sort of dissent or civil disobedience lacks any intelligibility in the world of normative cultural relativism.

A related problem with cultural relativism is its incompatibility with the notion of moral progress. How can we argue that a particular culture has achieved either moral progress or regression if we have no common yardstick by which to make such a judgment? It would be impossible to judge our own historic culture as a good one and to measure its social and moral progress, if there are no objective and transcultural standards of comparison. The best we can do is to criticize a society for not living up to the normative ideals it has chosen, but the ideals themselves cannot be criticized.[36]

Finally, cultural relativism is inattentive to the compelling philosophical arguments supporting our common humanity. The inescapable truth is that despite cultural and ethnic diversity we are all essentially similar as rational human beings. Skeptics and postmodernists may scoff at this line of reasoning. But if there is no human species and every human being is unique in kind we are vulnerable to the human rights abuses that often emerge from a separatist and racist mentality that sees superficial differences such as skin color as the mark of superiority. On the other hand, if we accept the highly credible assumption of a universally shared humanity that expresses itself in many cultural forms, we can quickly deduce that there must be *some* substantive, universal goods that we all seek out, such as friendship and knowledge. According to the philosopher, Philippa Foot,

> Granted that it is wrong to assume identity of aim between people of different cultures; nevertheless there is a great deal that all men have in common. All need affection, the cooperation of others, a place in the community, and help in trouble. It isn't true to suppose that human beings can flourish without these things—being isolated, despised or embattled, or without courage or hope. We are not therefore simply expressing values that we happen to have if we think of some moral systems as good moral systems and others as bad. Communities as well as individuals can live wisely or unwisely, and this is largely the result of their values and the codes of behavior that they teach. Looking at these societies, and critically also at our own, we surely have some idea of how thing[s] work out and they work out as they do.[37]

Some philosophers would go deeper than Foot by arguing for a rational nature as the metaphysical basis to our common humanity and profound equality. We cannot address this debate here, but surely our existential experience bears out Professor Foot's balanced conclusions about our shared humanity along with a common normative code of conduct that supports the needs and aspirations of all human persons. In addition, the notion of a common human nature is not confined to the Western philosophical tradition. The Confucian tradition gives prominence to the notion of *ren* or humanity, and some Chinese scholars regard the Mencian concept of common humanity as a critical link between classical Confucian philosophy and modern human rights discourse.[38]

Of course, any postulation of a common humanity and universal goods defies the popular postmodern paradigm. Challenging the postmodern critique that has provided such strong support for moral conventionalism and nihilism is well beyond the limited scope of this book. But let it suffice to say that we should not be intimidated by postmodernity's renunciation of objective truth and objective morality. The denial of metanarratives seems to refute itself since that very denial and its rationale is also a metanarrative, articulating a truth presumably universal in its significance. When these philosophers claim that there is no truth, either they are claiming to inform us of a truth, what really *is* the case, or their assertion is also culturally, historically, and linguistically conditioned such that this statement too is relativized, just another opinion that need not really concern us.[39] As Bernard Williams has observed, the postmodern skeptic "holds up before the reader's lens a sign saying that something is true or plausible or worth considering, and then tries to vacate the spot before the shutter clicks."[40]

Yet, even in the face of these potent criticisms, extreme cultural relativism still has its vocal defenders. However, it has arguably not succeeded so well as a sound philosophical doctrine since few philosophers are willing to follow this line of reasoning to its logical conclusion of pure moral nihilism. Far more plausible and defensible is the more nuanced doctrine of modified cultural relativism. This thesis maintains that there are at least some cross-cultural norms, some common elements of morality, though there is a large gray area where cultures disagree over what is right and wrong. There are certain universal moral rules or rights that apply to all nations and peoples. The key question is not whether there are objective cross-cultural norms that constrain the behavior of all international agents (including multinational corporations), but what is the content and scope of those obligations?[41]

Donaldson and Dunfee prefer to speak about these cross-cultural objective standards as "hypernorms," which represent the norms by which all others are to be judged. Hypernorms constitute a "thin universal morality," but they also respect intercultural diversity by setting broad parameters for a "moral free space."[42] They argue for procedural hypernorms such as the "right of voice," structural hypernorms such as the right to property (which may be defined differently by different societies), and substantive hypernorms such as respect for human dignity and promise-keeping. While these various hypernorms might reflect what human beings tend to have in common, they are not grounded in human nature. Rather, they depend on "widespread consensus:" conformity with global industry standards, conformity with the standards of regional government organizations, and a general consistency with the precepts of major religions and philosophies. This approach is pluralistic in its acceptance of a broad range of ethical viewpoints that may be chosen by a culture, yet it rejects the relativistic notion that any cultural norm is routinely permissible.[43]

This pluralistic moral philosophy supports a minimal set of universally biding moral principles as an antidote to moral relativism, and it recognizes the need for an appropriate balance between "ethical universality" and the "cultural particularity," that is ignored by normative cultural relativism. At the same time, it repudiates extreme universalism (or moral absolutism) which argues for a single set of universally binding moral principles that capture and define *all* normative issues of global significance. Hypernorms give some recognition to our shared humanity, while the zone of moral free space respects the unique identity of particular peoples or cultures.[44] Despite the clear advantages of this nuanced theory, it still raises some pressing questions. Is it adequate to ground these universal moral norms in an overlapping consensus when such consensus is always subject to change? Or can we find a stronger basis for a moral objectivism that can serve as a more potent defense against moral nihilism and the hegemony of cultural consensus? In the next chapter we argue for a *moderate universalism*, a set of universal natural rights that express *many* normative issues of global significance, grounded not in overlapping consensus but in fundamental human goods. This perspective is less pluralistic than the theory proposed by Dunfee and Donaldson, since it offers a thick set of natural trans-cultural rights and rejects some ethical theories as unworkable or impractical. Nonetheless, there is still some room for moral free space in the interpretation and implementation of these basic rights. Also, when fundamental rights are not at stake, moral decisions can be based on prudential judgments that take cultural factors into account.

Conclusions

Managers and executives of multinational corporations must often confront the reality of moral and cultural diversity when they do business abroad. This is part of the liability of foreignness that makes crossing borders so tenuous, even for well-prepared corporations. The extent of this liability correlates to the distance between the home economy of a multinational and the host economy. There are four dimensions of this "distance:" political, geographic, economic, and cultural. Our primary concern has been cultural distance, which is sometimes exceedingly difficult to bridge.

Multinationals must assess the effects of their transactions on the integrity of local cultures and factor this assessment into their strategic decisions. Corporate strategies should always reflect a suitable appreciation for cultural diversity. A more daunting challenge for multinationals is how to deal with the normative diversity that can exist between two different cultures. Multinationals often find themselves in awkward situations where the moral norms in the host country conflict with their own moral standards and the standards of their home country. Yahoo, for example, must contend with a Chinese government that wants to control free expression on its email platform. Should Yahoo adapt to the host country's norms or should the Internet company abide by its own standards, even if it means imposing its own morality in another cultural context? While this is a matter of intense debate, most people would probably agree that companies should avoid two obvious extremes. According to one extreme, caricatured as the Empire Type, the multinational always exports home country values regardless of the consequences. At the other extreme, called the Foreign Country Type, the multinational always adapts its standards to host-country values, even if those values entail human rights violations. Responsible multinationals will stake out a more reasonable middle ground that acknowledges the local community's prerogative to set its own moral standards, while recognizing that there are limits to such local sovereignty.

In order to appreciate the theoretical underpinnings of these practical questions, we explored in some depth the issue of moral relativism, especially the more popular form of cultural relativism. Descriptive cultural relativism asserts that moral values and practices differ in a significant way from one culture or social group to another and that these differences generate irreducible moral disagreements. Our main concern has been the topic of normative cultural relativism which insists that moral rightness or wrongness differs from one society or culture to another and that prevailing moral standards are equally valid. There are no universal moral standards, only a cultural consensus on what is right or wrong. We demonstrated the philosophical problems with this approach since it implies that any behavior, no matter how indecent or extreme, is morally permissible so long as it meets with cultural approval. Far more intellectually coherent is the thesis of modified cultural relativism, which acknowledges a minimal set of moral standards that have normative force across different cultures. Those standards can be expressed in terms of hypernorms that constitute some limits on cultural consent. Instead of this more pluralistic approach, we prefer a moderate universalism that sees morality in terms of basic goods and the natural rights that protect those goods. Multinational corporations can rely on these fundamental rights as a moral compass for dealing with the conflicting claims of contending cultures.

Moral systems predicated on a minimal normative code of hypernorms or even on a strong set of universal natural rights are not attempting to negate cultural differences or promote dogmatic ethnocentric standards that will homogenize diverse cultures. Rather, they seek to recognize and respect both cultural particularity and universal humanity. The challenge for the fair-minded multinational corporation and its managers is to combine respect for people in their cultural diversity with a steadfast refusal to tolerate any injustice. Cultural diversity does not deserve respect when it appears to manifest itself as ethnic cleansing, forced labor, or torture.[45] To be sure, this is difficult terrain even for the most savvy and nimble multinational enterprise.

Notes

1 Arthur Schlesinger, "The Opening of the American Mind," *New York Times Book Review*, July 23, 1989, 1, 26–7.
2 Despite the claims of some contemporary Aristotelian scholars, Aristotle, who described virtue as the capacity to choose the intermediate or the mean between the vices of defect or excess, was particularly clear that certain actions are always wrong. According to Aristotle: "But not every action nor every passion admits of a mean; for some have names that already imply badness, e.g., spite, shamelessness, envy, and in the case of actions, adultery, theft, murder. It is not possible, then, ever to be right with regard to them; one must always be wrong." *Nicomachean Ethics* trans. William Ross, John Ackrill, and W. Urmson (Oxford: Oxford University Press, 1934), 2.6.
3 S. Zaheer, "Overcoming the Liability of Foreignness," *Academy of Management Journal* 38 (1995): 341–63. See also Geoffrey Jones, *Multinationals and Global Capitalism* (Oxford: Oxford University Press, 2005), 4–6.
4 Pankaj Ghemawat, "Distance Still Matters: The Hard Reality of Global Expansion," *Harvard Business Review*, Sept–Oct (2001): 138–52.
5 James Hagerty and Paul Sonne, "Paper Titan's Big Bet Hits a Frosty Siberia," *The Wall Street Journal*, July 17, 2013, A1, A12.
6 Ghemawat, "Distance Still Matters," 140–6.
7 "The Power of Tribes," *The Economist*, January 28, 2012, 68.
8 David Turner, "Toys 'R' Us Goes to Japan," *The Wall Street Journal*, February 7, 1990, B1.
9 Daniel Litvin, *Empires of Profit* (New York: Texere, 2003), 192–5.
10 See John Kline, *Ethics for International Business* 2nd ed. (New York: Routledge, 2010), 195–8.
11 Amol Sharma, "Google, Facebook Fight India Censors," *The Wall Street Journal*, March 18, 2012, B1–2.
12 George Enderle, "What is International? A Topology of International Spheres and its Relevance for Business Ethics," Paper presented at the annual meeting of the International Association of Business and Society, Austria, July, 1995. See also Thomas Donaldson and Thomas Dunfee, *Ties*

that Bind: A Social Contract Approach to Business Ethics (Boston: Harvard Business School Press, 1999), 217–20.
13 Gilbert Harman, "Is there a Single True Morality," in *Moral Relativism: A Reader*, ed. Paul Moser and Thomas Carson (New York: Oxford University Press, 2001), 165–84.
14 Johann Herder, *Herders Sämtliche Werke*, ed. Bernard Suphan 15 volumes (Berlin: Weidmann, 1913), vol. 13, 291.
15 Richard Brandt, "Ethical Relativism," in *Moral Relativism*, 26.
16 Jean-Francois Lyotard, *The Post-Modern Condition: A Report on Knowledge* (Minneapolis, MN: University of Minnesota Press, 1984), xix.
17 Zygmunt Bauman, *Life in Fragments: Essays in Postmodern Morality* (Cambridge: Blackwell, 1995), 8.
18 Michael Freeman, *Human Rights* (Cambridge: Polity Press, 2011), 62.
19 Harman, "Is there a Single True Morality?," 170.
20 Charles Taylor, *Multiculturalism and the Politics of Recognition: An Essay by Charles Taylor* (Princeton, NJ: Princeton University Press, 1992), 42.
21 Harman, "Is there a Single True Morality?," 172.
22 According to Coleman and Leiter, "what counts as law in any particular society is fundamentally a matter of social fact or convention." See Jules Coleman and Brian Leiter, "Legal Positivism," in *A Companion to Philosophy of Law and Legal Theory* ed. Dennis Patterson (Oxford: Oxford University Press, 1996), 241. See also John Finnis, "Natural Law Theories," *Stanford Encyclopedia of Philosophy* at http://plato.standord.edu/entries/natural-law-theories (accessed March 14, 2013).
23 J.L. Mackie, *Hume's Moral Theory* (London: Routledge & Kegan Paul, 1980), 150.
24 James Rachels, "The Challenge of Cultural Relativism," in *Moral Relativism*, 55.
25 Michelle Moody-Adams, *Fieldwork in Familiar Places* (Cambridge: Harvard University Press, 1997), 15.
26 Ruth Benedict, *Patterns of Culture* (Boston, MA: Houghton Mifflin, 1934), 223.
27 Melville Herskovits, *Cultural Relativism: Perspectives in Cultural Pluralism* (New York: Random House, 1972), 32. See also Moody-Adams, *Fieldwork in Familiar Places*, 99.
28 Kenneth Goodpaster, "Note on Relativism in Ethics," in *Polices and Persons* Supplement eds. Kenneth Goodpaster, John Matthews, Laura Nash (New York: McGraw-Hill, 1991), 358–66. See also Richard Brandt, "Ethical Relativism," in *Moral Relativism*, 25–31.
29 Moody-Adams, *Fieldwork in Familiar Places*, 103.
30 Melville Herskovits, *Man and his Works* (New York: Knopf, 1948), 63.
31 John Ladd, *Ethical Relativism* (New York: Wadsworth, 1973), 1.
32 Goodpaster, "Note on Relativism in Ethics," 360–1.
33 Georg W. F. Hegel, *Die Vernunft in der Geschichte* ed. J. Hoffmeister (Hamburg: Niemeyer, 1955), 80.

34 Roger Moorhouse, "The League of Races," Review of *The SS: A New History*, *Financial Times*, July 24, 2011, F3.
35 Mary Midgley, "On Trying Out One's New Sword," in *Heart and Mind* (New York: St. Martin's Press, 1981), 69–75.
36 Rachels, "The Challenge of Cultural Relativism," 58.
37 Phillipa Foot, "Moral Relativism," in *Moral Relativism*, 195–6. See also Steven Rockefeller's "Comment," in *Multiculturalism and the Politics of Recognition*, 87–98.
38 See Grace Kao, *Grounding Human Rights in a Pluralist World* (Washington, D.C.: Georgetown University Press, 2011), 24–5. See also Irene Bloom, "Fundamental Intuitions and Consensus Statements: Mencian Confucianism and Human Rights," in *Confucianism and Human Rights* ed. Wm. Theodore De Bary and Tu Weiming (New York: Columbia University Press, 1998), 94–116.
39 See W. Norris Clarke, *Explorations in Metaphysics* (Notre Dame: University of Notre Dame Press, 1994), 154–5.
40 Bernard Williams, *Truth and Truthfulness: An Essay in Genealogy* (Princeton, NJ: Princeton University Press, 2002), 19.
41 Thomas Donaldson, *The Ethics of International Business* (New York: Oxford University Press, 1989), 17–18. See Donaldson's insightful discussion of normative cultural relativism, which influenced my own views on this subject.
42 Donaldson and Dunfee, *Ties that Bind*, 43.
43 Donaldson and Dunfee, *Ties that Bind*, 49–82.
44 Donaldson and Dunfee, *Ties that Bind*, 79.
45 See John Finnis, "Virtue and the Constitution of the United States," *Fordham Law Review* 69 (2001): 1596. I am indebted to Finnis' analysis of civic virtue for helping me formulate some of the issues in this chapter.

4

LAW, ETHICS, AND CORPORATE SOCIAL RESPONSIBILITY

Introduction

Multinational corporations (MNCs) are the primary drivers of globalization. Their investments have created many positive effects, including higher employment, and accelerated transfers of technology and management skills. As we have seen, however, these corporations have sometimes acted without restraint. The result has been a series of ethical morasses that have damaged corporate reputations and cast a shadow over global capitalism itself. These scandals range from bribery and corruption to unsafe sweatshops and environmental degradation. To the casual observer, the multinational corporation seems to be an entity with unchecked and limitless power, an amoral "empire of profit" which seeks to extend its tentacles into foreign countries to exploit workers and find incremental markets for its goods. Critics of multinationals worry with good reason over the scope and reach of these sprawling organizations that often seem obsessed with lowering costs through finding cheap labor. It is not uncommon to see multinationals castigated as "increasingly rapacious" and predatory.[1] As Barnet and Muller presciently opined decades ago, the MNC is "the most powerful human organization yet devised for colonizing the future."[2]

While some multinational corporations have acted responsibly abroad by investing in green technologies and attending to the needs of the workforce, there is room for significant progress. Corporate social responsibility may be a matter of enlightened self-interest, nothing more than good business practice that can contribute to a corporation's competitive advantage. However, it is still instructive to think about that responsibility in terms of constraints on the wealth-creating activities of the multinational enterprise. In this chapter we review those constraints that take the form of legal and moral obligations. Some might argue that the law is a sufficient guide to responsible behavior, a worthy surrogate for corporate integrity. But there are often legal and regulatory vacuums, especially in developing countries; hence the need for ethical self-regulation and a corporate ideology of solidarity. In the previous chapter we demonstrated the logic and credibility of moral objectivism. It is possible to speak intelligibly of hypernorms or universal natural rights that are not culture-specific. We now consider more specifically the moral expectations for multinationals which operate so extensively outside their home country's borders. Above all, multinational corporations, like all moral agents, have an obligation to do no harm to anyone. Behind the concept of harm lies the more fundamental concept of human good, and goods need to be protected by rights.

Thus, we claim that the best avenue for specifying the obligation to do no harm is respect for basic human rights and the correlative duties associated with those rights. Given this premise, we lay out a modest list of rights that is neither thick nor thin, but moderate and adequate to ensure the most basic requirements of international justice. We also verify the necessity of those rights for protecting intrinsic human goods. Universal human rights must ultimately depend on human equality that derives from our membership of the human species. Therefore, these rights are most cogently grounded in a theory called the new natural law, which addresses the features of human reality that make us equal to one another.

Finally, it is important to briefly consider the extent of a corporation's social responsibility beyond common decency and respect for basic human rights. Should a multinational enterprise also have a social agenda and aspire to even higher levels of corporate goodness? Specifically, should it be concerned about social justice issues such as distributive inequities and should it contribute resources to rectify those inequities?

Legal and Moral Obligations

All corporations have three basic duties: to create value and wealth for their stakeholders, to follow society's laws and regulations, and to observe ethical standards of justice and decency. This triad of responsibilities creates a framework within which executives and corporate CEOs are expected to govern their organizations and develop strategies for sustainable competitive advantage. The first obligation is to create wealth or value in the marketplace. According to traditional economics, value is added by creating the biggest differential possible between willingness to pay for a product and the cost of the supplies needed to make that product. Corporations must be adept in creating value and appropriating that value or they will be disciplined by the market. If customers are not willing to pay for a company's products, at a price that allows it to make an adequate return on its investment, it cannot prosper and probably will not survive very long. Corporations must also sustain their competitive advantage by counteracting the threats to their value-adding activities. Wealth creation is the primary contribution that the multinational enterprise makes to society.[3]

Multinationals and the Law

These value-added activities must be carried out within the rules of the game, general laws and specific regulations that govern a particular industry. Corporations are legal entities—"artificial persons" in the eyes of the law. Like all persons they are agents, which must follow society's laws. Basic legal requirements of corporations would include honoring contracts, avoiding fraud, and refraining from the payment of bribes. In foreign countries multinational corporations are governed by the national laws of the host country. Thus, if a multinational operates a manufacturing plant in India through a subsidiary, that operation must follow Indian law. Executives welcome law's transparency, but multinationals with operations in many different countries must be prepared to deal with a bewildering array of legal and regulatory frameworks.

In developing countries, laws can be weak and inadequate, or the rule of law arbitrary and unfair. A weak or deficient legal system opens the door for opportunistic behavior. But companies cannot exploit their workers and pillage the environment just because the host country laws are weak or the legal infrastructure has poor enforcement mechanisms. Rather, multinationals must resist such behavior and abide by internal ethical standards that go beyond the external guidance provided by law.

In some cases, home governments will introduce laws or regulations to control the behavior of their firms operating abroad. The United States government was especially apprehensive about the damage being done by American multinational firms engaged in bribery to win foreign contracts. During the 1960s and 1970s, there were countless corruption scandals. United Fruit, for example, made payments to Honduran government officials in order to lower the country's export tax on bananas. In a highly publicized case, Lockheed executives admitted making payments of $12.5 million to Japanese government officials to win a lucrative contract from Nippon Air for its TriStar plane. When word of these bribes leaked out, Lockheed rationalized these payments as an "acceptable" way of doing business in Japan, where bribery was supposedly a common practice. Yet in Japan the payments caused a public scandal, so it is doubtful that this practice was as customary or acceptable as Lockheed had claimed.[4]

As a result of the Lockheed scandal and many others of smaller scale, The Foreign Corrupt Practices Act (FCPA) was passed into law in 1977. The FCPA essentially outlaws the payment of bribes to government officials and political parties. According to this law these companies are prohibited from making payments to "foreign officials" in order to "influence any act or decision of such official in his official capacity . . . [or] inducing such foreign official to use his influence with a foreign government or instrumentality thereof to affect or influence any act or decision of such government . . ."[5] The law applies to any U.S. company, any company listed on the U.S. stock exchange, and to any foreign firms operating on American territory. A later amendment to the law exempts "facilitation payments," that is, small payments made to expedite routine things such as clearing some goods through customs. The problem with this exception is that it's not always clear how facilitation payments differ from a bribe.[6]

Thanks to the impetus provided by the FCPA, many companies have been diligent about eradicating bribery from their overseas operations. Procter & Gamble, for example, closed a Pampers plant in Nigeria rather than pay a bribe to customs inspectors.[7] But there have also been many corruption scandals since the passage of the FCPA, which was not well enforced until the turn of the century. In Indonesia, Monsanto allegedly paid $750,000 to the country's Environment Minister and other officials to persuade them to grant permission to sell its genetically modified seed.[8] In 2008, Siemens AG agreed to pay $800,000 in U.S. fines to settle cases involving the alleged payment of $1 billion in bribes to government officials around the world.[9] And in 2012, Wal-Mart disclosed the likelihood that bribes had been paid to Mexican bureaucrats to smooth the way for expansion of its operations in Mexico.[10]

Critics of the FCPA frequently complain about the high cost of compliance. They also contend that it has put American firms at a disadvantage because other countries do not enforce their laws against bribery, so their multinationals are freer to bribe their way to lucrative contracts. This uneven playing field could mean lost investment and export potential for U.S. firms. But the law, for all its flaws and ambiguities, has a sound moral basis, since bribery is unjust. Bribes and payoffs are a means of getting preferential treatment and creating an unfair advantage. Bribery is also wrong because it often interferes with the fiduciary duty of government officials to act in the best interest of the government or government agency that employs them. A multinational that aspires to integrity and high moral ideals will make sure that it has a clear "no bribery" policy which is properly implemented throughout the organization.

Multinationals are also subject to international laws and regulations. However, since there is an inability among national governments to reach consensus on most issues, there is a lack of codified international law that governs interactions between host governments and multinationals. One of the few examples of multilateral regulation is Trade Related Aspects of Intellectual Property Rights (TRIPS). TRIPS, which harmonizes patent laws as well as other intellectual property standards, is controversial and will be discussed more thoroughly in Chapter Seven. There are also codes of conduct for multinationals such as the guidelines published by the Organization for Economic Cooperation and Development (OECD). These guidelines direct multinationals to refrain from bribery, to avoid any meddling in local politics, and to make contributions to local economies by training employees. But this code is voluntary and not legally binding.[11]

The lack of international law and global standards has prompted victims of multinational transgressions to rely on the arcane Alien Torts Claims Act (ATCA) of 1789. This concise law states that "The district courts shall have original jurisdiction of any civil action by an alien for a tort (civil wrong) only, committed in violation of the law of nations or a treaty of the United States."[12] Previous interpretations of the law allowed non-citizens to sue in U.S. courts for violations of international law that were committed overseas. In 1980, a Paraguayan immigrant successfully used the ATCA to sue a former Paraguayan police officer for torturing and killing her brother in Paraguay. The ATCA was also used to sue Unocal for human rights violations committed during its construction of a pipeline in Burma. However, a recent Supreme Court ruling in a case involving Royal Dutch Shell and Nigeria decided that the statute only covers violations of international law in the United States. But the Court left open the possibility that some acts abroad could so severely "touch and concern the territory of the United States," to thereby "displace the presumption" against the statute's use.[13]

Ethical Standards

Corporations must also abide by moral norms that are not codified in laws or regulations or even in voluntary codes of conduct. Law is reactionary and sometimes fails to protect basic human rights. But a morally responsible multinational is attuned to the demands of justice regardless of what the law allows. As moral agents, corporations can and should be held accountable for moral transgressions that inflict harm on others. Arguably, a multinational that is able to create value while staying within the boundaries of law and morality will be better able to sustain its competitive position in the world, by avoiding scandal and reputational damage.

But what precisely are the moral principles by which moral agents such as corporations should be guided? This is a controversial issue over which philosophers and ethicists have had profound disagreements. It is impossible to consider all of the normative theories of ethics and justice that have been proposed. Instead, we will review only the most prominent theoretical avenues for addressing moral dilemmas in corporate environment.

One immensely popular approach for resolving ethical dilemmas centers on the argument that justice can be expressed by the theory of utilitarianism, sometimes called consequentialism. According to this theory, the right or just course of action is to promote the general good or maximize happiness. The general good can be described in terms of "utility," and this principle of utility is the foundation of morality and the ultimate criterion of right and wrong. The term "utility" simply refers to the net benefits (or good) created by an action. According to Frankena, utilitarianism is the view that:

> the sole ultimate standard of right, wrong and obligation is the *principle of utility* or *beneficence*, which says quite strictly that the moral end to be sought in all that we do is *the greatest possible balance of good over evil* (or the least possible balance of evil over good).[14]

Thus an action or policy is right if it will produce the greatest net benefits or the lowest net costs (assuming that all of the alternatives impose some net cost) for all the parties affected by that action.

Consequentialism turns morality into a pseudo-science. The moral agent typically engages in a cost benefit analysis in order to determine which option would optimize the consequences or produce the greatest net benefits. For example, let's assume that a manager who runs a plant that makes telecommunications equipment is considering outsourcing jobs to cut costs and wants to focus on the moral dimension of that decision. There are two options: outsource jobs to Malaysia and cut production costs by 60 percent or keep the jobs in the U.S. The first option will mean higher profits, more money to invest in R&D, and a more secure future, but it will lead to social costs such as layoffs, hardships for workers and their families, and economic chaos for the local community. The second option will avoid those hardships but the company's high operating cost structure will make it more difficult to compete with Japanese and European companies that have already outsourced many of their jobs. The conscientious manager must weigh all of these diffuse costs and benefits and choose the alternative that maximizes net benefits.

Critics of consequentialism are quick to identify its vulnerabilities, including an insensitivity to basic human rights and justice. There are no intrinsically unjust or immoral acts since any act can be justified if it maximizes the good. When human rights conflict with utility they can be compromised or put aside. Basic liberties, such as freedom of speech, can be suppressed for the sake of the general good. Even an act of torture or rape can be justified if utilitarian calculation demonstrates that it will promote the greater good. There is nothing in utilitarianism that would prevent these abuses from happening, as long as a cogent and objective case is made that the benefits flowing from these moral choices would exceed the costs.

Consequentialism is also fraught with an array of practical problems. How can subjectivism be avoided in the evaluation of consequences? Are managers capable of putting aside self-serving assumptions and prejudices when they engage in a utilitarian calculus? Are they likely to take into account general issues such as the action's contribution to the undermining of trust in society? Moreover, whose interests should be considered in this type of analysis? To what extent should consequences be investigated? How do remote consequences relate to more immediate ones? These questions have vexed proponents of consequentialism for a long time, and yet no satisfactory answers have been forthcoming. As Paine concludes, "for all its aura of objectivity and precision, cost-benefit analysis is highly vulnerable to distortions and biases that cloud the moral issues."[15]

Despite these deficiencies, corporations remain inspired by utilitarian reasoning to justify their strategic plans and policies. However, reliance on this pragmatic form of reasoning led to a *faux pas* for one multinational operating in East Europe. The stigma of cigarette smoking has generally bypassed Eastern European countries, where smoking remains quite popular. When the Czech Republic government announced a big tax increase on cigarette purchases to counter the rising health costs associated with smoking, the U.S. cigarette giant Philip Morris sprang into action. The company commissioned a cost–benefit analysis of the effects of cigarette smoking in the Czech Republic. The study results, which Philip Morris shared with some enthusiasm, showed that smoking actually helped the economy because smokers usually die early and save the government some money. Thus, the study concluded, smoking is actually justified in social welfare terms as it saves society money. Philip Morris was rebuked for relying on this sort of moral reasoning and eventually apologized for implying that smoking was defensible on economic grounds because it saved the taxpayers some money. The Philip Morris case illustrates the pitfalls of deploying the blunt instrument of utilitarian logic in the boardroom when sensitive moral issues are at stake.[16]

A second popular normative framework derives from the philosophy of Immanuel Kant. Kant's "pure moral philosophy" is based on the "common idea of duty." According to Kant, actions only have moral worth when they are done for the sake of duty, not when they optimize consequences. Only the motive of duty bestows moral worth on an action because only then does a moral agent do the right thing for the right reason. But what is our duty? For Kant, the answer is simple. Our moral duty is to follow the moral law, which, like all rational laws, must be universal, since universality represents the common character of rationality and law. And this universal moral law is expressed as the categorical imperative: "I should never act except in such a way that I can also will that my maxim should become a universal law." The imperative is "categorical" because it is unconditional and does not allow for any exceptions.[17]

A "maxim," as referred to in Kant's categorical imperative, is an implied general principle or rule underlying a particular action. If, for example, I usually break my promises, then I act according to the private maxim that promise-breaking is morally acceptable when it is in my best interests to do so. But can one take this maxim and transform it into a universal moral law? As a universal law this particular maxim would be expressed as follows: "It is permissible for everyone to break promises when it is in their best interests to do so." Such a law, however, is invalid since it entails both a pragmatic and a logical contradiction. There is a pragmatic contradiction, because the maxim is self-defeating if it is universalized: if everyone could break promises they would never be made in the first place. The act of breaking a promise without losing credibility can only be accomplished if it is an exception to the rule of promise-keeping. Universal promise-breaking also implies a logical contradiction (like a square circle). A world of universalized promise-breaking is conceptually absurd, and hence inconceivable. In view of the contradictions involved in universalizing promise-breaking we have a perfect duty to keep all of our promises.[18]

Also, from the categorical imperative we can derive other duties, such as the duty to keep contracts, to tell the truth, to avoid injury to others, and to refrain from taking another's property. For example, no one would enter into a contract if he or she believed that the other party had no intention of honoring that contract. Kant maintains that each of these duties is also categorical, admitting of no exceptions, since the maxim underlying such an exception cannot be universalized. Thus, Kant's universalizablity principle, embodied in the categorical imperative, can be used to test the moral legitimacy of specific corporate actions. If such immoral actions "cross a critical threshold, the business institutions that presuppose norms of trustfulness and fairness will become unstable and in extreme circumstances even cease to exist."[19]

Kantianism does not suffer from the sort of soft relativism that undermines utilitarianism. However, this theory has its own peculiar difficulties. Perhaps the most serious problem with Kant's moral philosophy is its rigidity: the absolute norms derived from the categorical imperative allow for no exceptions. Thus, even if lying will prevent injury to someone else, I am still forbidden from doing so, since the maxim, "it's permissible for me to tell a lie," cannot be universalized. According to Kant, "Truthfulness in statements that cannot be avoided is the formal duty of man to everyone, however great the disadvantage that may arise for him or for any other."[20] This lack of flexibility along with the theory's sheer abstractness has probably militated against the more widespread use of this reasoning as a promising avenue for addressing moral issues.

A third approach to ethics focuses on basic human rights. According to this perspective, moral reasoning should be governed by respect for individual rights and a philosophy of fairness. A rights-based analysis of moral dilemmas considers whether a particular action or policy violates an individual's human or legal rights, such as the right to privacy, the right to own property, or the right to subsistence-level wages. And where two rights conflict, ethical reasoning must determine which right should take precedence. In the following section we explain why we favor a rights-based approach, supported by the theory of new natural law, as a productive way of thinking about the moral obligations of multinationals.

Rights: Thick or Thin?

We opt for a rights-based perspective on morality for several reasons. First, a rights-based approach does not suffer from the indeterminacy and complications of utilitarianism. At the same time, it is not rigid and abstract like Kantianism. Managers and policymakers are unlikely to think about their obligations in terms of Kant's categorical imperative or apply his universalizability test every time they face a moral dilemma. The language of rights, on the other hand, is concrete and easily understandable. Rights can serve as an effective instrument for accurately conveying the requirements of justice. According to Lord Bingham, one of the most important criteria for assessing a legal system is whether that system provides adequate protection for fundamental human rights.[21] Moreover, the general thesis that persons have rights coheres with the assumptions of liberal capitalism, which presupposes the rights of economic liberty and property.

Rights language is at the center of many national and international constitutions. Prominently enshrined in the United States Constitution is a Bill of Rights that guarantees every citizen certain rights, such as the right to freedom of speech and religion. The Universal Declaration on Human Rights (UDHR), ratified by the General Assembly of the United Nations in 1948, boldly declares that every human person should be guaranteed certain fundamental rights and freedoms. The U.N.'s declaration on rights has been widely endorsed and it was the model for European Convention for the Protection of Rights and Fundamental Freedoms (1952). Article One of the UDHR declares that all human beings are equal in dignity and rights. The UDHR goes on to stipulate a plethora of basic human rights, such as the right to freedom of movement, the right to be free from slavery and torture, the right to work, the right to own property, and the right to just remuneration. While not everyone may agree with every right on this extensive list, the UDHR warrants our close attention and serious consideration.

Thus, the concept of a right or entitlement quite often serves as the foundation of our moral discourse about complex issues. Rights, provided that they are properly specified, offer an important means for dealing with cross-cultural conflicts. The revival of interest in natural rights, inspired by the United Nations, represented a major shift in world politics. The notion of interdependent and universal human rights, that are not contingent on some aggregate collective good, also opens an avenue for moral reasoning that can resonate with all international moral agents, including multinationals.

However, discussions about rights can sometimes be facile, imprecise, and self-centered. Rights claims have proliferated over the years and some people now argue for all sorts of questionable rights. In addition, sometimes reflecting upon social and moral issues in terms of rights is counterproductive because it obscures complicated issues. To declare that one has a right to a perfectly pristine environment is too simplistic, since it ignores the societal costs of providing such comprehensive protection. This difficulty does not imply that a rights-based approach is fruitless, but only that rights must be adequately specified and properly limited.

Concerns also persist about the validity of universal human rights. Some philosophers argue that rights are a Western invention, and so they cannot be equally applied to all peoples and cultures. According to Fox:

> If we add up China, North Korea, most of Southeast Asia, and the whole Muslim world from Morocco and Nigeria to Indonesia, we have a vast majority of the international community that does not subscribe to the liberal, democratic Enlightenment values of the UDHR, whatever documents their governments might have endorsed.[22]

As we noted earlier, any plausible defense of *universal* human rights must be contingent on arguments for human equality. But are those arguments sound and convincing? Furthermore, it is noteworthy that neither the United States Constitution nor the United Nations Declaration provides any foundation or normative justification for the rights they declare. These rights are merely asserted as necessary and self-evident. Thus, while the U.N. declaration remains influential, its efficacy is limited by the fact that the rights it proposes are philosophically ungrounded.[23]

Nonetheless, is it still possible to defend the UDHR's extensive or "thick" set of rights, or can we only defend a minimal or "thin" list of rights in the face of cultural pluralism? Can we overcome the apparent

Western bias of the UDHR, some of which appear to be based on liberal principles and premises? Before we evaluate these various options, it is necessary to briefly review two other principal issues: the nature of a right, and the difference between legal and moral rights. A right is generally regarded as an entitlement to something, but we must be more precise about the normative significance of a right and consider whether there are rights even if they have not been legally recognized.

W. H. Hohfeld, in a classic work on rights theory, distinguishes between a "claim right," or right in the "strict sense," and a liberty right. According to Hohfeld, A has a claim right that B should do Ø if and only if B has a duty to A to do Ø.[24] The key point is that when claim rights are at stake, the action in question is an action on the part of others and not on the person who has the right. A claim right is either a right to be given something, to be "assisted in some way," or a right not to be interfered with or dealt with in a certain way.[25] Otherwise, in Hohfeld's terms, we would be talking about a liberty or a "privilege" instead of a claim right.

Thus, rights are *justified claims* that a person or group of persons can make upon other individuals or upon society. These claims entail *correlative duties* on the part of other individuals. If one possesses a right, one is in a position to determine, by one's choices, what others should or should not do. In Hohfeld's framework, for example, privacy would be considered a claim-right such that one individual (the right-holder) has a claim on another (the duty-bearer) to assist in the process of restricting access to the right-holder's personal information or not to interfere with the right-holder's efforts to restrict such access.

Now that we understand the nature of a right, we must consider a second general issue. What is the authority behind the assertion of a right, and what is the difference between a legal right and a natural or moral right? A legal right is simply a right someone has by virtue of the civil law, whereas a moral right is a right one has by virtue of the demands of morality or justice. Legal positivists contend that only legal rights have authority since they are supported by the weight of the law and the sovereignty of the state. According to hard core positivists, like Kelsen, the only source of normativity is the willing of a particular norm by a sovereign state or superior which makes that law a norm. "In general terms," writes Kelsen, there is "no Ought without a will."[26] Legal positivism remains popular, but as Glendon has pointed out, the heinous war crimes of Nazi Germany has "caused many people to reevaluate the proposition that there is no higher law by which the laws of nation-states can be judged."[27]

Hence it is not possible to rely only on the law and the civil authorities as a source of rights, since laws do not always promote human flourishing or express the principles of justice which can best be defined as the willingness to give others their due.[28] There must be natural or moral rights antecedent to just laws. A natural right has its own moral authority, which must be asserted even if that right is not reflected in the legal structure of a particular political community. But how is it possible to specify those rights for peoples across the globe within different historic cultures and holding conflicting moral beliefs? And how can we avoid the dangers of a purely West-centric approach to rights that obscures those differences?

After elaborating his conception of justice as fairness, John Rawls developed a theory of international rights according to the political role they play in the world. In the *Law of Peoples*, Rawls articulates an account of justice between and among "peoples," and thereby enters the contentious debate about universalism. The Law of Peoples constitutes political principles of international law that govern interactions among different societies. Rawls is concerned not so much with individual persons but with "peoples" and their inter-relationships. He uses the term "people" to refer to what is commonly called a nation or political community. He assumes that a shared culture is central to being a certain people who are united among themselves by certain common traits and "sympathies" which they do not share with others. Rawls differentiates between reasonable, liberal peoples and decent peoples. Liberal societies such as those in the West must tolerate decent societies even if the latter do not subscribe to the tenets of classical or social democratic liberalism.[29]

But what makes a society "decent," rather than an outlaw state that deserves to be shunned by other nations? Rawls argues that there are two broad conditions necessary for decency. First, this society does not have aggressive ambitions and it recognizes that it must achieve its objectives through diplomacy and other peaceful means. Second, a decent society secures for all of its citizens basic human rights. A social system that violates rights cannot postulate a just or "decent" scheme of political and social cooperation. A decent society may not be quite as just and reasonable as a well-ordered liberal one, but its decency wins it the prerogative to be tolerated and left alone by other peoples or nations. Liberal societies must tolerate and cooperate with all decent peoples in good standing.[30]

Rawls presents a list of core human rights that every decent society would agree to no matter what its cultural heritage happens to be. This set of rights represents universal rights since both liberal and decent societies accept them, even if they are only a subset of the rights accepted in liberal societies. Since these universal rights cannot be peculiarly liberal or unique to Western cultures, Rawls recognizes only a "special class of urgent rights" as moral rights in the proper sense.[31] This severely limited list includes "group rights," such as the right to be free from mass murder and from genocide. It also includes individual rights, such as the right to life (to the means of subsistence and security), to liberty (understood as freedom from slavery, serfdom, and forced occupation), to property (but only personal property), to a "sufficient measure" of liberty of conscience to protect freedom of religion and thought, and to formal equality as expressed by the rules of natural justice (that is, similar cases must be treated similarly).[32] Conspicuously absent from this list is the right to freedom of speech and association, the right of political participation, or the right against discrimination. The reason for this exclusion is that international rights must be subject to the "criterion of reciprocity," which implies the disqualification of any rights reflecting a Western bias or liberal conviction.[33]

Contrary to the natural law or other philosophical traditions, Rawls does not base his set of "urgent" human rights on any concept of the person. He also gives priority to the rights of peoples or nations rather than individual persons. Thus, he claims that the Law of Peoples "is fair to peoples and not to individual persons."[34] But this approach, which gives priority to the state over the individual for the sake of world harmony, sanctions the discriminatory treatment that religious minorities and nonconformists might expect to receive in a decent society. This discrimination puts minorities in a more vulnerable position, which hardly seems just. More fundamentally, aren't persons the bearers of rights rather than nations? And shouldn't rights be regarded as what is justly owed to each individual person as a requirement of justice?[35]

Despite its limitations, Rawls' theory of thin universal rights is not unique. Michael Walzer adopts a similar minimalist approach to human rights. Like Rawls, he rejects any thick versions of morality and favors instead a thin set of moral principles. Minimalism does not imply a morality that is shallow but one that has a compelling depth. In moral discourse, "thinness and intensity go together, whereas with thickness comes qualification, compromise, complexity, and disagreement."[36] According to Walzer's moral scheme, there are only a few "standards to which all societies can be held—negative injunctions, most likely, rules against murder, deceit, oppression, torture and tyranny."[37] While Walzer does not express these standards in terms of rights the implications are clear enough. Thus, both Rawls and Walzer believe that if we are to be realistic about universal moral codes or human rights that all peoples can embrace, we cannot overreach. Rather, we must find the "lowest common denominator" that is, a small set of rights or hypernorms that all diverse cultures, East and West, can readily agree upon.

In contrast to Walzer and Rawls, we join with those ethicists who propose a broader set of rights, and interpret a multinational's obligations in terms of fundamental natural rights that all international moral agents should endorse and respect. But how can we determine which rights should be included in such a list? The UDHR list is too thick because it includes too many questionable economic rights, such as rights to social security insurance or the right to "periodic holidays with pay" (art. 24). Nickel suggests stricter criteria and argues that an international right must satisfy three conditions to have full legitimacy:

1. The right must protect something of great importance.
2. The right must be subject to substantial and recurrent threats.
3. The obligations or burdens imposed by the right must satisfy the fairness–affordability test.

The first condition implies that rights refer to goods of critical importance. Second, Nickel believed that rights must involve goods subject to threats or the list of rights would be too expansive. Donaldson interprets the fairness–affordability test to mean that international agents, including multinationals, must be able under ordinary circumstances to assume the burdens and duties that fall upon them in honoring a particular right. And for any right to qualify as a valid right, there must be some fair arrangement for sharing the duties and burdens among those whose duty it is to honor this right. Satisfying all three conditions qualifies a presumptive right as a "fundamental international right" which must be respected by individuals, corporations, and nation states.[38]

A somewhat similar approach to rights is reflected in the work of legal philosophers like H.L Hart and John Finnis, whose works confirm the first and most important of Nickel's conditions for the classification of something as a right. According to Hart, "the core of the notion of rights is neither individual choice nor individual benefit, but basic or fundamental individual needs."[39] In Finnis' terms, rights involve basic aspects of human flourishing. They protect basic human goods, without which human flourishing is impossible. Hart and Finnis, therefore, concur with the logic of rights implicit in Nickel's analysis. Rights proceed from our understanding of basic human goods and protect those goods, which are "something of great importance" for human well-being. Rights provide a way of speaking about what is just "from the viewpoint of the other to whom something is owed or due, and who would be wronged if denied that something."[40] In contrast to Rawls, rights are not detached from the person, and there is no basis to exclude traditional liberal rights if that right protects a good fundamental for human well-being. Our own proposed list of rights is more expansive than Rawls' and Walzer's, because it gives priority to Nickel's first condition and has a more subtle view of how rights are threatened.

Given these conditions, and mindful of the fact that our focus is on rights that all international agents must honor, we propose a list of 14 basic rights. Some of these rights are suggested by Donaldson and Nickel, though we sometimes formulate them differently, and virtually all of them are included in the United Nations' UDHR. This list is not necessarily exhaustive, but the rights enumerated here express quite well the most basic demands of justice:

- Right to freedom or political liberty
- Right to be free from slavery or servitude
- Right to freedom from torture
- Right to life, health, bodily integrity, and security of person
- Right to equality before the law and to a fair trial (due process)
- Right not to be subject to arbitrary arrest or detention
- Right to nondiscriminatory treatment
- Right to freedom of speech and association
- Right to political participation
- Right to minimal education
- Right to privacy
- Right to freedom of thought, conscience, and religion
- Right to ownership of property
- Right to subsistence ("a standard of living adequate for health and well-being," Art. 25, UDHR).

These rights, of course, must all be properly specified and limited by other rights and by certain aspects of the common good. The right to free speech, for example, is not absolute but must be properly configured to protect morally justified secrecy and security concerns. Specification for all of these rights is beyond the scope of our analysis, but a few words are in order about which of these rights might be considered absolute. Given the great importance of the fundamental good of human life, a strong case can certainly be made for the absolute right of an innocent person not to have his or her life taken directly either as a means or as an end. Similarly, the right not to be tortured should be subject to no exceptions. Physical torture involves intentional damage to a person's bodily integrity or health, which is intrinsically morally wrong. The absolute right not to be tortured conveys this requirement that these goods of bodily integrity and health should never be damaged or interfered with by others in this way.[41]

As we noted earlier, duties are correlative to rights, and, according to Shue, there are three classes of duties for every basic right, all of which must be performed if the right is to be fully honored, but not necessarily performed by the same individuals or institutions. These correlative duties include: 1) Duties to avoid depriving; 2) Duties to protect from deprivation; and 3) Duties to aid the deprived.[42] For example, with respect to the right of physical security, there is a duty not to directly abolish a person's security (by assaulting or raping that person), a duty to protect people against deprivation of security by other people, and a duty to provide security for those unable to provide their own. While all of these generic duties might apply to certain institutions such as the state, we can safely assume that a multinational corporation's duty should only fall within the first two categories. Corporations are not required to assist those deprived of rights and correct rights abuses, since they are unsuited for this task, which may sometimes require them to educate the young and care for the sick. Thus, a multinational corporation should *avoid depriving* people of the object of these rights and avoid cooperation in such deprivation by another party. This means that a multinational corporation cannot cooperate with a government that denies freedom of speech to some of its citizens. In many cases, where corporate activities are concerned, multinationals must also help *protect* rights from being deprived. A corporation that uses an overseas contractor employing very young children is not directly depriving those children of an education. But given its leverage over that contractor, that corporation has a duty to take reasonable actions to protect the right to a minimal education from being deprived.[43]

The advantage of this modest but more person-centered approach to rights is that it strikes a reasonable balance between the maximalist scheme proposed by the United Nations in its Declaration (which includes 29 rights) and the minimalism recommended by Walzer and Rawls. This moderate universalism goes beyond more pluralistic approaches, which allow for a broader range of ethical viewpoints and which predicate transcultural hypernorms on overlapping consensus. On the contrary, these universal rights are firmly grounded in a theory of the good. Yet moderate universalism respects cultural diversity because it recognizes that cultural factors can play *some* reasonable role in the specification of these rights. Cultures also enjoy considerable moral free space when these rights are not at stake. Moreover, a commitment to natural rights and equality of respect for those rights does not imply in any way the impropriety of a corporate social agenda that goes beyond this minimal duty. However, given the lamentable history of rights abuses by multinationals, fostering consistent and sincere respect for these basic international rights, regardless of the exigency of the circumstances or the laxity of local law, is a pivotal step in the evolution of corporate integrity.

Natural Law and Natural Rights

The list of rights we have proposed offers a clear and concrete delineation of a multinational's basic obligations as a moral agent. It is a fairly thick set of rights that exceeds the minimalism of the Rawlsian approach. It does not exclude certain liberal rights merely because they seem to originate from a liberal bias. These universal rights proceed from an understanding of basic human goods ("something important" in Nickel's words), and we must now demonstrate the relationship between these goods and human rights. Our main contention is that more foundational than human rights are certain intrinsic goods valued for their own sake, which identify the basic reasons for our actions. A theory of rights is incomplete unless it attends to those goods, that are aspects of our well-being and necessary for our human flourishing. In order to complete our treatment of rights, therefore, we introduce the key principles of the new natural law, which unfolds a comprehensive theory of human flourishing without the metaphysical suppositions of traditional natural law.[44]

The word "goods" refers to what people want and desire. People desire many things but some goods are more basic and fundamental than others. Some of the goods we seek amount to definite or precise objectives: paint the house, finish college, go to a baseball game. But the most basic human goods in themselves (which include knowledge, friendship, health and life) are not definite objectives because they can never be fully attained and their pursuit never ends. Nevertheless, they guide and direct our actions by providing reasons to consider certain choices as intelligible and "choice worthy." These "basic human goods" are basic, not because we need them to survive but because we cannot flourish as human beings without them. Hence these goods are intrinsically valuable, and we recognize that they are choice worthy, not as means to other ends buts as ends-in-themselves. These goods, which are aspects of human well-being and fulfillment, are the primary reasons for action and the ultimate source of normativity.[45]

If a good is not intrinsic to human fulfillment, it cannot qualify as a basic human good. External or material goods are important, but they are not basic for fulfillment. Even freedom cannot be classified as a basic human good. Freedom is an extremely important good, but it's an instrumental one, since individuals are not ultimately fulfilled or perfected by freedom. Rather, they want freedom to pursue other fulfilling goods, such as knowledge of truth, marriage, or the worship of God in a way they deem proper.

What then are these basic human goods? Finnis, Grisez, and other natural law theorists argue for the following list of basic irreducible human goods. The list begins with several substantive goods: bodily life (including "component aspects of its fullness:" health, bodily integrity, and safety); knowledge and esthetic appreciation; skillful performance or excellence in work and play. In addition there are relational goods such as friendship or harmony between persons and groups of persons; marriage; religion or harmony with God; and harmony between human persons and the wider sub-personal reality or physical environment the person inhabits. And finally there is the good of self-integration, or inner harmony between one's judgments and behavior (authenticity) and between one's judgments and inner feelings (integrity).[46]

Each of these goods, such as health or knowledge, is worth pursuing and having for its own sake and does not necessitate the search for further reasons to explain a choice's intelligibility. If we ask someone why they are taking bad-tasting medicine and they tell us that they need the medicine for their health we know that person's choice makes sense. These goods are rationally directive and they constitute the ultimate basis for moral reflection, for considering what ought to be done. Intrinsic goods are self-evidently worthwhile, and they exclude as "unchoiceworthy" pointless activities, such as the activity of breathing stale air in a windowless classroom, which do not aim at an intelligible end. We participate in these basic goods, which "are no more and no less than opportunities of being all that one can be . . . they outline the worthwhile self that one may constitute by one's self-determination."[47]

These goods are disclosed to us through experience, which is the basis of practical reason. In our experience of friendship, for example, we discover the intelligibility and value of having and being a friend.[48] However, reliance on experience does not mean that these goods are subjective or detachable from our human nature. The intrinsic goods are not mere accidents of history, nor are they contingent psychological phenomena. Rather, these goods, which we all seek, represent basic aspects of human well-being that reveal the permanent features of human reality that make each of us the equal of other human beings. If human nature, which is prior in reality to these goods that fulfill it, were radically different, so would be the basic human goods. Human nature is not completely static, however, since it changes over time, in the sense that human flourishing, as realized through human actions, evolves through the unfolding of human potentialities. There are countless ways of participating in or sharing basic human goods. Knowledge will always be a basic human good but the scope and quality of humanity's knowledge, along with methods for appropriating and disseminating that knowledge, have clearly evolved throughout the course of history.[49]

Morality can begin to claim objectivity because the good—that is, this discrete set of basic human goods—is not subjective: subject to cultural differences or individual whims. Each good, such as knowledge, life, or friendship, is an *objective perfection* because it fulfills any human person and makes that person better off. Although the practical principles flowing from these goods ("life and health are worthy of our pursuit") represent the ultimate directives for practical reasoning, they are insufficient for directing people to make the right choices. They are at best incipiently moral principles. So we must differentiate between choices that are morally good or morally bad. First we assume that morality's foundation is to be found in the goods of human persons as individuals and as communities, and rightness or wrongness depends on one's attitude to the whole set of basic human goods instantiated in ourselves and in others. Moral rectitude implies that one is well-disposed to this entire moral foundation: that is, to all of the basic human goods in all of their aspects. The morally upright person regards the chosen good (such as marriage) as part of a larger whole and chooses that good in such a way that he or she respects the other goods that constitute the moral foundation. Thus, sound moral judgment always reflects a positive orientation to the human good "integrally conceived."[50]

A morally bad choice, on the other hand, is one that unnecessarily or arbitrarily forecloses possibilities of fulfillment for others or for oneself. Any choice contrary to one good (either my good or my neighbor's good) is unreasonable and morally wrong, even if it is done for the sake of another good. Bad choices often occur by absolutizing or fixating on a particular concrete good to the detriment of other goods. For example, marriage is a worthwhile good worthy of our pursuit, but if Joe's misguided choice to marry Jane will undermine the harmony and community of Jane's current marriage to Bob, Joe is acting immorally by fixating on the particular good of marriage-to-Jane. Whenever one negates (or destroys) an instantiated good which should be allowed to be, whether in oneself or another, there is moral evil, which consists precisely in such an act of negation.

A morally upright choice, therefore, is a completely reasonable choice, since it is fully respectful of the goods, persons, and communities involved. But an immoral choice is not fully reasonable. It often exhibits favoritism among various goods, persons, and communities. Moreover, an immoral choice typically entails the damage, impediment, or destruction of an instantiated good that any reasonable person would perceive as an intrinsic good worthy of pursuit.[51]

Once we see the need for a proper appreciation or disposition to this moral foundation of human goods as aspects of human persons, the First Principle of Morality becomes evident. This principle states that:

> in voluntarily acting for human goods and avoiding what is opposed to them, *one ought to choose and otherwise will those and only those possibilities whose willing is compatible with integral human fulfillment.*[52]

Integral human fulfillment must be carefully distinguished from individualistic self-fulfillment. It refers to the good of all persons and communities. We must recognize that all the goods in which we participate also can fulfill others, and some goods, such as friendship, can only be realized in communion with others.

This ideal of integral human fulfillment provides the general criterion for differentiating between morally right and wrong choices.

However, this first moral principle is too general and abstract to provide practical guidance. Therefore, it needs more specification, which comes in the form of intermediate moral principles or "modes of responsibility."[53] These can be derived from this first principle and they exclude as practically unreasonable (i.e., immoral) various types of willing inconsistent with a will that acts in good faith in a manner open toward all of the human goods. Three of these modes should be singled out for more elaboration because of their importance in the moral life. We will refer to them as the principal modes of responsibility. The first of these principal modes is the Golden Rule, or the principle of fairness, which plays a pivotal role in ethical decision-making. A will unduly influenced by egoism and partiality cannot be open to integral human fulfillment. Given the conflicts that arise in business and everyday life that cause us to render some harm to another (for example, striking a thug in order to rescue an innocent victim or laying off a few workers in order to prevent bankruptcy), this principle will surely be an important part of ethical decision-making. It requires that our actions and policies, which can sometimes be to the detriment of others, must pass the impartiality test imposed by the Golden Rule. Following this principle does not preclude a preference for oneself or one's family. But it does preclude preferences based on jealousy, or other emotions that prevent others from participating in basic human goods.

Respect for persons who are bearers and sharers of goods means more than treating them fairly. The second principal mode of responsibility forbids a moral agent from deliberately damaging, destroying, or impeding a basic good out of hostility, anger, or vengeance. Thus, even if an injury is inflicted upon someone, that person should not respond by injuring the perpetrator. Quite simply, one is obliged not to respond to injury with injury. A person or community motivated by revenge, resentment, or hostility does not have a will that is open to integral human fulfillment.

According to the third mode of responsibility, it is never right to act directly against some instance of a basic human good (such as life or health) even for the sake of a good end. This principle implicitly repudiates utilitarianism, which argues that evil can be done for the sake of sufficiently positive consequences. It is echoed in some modern ethical philosophies critical of utilitarianism. According to computer ethicist James Moor, for example, good ends or goals should not blind us to the injustice of the means—"[t]his is precisely what happens when the good becomes the enemy of the just."[54] These three modes of responsibility shape our specific moral responsibilities, which direct us to those choices compatible with integral human fulfillment.

Contrary to Rawls, the good is always prior to rights, since rights get their content and articulation from both intrinsic and instrumental human goods. Rawls' thesis of the priority of the right over the good is vital to his theory of justice, yet even he must admit that it is impossible to determine a framework for rights without reference to a set of "primary goods."[55] Accordingly, these basic human rights, which orient our choices to human flourishing, are derived from the basic goods, along with the modes of responsibility, that specify the first moral principle. For example, how might we derive the right to life? Life is an intrinsic good, and any act which intends as a means, or as end, to kill an innocent human person is in opposition to that good. There is no way to justify the intentional taking of an innocent human life according to the modes of responsibility. A moral agent cannot act in conformity with the Golden Rule if that agent, who values his own life, chooses to deprive an innocent person of his or her bodily life. Therefore, since there is a claim on others to respect the good of life, it logically follows that there must be a natural right to life, an entitlement required of others in justice. No one is permitted to act on the view that the life of another person is expendable, no matter what the circumstances or consequences.[56]

Each of the other rights proposed on our list of fundamental international rights can be defended more forcefully by reference to these intrinsic human goods, or to instrumental goods like freedom that enable the pursuit of various forms of fulfillment. All of these goods constitute the moral foundation for the precepts of justice. For example, since knowledge is indisputably a basic human good, essential for human flourishing, one should not choose in a way that is contrary to that good by depriving another person or group of persons of a basic or minimal education so that they can extricate themselves from a state of ignorance. Such choices (or moral inertia), which impede the good of knowledge, cannot be consistent with the Golden Rule. If there is a valid reason to promote the good of knowledge, it is discriminatory and unreasonable to promote my knowledge and yet fail to promote someone else's. Given the critical importance of knowledge for human well-being, there is a duty to educate all human persons, which can be expressed as the right to a minimal education. This right, unlike the right to life, is not absolute and so needs to be properly qualified and specified. The duty to educate belongs to the state, but in relevant circumstances, corporations have a duty to prevent this right to a minimal education from being deprived. Of course, there may be some legitimate debate on what constitutes a "minimal education," which to some extent is a matter of prudential judgment and can vary from one culture to the next.

Aside from providing a proper theoretical underpinning of these rights, the new natural law theory keeps our attention keenly focused on the critical importance of respecting the legitimate claims and interests of others. It prompts us to always ask the question "how does this corporate plan or project negatively affect the flourishing of others?" As we have seen, the principle of fairness, in the form of the Golden Rule, is a key intermediate principle which precludes partiality and arbitrary self-preference in the pursuit of one's goals. Similarly, the pursuit of integral human fulfillment reminds us of our interdependence—my flourishing is inextricably linked with the flourishing of my friends, colleagues, and the communities in which I participate. What better way to stress our interdependence than the ideal of integral human flourishing: no human being or community can flourish in isolation, but only in solidarity with others.

A Social Agenda?

One final word about a corporation's moral and social responsibility. Many ethicists and activists have maintained that corporations have obligations that exceed respect for international rights and rational moral principles such as the Golden Rule. They envision the multinational corporations as committed to a broad social agenda that includes rectifying social problems. According to this view, corporations are not just bound to avoid depriving people of their rights but they must also correct human rights abuses, even if this means working for the aim of distributive justice.[57] Corporations must pledge some of their plentiful resources for the sake of corporate charity, as a way of "giving back" to the community.

Although there is sometimes an overlap between these ethical and social obligations, it is useful to keep them distinct. Ethical obligations, as we have presented them, primarily involve respect for basic human rights that protect intrinsic and instrumental goods. But social obligations, in the thick sense, are more philanthropic and proactive in nature. They go beyond the demands of decency and respect for human rights, and involve large commitments of time and resources to charitable activities or the correction of social injustice. Coca-Cola, for example, does not just conserve water in its own operations, but is also committed to promoting water conservation and collaborates with environmental groups to conserve seven major freshwater river basins. Several major Indian firms like Tata are quite active in providing vital services, such as education and health care, for impoverished Indian communities.[58]

However, not everyone concurs that corporations should have such a social agenda. Milton Friedman, and those who endorse the doctrine of shareholder primacy, resisted the idea that a corporation is obliged to resolve social problems or contribute resources for such solutions. According to Friedman, "there is one and only on[e] social responsibility of business—to use its resources and engage in activities designed to increase its profits so long as it stays within the rules of the game, which is to say, engages in free and open competition, without deception or fraud ..."[59] Thus, the only responsibility for corporations is to increase long-term profits, within the framework of the law and within certain bounds of ethical probity that preclude fraud and deception. Friedman also believed that the markets themselves would solve many of the "social" problems that resulted from market failures, such as negative externalities. When this doesn't happen, laws may be necessary to fix the problem so that resources are directed to their optimal social use. Hence, corporations can count on markets and the law as a guide to their proper social behavior. For Friedman, correcting market failures is the government's domain. The problem, of course, is that markets and government regulators often react too slowly to failures, and in developing countries sometimes they don't react at all. In some countries the rule of law is not upheld. Since economic regulation is so reactive and sometimes unenforced, we have argued that in most circumstances corporations have an ethical obligation to do something about market failures caused by their actions and policies, especially when those failures lead to the abridgement of rights. A corporation has a duty to inform its customers about the risks of using its products, regardless of what the market or the law allows, because basic human goods like health are at stake. It's not completely clear what Friedman means by "rules of the game," but it seems that he does not go far enough in respecting the ethical dimension of a corporation's overall social responsibility.

However, the prime thrust of Friedman's critique is that corporate social responsibility in the strong sense is invalid. His theory seeks to constrict a corporation's philanthropic impulses, its willingness to commit corporate resources to solve social ills. His reasoning is that these corporate executives are spending the shareholders' money and have no right to do so. These executives have a fiduciary obligation to make money for those shareholders and to allocate resources that will maximize long-term profits, rather than promote the social good. This is a more difficult issue that we cannot resolve in these pages. There is some merit to Friedman's argument, since corporate philanthropy does come at the expense of the firm's owners. Disputably, the generous CEO who gives away the owner's money is engaging in a questionable transaction. This is why some refer to corporate philanthropy as "borrowed virtue."[60] On the other hand, it is worth pointing out that many businesses have found a way to enhance their competitive position while also raising the level of social welfare. The good corporate citizen, for example, is often able to attract the most proficient and dedicated workers.

There are certainly many other sound arguments to support corporate social responsibility that involves philanthropy and good citizenship even if a corporation must sacrifice its profitability. However, while a social agenda is commendable, there are a few other caveats worth mentioning. First, social responsibility or corporate philanthropy programs should not distract corporations from their ethical obligations to respect human rights. Multinationals can't take credit for opening clinics in Bangladesh, but then allow their suppliers to pay below-subsistence-level wages in unsafe facilities. Second, in most situations corporations are not competent to advance the public good by trying to remedy distributive injustice or correct human rights abuses. They also lack the democratic credentials to engage in this sort of work, which is the function of government—the real custodian of public interest.[61] Third, in keeping with the concept of "conscious capitalism," it should not be forgotten that the pursuit of a profitable business does a service to society and advances the public good in its own right. By adding value, through the creation of goods and services people are willing to pay for, corporations enhance social welfare, and this primary obligation should not become a "sideshow" to more noble, philanthropic activities.[62]

Conclusions

All corporations, including multinationals, have at least three fundamental obligations to society: to create value or wealth, to follow the relevant law, and to observe ethical standards. The corporation's value-creating activities, which are aimed at maximizing the value of the owners' assets, are constrained by law and by moral norms. In most cases these constraints will not interfere with the corporation's economic objectives. Multinationals are obliged to follow the law of their host country, but sometimes their home country will regulate their behavior abroad. Thanks to several prominent corruption scandals, the United States implemented the Foreign Corrupt Practices Act, which forbids payment to foreign officials in order to get an unfair advantage in selling their goods or services. There are few multilateral regulations because of a lack of global consensus on social issues, along with a suspicion that international norms will be used to weaken the sovereignty of less developed nations.

We have argued that corporations must do more than follow the law, which is reactive, riddled with loopholes, and sometimes even unjust. Regulations do not promote moral conduct but often lead instead to "instrumental behavior," oriented towards how those regulations can be circumvented or how their effects can be mitigated.[63] Thus, in the marketplace companies should be guided primarily by appropriate ethical standards. But what are those standards? Should they be construed in terms of utility, duties (such as those derived from Kant's categorical imperative), or human rights, which amount to "rightful" entitlements? We contend that the framework of universal human rights is the most fruitful avenue for ethical analysis since it does not suffer from the indeterminacy of utilitarianism or the abstractness of Kantianism. This framework is simple, concrete, and applicable in almost every moral context. A company that sincerely respects rights will do no harm, follow the Golden Rule, and live up to the primitive moral standard of "common decency."

Many philosophers accept the validity of natural rights as well as legal ones, while international organizations like the United Nations have reaffirmed the universality of those rights. But can we accept the U.N.'s thick version of rights? Rawls argues that only a thin set of universal rights is warranted, because traditional rights, such as freedom of speech, have a liberal bias and are not universalizable. In contrast to Rawls, we made the case for a moderate universalism, a fairly thick set of rights that must be honored by all international moral agents. Those rights are justified by the fact that they protect important goods that are in jeopardy, though the list is also tempered by the fairness–affordability doctrine, which precludes some of the economic rights of the UDHR. These rights are fitting transcultural norms that recognize our shared humanity and give normative recognition to the basic equality of all persons. At the same time this limited set of rights does not deny the validity of each culture's "moral free space."

Rights have three general correlative duties all of which must be carried out if a right is to be properly honored, but not all of which must be carried out by the same individuals or institutions. Multinational corporations have a duty not to deprive people of the object of their rights and in some cases to protect rights from being violated. But they do not have a duty to correct human rights abuses and resolve distributional inequities, since they lack the democratic qualifications and the competencies to deal with the demands of social justice.

We also demonstrated that these rights logically proceed from the irreducible human goods essential for human flourishing. Rights protect intrinsic goods, such as knowledge or life, along with instrumental goods like freedom, and they give normative acknowledgement to our human equality. Therefore, they are justified as the conditions for human flourishing. Intrinsically valuable goods, which are sought after as ends-in-themselves, are defended in the new natural law theory, which proposes integral human flourishing as an overarching moral standard. We contend that a viable theory of rights must be grounded in the intrinsic goods or basic aspects of human well-being, which permit us to identify important moral requirements that can express what is just or owed to someone in terms of natural rights, such as the right not to be tortured or enslaved.

Corporations may conceive their social obligations more broadly than the mandate to respect and protect the rights of others. They might opt for social responsibility in the strong sense, which involves a substantial commitment of time and money to advancing social progress. But they should bear in mind the complexity of acting in the public interest, and they should not let this social agenda distract them from more fundamental moral obligations.

There is a legitimate concern that globalization has undermined human rights and created economic insecurity. As we have seen, multinationals have behaved opportunistically and sometimes failed to honor basic human rights by degrading the environment of the host country or providing meager wages. Profit-seeking multinationals serve the public interest and benefit the poor by providing jobs and a higher standard of living. But ethically sensitive multinationals further enhance social welfare in the long run by also diligently upholding and protecting the human rights of their workers and other stakeholders.

Notes

1 Alan Wolfe, "The Snake: Globalization, America and the Wretched Earth," *The New Republic*, October 1, 2001, 31.
2 Richard Barnet and Ronald Muller, *Global Reach: The Power of Multinational Corporations* (New York: Simon and Schuster, 1974), 363.
3 Lynn Sharp Paine, "Guide to Leadership and Corporate Accountability," (Boston, MA: Harvard Business School Publications, 2007).
4 Edwin Reischauer, "The Lessons of the Lockheed Scandal," *Newsweek*, May 10, 1976, 20–1. For a more detailed account of this scandal see David Boulton, *The Grease Machine* (New York: Harper & Row, 1978).
5 The Foreign Corrupt Practices Act, Pub. L. No. 95–213, 91 Stat. 1464 (1977) codified at 15 U.S.C. § 78, 78m, 78dd-1, 78ff.

6 "Bribery and Business: The Short Arm of the Law," *The Economist*, March 2, 2002, 63–5.
7 "Bribery and Business," 64.
8 Peter Fritsch and Timothy Mapes, "In Indonesia, a Tangle of Bribes Creates Trouble for Monsanto," *The Wall Street Journal*, April 5, 2005, A1, A6.
9 Joe Palazzolo, "The Business of Bribery," *The Wall Street Journal*, October 2, 2012, B1.
10 Miguel Bustillo, "Wal-Mart Faces Risk in Mexican Bribe Probe," *The Wall Street Journal*, April 23, 2012, B1.
11 Geoffrey Jones, *Multinationals and Global Capitalism* (Oxford: Oxford University Press, 2005), 222–4. See also P. Muchlinski, *Multinational Enterprises and the Law* (Oxford: Oxford University Press, 1995).
12 Alien Tort Claims Act 28 U.S.C. § 1350.
13 Jess Bravin, "Justices Limit Law's Reach for Acts Overseas," *The Wall Street Journal*, April 18, 2013, A5. The case is *Kiobel v. Royal Dutch Petroleum Co.* 133 U.S. 1659 (2013). See also *Doe v. Unocal Corp.* 963 F. Supp 880 [C.D. Cal 1997]. In the *Kiobel* case, the Court affirmed that "there is no indication that [ATCA] was passed to make the United States a uniquely hospitable forum for the enforcement of international norms," 1685.
14 William Frankena, *Ethics* (Englewood Cliffs, NJ: Prentice-Hall, 1963).
15 Lynn Sharp Paine, *Value Shift* (New York: McGraw-Hill, 2003), 222.
16 Gordon Fairclough, "Philip Morris Notes Cigarette's Benefits for Nation's Finances," *Wall Street Journal*, July 16, 2001, A2. See also Michael Sandel, *Justice* (New York: Farrar, Straus, and Giroux, 2009), 42–3.
17 Immanuel Kant, *Grounding for the Metaphysics of Morals* (Cambridge, MA: Hackett Publishing, 1993).
18 Norman Bowie, *Business Ethics: A Kantian Perspective* (Oxford: Blackwell, 1999), 19–25.
19 Norman Bowie, *Business Ethics*, 23.
20 Immanuel Kant, *On the Supposed Right to Lie for Philanthropic Concerns* (Cambridge, MA: Hackett Publishing, 1993), 64.
21 Lord Thomas Bingham, *The Rule of Law* (London: Blackwell, 2010). See also Niall Ferguson, *The Great Degeneration* (New York: Penguin Press, 2013), 79–80.
22 Robin Fox, "The Ground and Nature of Human Rights: Another Round," *The National Interest*, 68 (2002), 113–23.
23 Michael Freeman, *Human Rights* (Cambridge: Polity, 2011), 41–2. Philosopher Jacques Maritain, who helped craft the UDHR, called attention to this glaring deficiency but hoped that agreement would be reached "not only on the enumeration of human rights, but also on the key values governing their exercise." Jacques Maritain, "Introduction," in *Human Rights: Comments and Interpretations* ed. UNESCO (Westport, CN: Greenwood Press, 1949), 17.
24 W. H. Hohfeld, *Fundamental Legal Conceptions* (New Haven, CT: Yale University Press, 1919), pp. 140–4.

25 John Finnis, *Natural Law and Natural Rights* (Oxford: Oxford University Press, 1980), p. 200. I am indebted to Finnis' treatment of rights throughout this brief discussion.
26 Hans Kelsen, *General Theory of Norms* (Oxford: Oxford University Press, 1990), 6. See also John Finnis, "Propter Honoris Respectum: On the Incoherence of Legal Positivism," 75 *Notre Dame Law Review*, 1597 (2000).
27 Mary Ann Glendon, *A World Made Anew: Eleanor Roosevelt and the Universal Declaration of Human Rights* (New York: Random House, 2001), 176.
28 See, for example, St. Thomas Aquinas, *Summa Theologiae*, II–II, q. 58, a. 1c. Following Aristotle, he defines justice as "a habit whereby a man renders to each one his due by a constant and perpetual will."
29 John Rawls, *The Law of Peoples* (Cambridge, MA: Harvard University Press, 1999), 62–5. See also Grace Kao, *Grounding Human Rights in a Pluralist World* (Washington, D.C.: Georgetown University Press, 2011), 58–68.
30 Rawls, *The Law of Peoples*, 64–5.
31 Rawls, *The Law of Peoples*, 79.
32 Rawls, *The Law of Peoples*, 65.
33 Rawls, *The Law of Peoples*, 80. See also Kao, *Grounding Human Rights in a Pluralist World*, 63.
34 Rawls, *The Law of Peoples*, 17n.9.
35 Kao, *Grounding Human Rights in a Pluralist World*, 63–4.
36 Michael Walzer, *Thick and Thin: Moral Argument at Home and Abroad* (Notre Dame: University of Notre Dame Press, 1994), 6.
37 Walzer, *Thick and Thin*, 10.
38 James Nickel, *Making Sense of Human Rights: Philosophical Reflections on the Universal Declaration of Human Rights* (Berkeley, CA: University of California Press, 1987), 107–108. See also Thomas Donaldson, *The Ethics of International Business* (New York: Oxford University Press, 1989), 72–77.
39 H. L. Hart, "Bentham on Legal Rights," *Oxford Essays in Jurisprudence: Second Series*, ed A. Simpson (Oxford: Oxford University Press, 1971), 171–185.
40 Finnis, *Natural Law and Natural Rights*, 223–226.
41 Patrick Lee, "Interrogational Torture," *American Journal of Jurisprudence*, 51 (2006), 131. See also Finnis, *Natural Law and Natural Rights*, 205.
42 Henry Shue, *Basic Rights: Subsistence, Affluence, and U.S. Foreign Policy* 2nd ed. (Princeton, NJ: Princeton University Press, 1996), 52–3. See also Donaldson, *The Ethics of International Business*, 83–84.
43 For Donaldson's full argument on why corporations do not have duties to aid the deprived, see Thomas Donaldson, "The Perils of Multinationals' Largess," *Business Ethics Quarterly*, 4(3) (1994), 367–371.
44 John Finnis, "Natural Law: The Classical Tradition," in *The Oxford Handbook of Jurisprudence* eds. Jules Coleman and Scott Shapiro (Oxford: Oxford University Press, 2002), 24–25.
45 Germain Grisez, "A Contemporary Natural Law Ethic," *Normative Ethics and Objective Reason* ed. G. McLean; available at http://216.255.45.103/

book/Series01/1–11/chapter_xi.htm (accessed October 17, 2008). See also Robert George, "Natural Law," *American Journal of Jurisprudence*, 52 (2007).
46 John Finnis, "Liberalism and Natural Law Theory," *Mercer Law Review*, 45 (1994): 691–92. See also Grisez "Contemporary Natural Law Ethic."
47 John Finnis, *Fundamentals of Ethics* (Washington, D.C.: Georgetown University Press, 1983), 125.
48 Robert George, *Conscience and its Enemies* (Wilmington, DE: ISI Books, 2013), 74–75.
49 Germain Grisez, "Natural Law and Human Fulfillment," *American Journal of Jurisprudence*, 46 (2001), 3–21. See also Finnis, "Natural Law: The Classical Tradition."
50 George, *Conscience and its Enemies*, 89. See also John Finnis, "Aquinas' Moral, Political, and Legal Philosophy," *Stanford Encyclopedia of Philosophy*, 2005; available at http://plato.stanford.edu/entries/aquinas-moral-political/ (accessed March 6, 2014)
51 John Finnis, "Aquinas' Moral, Political, and Legal Philosophy."
52 John Finnis, Joseph Boyle and Germain Grisez, "A Sounder Theory of Morality," in *Nuclear Deterrence, Morality, and Realism* (Oxford: Oxford University Press, 1987), 283.
53 For a more elaborate discussion on these modes of responsibility see Finnis, "Natural Law: The Classical Tradition," 27–30 and Grisez, "A Contemporary Natural Law Ethic."
54 James Moor, "Just Consequentialism and Computing," in *Readings in Cyberethics* ed. Richard Spinello and Herman Tavani (Sudbury, MA: Jones & Bartlett, 2001), 103.
55 See W. Norris Clarke, "Freedom as Value," in *Freedom and Value* ed. Robert Johann (New York: Fordham University Press, 1975), 1–19.
56 Aquinas expresses this moral norm against taking innocent life quite precisely and implies that we have the right (*ius*) to life by virtue of the natural law. See the *Summa Theologiae*, II–II, q. 64, a. 6. See also John Finnis, *Aquinas* (Oxford: Oxford University Press, 1998), 141–43.
57 See, for example, Kevin Jackson, "Distributive Justice and the Corporate Duty to Aid," *Journal of Business Ethics*, 12 (1993): 547–551.
58 "Just Good Business," A Special Report on Corporate Social Responsibility, *The Economist*, January 19, 2008, 6, 20.
59 Milton Friedman, *Capitalism and Freedom* (Chicago, IL: University of Chicago Press, 1962), 133. See also Friedman's celebrated article, "The Social Responsibility of Business is to Increase its Profits," *New York Times Magazine*, September 13, 1970, 32–33, 122–26.
60 "The Good Company: A Survey of Corporate Social Responsibility," *The Economist*, January 22, 2005, 8–9.
61 "The Good Company," 22.
62 "Just Good Business," 8.
63 Colin Mayer, *Firm Commitment* (Oxford: Oxford University Press, 2013), 59–60.

PART II
DOING BUSINESS IN A GLOBAL ENVIRONMENT: INDUSTRY ANALYSES AND CASE STUDIES

5

MULTINATIONAL CORPORATIONS AND INTERNET FREEDOMS

Cisco, Yahoo, and Google in China

Introduction

It is no secret that authoritarian regimes have adopted technologies that enable them to stifle dissent through censorship and surveillance. Over concerns about "subversive" content, some countries have made Herculean efforts to close off parts of cyberspace and the World Wide Web from their citizens. The Iranian Government, for example, is taking the extreme step of implementing its own national Internet that would effectively disconnect Iranian cyberspace from the rest of the Internet. The regime has already introduced *Mehr*, the country's version of YouTube. Authoritarianism is incompatible with the political dynamics of the social media age. As a result, countries like China, Syria, and Egypt have aggressively used technology both to insulate their citizens from the "invasion" of Western ideas and culture and to limit the activities of dissidents. These regimes also like to keep a close eye on dissidents, and mobile phones, linked with the right software, provide an unprecedented opportunity for monitoring and tracking.

Less well known perhaps is the essential role that United States and European multinationals have played as the purveyors and architects of these censorship and surveillance technologies. Companies such as Yahoo, Google, and Microsoft, ostensibly committed to promoting free expression and open communication, have been implicated in efforts to censor the Internet in China. Siemens' joint venture with Nokia, known as NSN, provided Iran's largest telecom company with a monitoring center that can intercept and record calls made over mobile networks.[1] Similarly, products from Great Britain's Gamma International UK have been marketed to countries anxious to stifle the use of Skype as a tool for dissent. During the Middle East uprisings in 2011 protesters relied on Skype for confidential video conferencing and instant messages. Gamma markets software called FinSpy that eavesdrops on Skype by intercepting its audio stream and bypassing its encryptions. Egypt's Secret Service tested the product and the Interior Ministry approved its purchase, but the deal was never consummated as a result of the Egyptian revolution.[2]

United States companies that pioneered the design and manufacture of censorship or filtering software to protect children from pornography now actively sell that software to authoritarian Middle East governments, in countries like Bahrain, Qatar, Saudi Arabia, and Yemen. Products like Websense, McAfee's Smartfilter, and Bluecoat (from Palo Alto Networks), are now configured to filter out social and political content, "effectively block a total of over 20 million Internet users from accessing such websites."[3]

China has transformed the Internet into a "giant cage," and the cage metaphor suggests the extent to which the Chinese government has infused regulatory controls into the Internet's architectures and processes. As Schmidt and Cohen point out, "China is the world's most active and enthusiastic filterer of information."[4] However, with hundreds of millions of Internet users, China also represents an attractive investment opportunity for multinational high-tech companies like Google, Yahoo, Twitter, and Facebook. But the Chinese government demands that companies investing in China play by their rules, and their rules include cooperating with its strict censorship and surveillance laws. As a result, multinationals like Yahoo and Google have had to navigate an ethical minefield in China, and many would argue that their navigation has been quite poor. Other companies like Twitter have refused to comply with China's censorship laws: "We are not going to make the kinds of sacrifices . . . [necessary] to be unblocked in China," declares Twitter CEO Dick Costolo.[5] Although many authoritarian regimes besides China censor the Internet aggressively, our focus of attention will be primarily on Chinese policies.

The theme of this chapter is the ethical risk that Internet companies must assume when they invest in countries like China or Iran, which are committed to the censorship and surveillance of Internet activities. The principal ethical question is straightforward: to what degree can these companies cooperate with a government's Internet-monitoring efforts or online censorship policies that deny people the right to protest or to criticize their own government? Is this an area where the host country culture should enjoy extensive free moral space? Sometimes the assistance provided by multinationals is direct. For example, in China, Microsoft configured its blog-creating product, "MSN Spaces," to prohibit any blog site titles such as "freedom" or "democracy." In other cases the cooperation is more subtle and indirect. Cisco sells routers to China as it does to all countries connected to the Internet. But China equips those routers with filtering software to block an array of unwanted speech. Is Cisco accountable if its product is used in a way that Cisco did not intend it to be used? There are many high-tech multinationals that enable the extensive censorship and surveillance regime of China, but we will concentrate primarily on the experience of three major U.S. firms: Cisco, Yahoo, and Google.

Censorship and Digital Technologies

Before we sort out these complex issues it would be instructive to review, at least briefly, the nature of censorship and the technological weapons of the censor. Censorship has been broadly defined by philosophers as the intentional suppression or regulation of expression based on its content. Also, according to Williams, the activity in question "has at least to be publicly recognized in order to count as censorship."[6] Thus, it is usually associated with a government or a "legally constituted" authority's prohibition of a publication or speech that has a certain content. But censorship should include any act that is intended to restrict, encumber, limit, or deter in some way the expression of another. It is possible to restrict and limit another's expression in a non-transparent fashion, especially given the tools of digital technology. It is also possible for private individuals or organizations to suppress expression. When a library installs filters on its computers to prevent access to pornographic material it is engaged in a form of censorship. Therefore, a modification of the traditional definition seems appropriate: censorship is the public or covert suppression or regulation of speech, based on its content, conducted by a legally constituted authority or by private parties, including individuals and institutions.

It was once presumed that the Internet's distributed and anarchic architecture made it strongly resistant to government regulation, including traditional types of censorship. Conventional wisdom was that this international network would eventually erode the state's sovereignty and self-sufficiency. The virtues of this distributed network were resiliency, contingency, interoperability, flexibility and heterogeneity, along with a capacity to operate according to the simple principle, "Accept everything, no matter what source, sender, or destination."[7] Nonetheless, governments have found ways to control and censor the network, often under the pretense that regulated access will "protect" their citizens from corrupting foreign influences located in cyberspace. These governments justify censorship by claiming that they must safeguard vulnerable citizens from alien and corrupting cultural influences, but most often their main goal is to cut off dissenting political discourse.

What sorts of tools do the censors have at their disposal? We have already alluded to some of these tools, but Larry Lessig, following the work of Langdon Winner, provides us with a framework that can answer this question comprehensively. We are constrained in cyberspace by four modalities of regulation: law, code (including hardware and software applications), social norms, and the market.[8] Laws, such as those that provide copyright and patent protection, regulate cyberspace behavior by proscribing certain activities and by imposing *ex post* sanctions for violators. Markets regulate behavior in various ways—the pricing policies of Internet Service Providers will determine who can afford access to the Internet, while e-commerce websites come and go depending upon their marketplace acceptance. There are also norms that regulate cyberspace behavior, including Internet etiquette and social customs. But code, or the "architectures" of cyberspace, is by far the most effective regulator, thanks in part to the opacity of information technology systems. Sophisticated encryption code is used to protect sensitive data from thieves and snoops, and software programs such as CyberPatrol filter out pornographic material from a young child's personal computer. Code represents a "new form of necessity," as logical constraints take the form of "social constraints."[9]

Censorship of online information is most effectively accomplished by code or by laws, and sometimes by reliance on the interaction of code and law, that is, code supported by law. Code creates new opportunities for the censor, who can inscribe restrictions on speech into technologies by means of software filters, firewalls, and similar architectures. Code also creates unprecedented opportunities for online surveillance. Ordinary users have little recourse and usually offer no resistance to this extension of surveillance and content controls into their networked space. Thanks to the proliferation of filtering and monitoring technologies, the Internet in some countries has been transformed from a networked information society into a "society of control."[10]

This suppression of speech is antithetical to the philosophy of the Internet's original design. Cyberspace was supposed to be an open environment where anyone could express their opinions, protest corruption, or engage in digital activism without reprisals from the state. Its end-to-end design created an environment conducive to liberty and democracy, with unfettered access to all types of information in different digital formats. As the U.S. Supreme Court eloquently wrote in its *Reno v. ACLU* decision, the Internet enables an ordinary citizen to become "a pamphleteer, . . . a town crier with a voice that resonates farther than it could from any soapbox."[11] But this potent combination of law and software code, such as monitoring and filtering programs, has enabled authoritarian societies to effectively undermine the Internet's libertarian ethos.

Virtual space still offers abundant opportunities for political participation and dissent, but the technologies of control can dramatically increase a dissenter's vulnerability. Access to the virtual world certainly facilitated the Arab Spring, but governments like Egypt and Iran fought back by shutting down the Internet to short circuit growing opposition. Also, repressive regimes have proven to be quite resourceful in intensifying the utilization of Internet surveillance technologies or spreading misinformation to websites designed to mobilize protesters.[12]

China, the Internet, and the Great Firewall

The People's Republic of China is the world's most heavily populated country, with over 1.35 billion people. China's political regime regards itself as a "central democracy." China is a single party state, ruled and governed by the Chinese Communist Party. China has the second largest economy in the world with an annual GDP of over $8 trillion. The country continues to be the developing world's largest recipient of foreign direct investment (FDI). Market-oriented reforms began in the late 1970s, when China embarked on the road to modernity. It dismantled collectives and strongly encouraged private enterprise. However, as discussed in Chapter Two, China is a prime example of state capitalism, with the economy firmly in the grip of the Communist Party. This party, which controls the Chinese legislature, is known for its intolerance of internal political dissent. The country has vigorously suppressed spiritual cults like Falun Gong, and it has clamped down on citizens seeking independence for Tibet. Any internal criticism of China's despotic government is regarded as "subversive" speech. These restrictive policies are consistent with a nationalistic sentiment that regards social order and political stability as necessary for the restoration of the country's lost wealth and power.

The use of computer technology in China has grown exponentially over the last two decades. In 1995, the same year that Bill Gates declared the Internet to be a "tidal wave" that changes all the rules, China offered Internet service to the public. According to recent estimates, China now has approximately 591 million Internet users, which amounts to 44 percent of the population.[13] Thanks to its ambitious broadband strategy, over 90 percent of these users have broadband access.[14] Penetration is particularly strong in Eastern cities like Shanghai and Beijing. In 2000, the number of Internet users had been less than 17 million, so there has been phenomenal growth in a relatively short time frame.

China's Ministry of Information Industry (MII) controls several state-owned government companies that operate networks which connect to the global Internet. These are the backbones or hubs through which all Internet traffic must pass, including all data files and communications such as email. Chinese users can access the Internet through the services provided by several state-licensed Internet Access Providers (IAPs), including China Telcom and China Netcom. Thanks to this system, the Chinese government controls the whole physical infrastructure that permits connectivity to the outside world.

The Internet has given rise to many business opportunities for companies involved in the Internet infrastructure. In addition to the Chinese IAPs there are Web portals such as Netease, Sina, and Sohu. In 2001 a Chinese search engine, Baidu.com, was introduced throughout the country to compete with Yahoo. There are also social networking sites and a very popular microblogging service called Sina Weibo, which is the Chinese version of Twitter. Microblogging has had a profound impact on daily life in China, since it has facilitated the spread of news and information in ways that were not possible in the past. It has also enabled spontaneous protests that are difficult for the government to moderate or repress. After a series of deadly school bus crashes, microblogging sites became an active platform for expressions of discontent about the State's neglect of safety issues. Thanks to the rapid postings that continually occur on these *weibos*, the Chinese government may not be able to control the news cycle as efficiently as it has done in the past.[15]

The Internet has also created opportunities for new domestic industries in China, such as online gaming. Foreign companies had little chance of success once China's Ministry of Culture classified online games as "cultural products." Online games, the ministry believed, should be based on Chinese stories and fables, not American ones. As a result, the Chinese gaming market is currently dominated by companies like Tencent, NetEase, and Shanda. Many foreign games are excluded from the market by regulatory barriers or censorship. China's success in gaming is a "metaphor" for how China works: copy Western technology with the help of joint ventures and erect barriers against foreign competition.[16]

China began blocking Internet content in August 1996, only a year after it made the Internet service available to its citizens. Among the first websites to be blocked was Voice of America. China's comprehensive censorship standards are now among the most restrictive in the entire world. The Net's distributed and anarchic architecture make it resistant to most forms of government regulation. Nonetheless, despite the difficulties involved with censoring this borderless global technology, China has been fairly successful at directing and regulating its citizens' use of the Internet. In the words of one U.S. congressman, the Internet in China has become "a cyber sledge hammer of repression."[17]

China believes that the Internet must be tightly controlled in order to ensure social harmony and economic stability. It makes no secret of its commitment to active censorship and shows no reluctance to aggressively enforce its Draconian censorship laws. But China relies even more heavily on simple digital technologies. In the late 1990s, the Chinese Government put in place an impressive filtering system, known as the "Great Firewall of China," by which it blocks hundreds of thousands of websites from the view of Chinese citizens. The second pillar of control is the Golden Shield, for domestic surveillance, which was initiated in 1998 by the Ministry of Public Security.[18]

The firewall blocks any speech that is not considered to be socially beneficial, such as content related to the Falun Gong spiritual movement. It blocks references to the Tiananmen Square incident in 1989, when young Chinese citizens sought to defy the government by demanding a more open political society. The famous image of a young man confronting a tank in the square can be downloaded almost anywhere in the world except China. Information on Tibet's political autonomy, the Dalai Lama, and Taiwanese independence is also filtered by the firewall. According to a study conducted by the Open Net Initiative (ONI), China has persistently and effectively blocked all websites with content about these topics. Here is a sample of the sites that were actually blocked: www.faluncanada.net, www.falun.org, www.tssquare.tv, www.hrchina.org [a site about human rights issues in China focusing on Tiananmen Square], www.taiwan.com, www.taiwanindependence.com, www.taiwanese.com/protest, www.tibet.com, www.dalailama.com, www.freetibet.org, www.tibetanliberation.org.[19]

Many media and news websites are also subject to government censorship. For example, the website of the British Broadcasting Company (BBC) is blocked [www.bbc.co.uk], and the international news website of Voice of America [www.voa.gov] remains off limits. Sometimes the *New York Times* website is blocked and sometimes it isn't. Bloomberg News was blocked in 2012 after it ran a story about the finances of vice-president Xi Jinping. If Chinese users try to access popular and influential human rights sites, like Amnesty International or Human Rights Watch (http://hrw.org), they will be disappointed.[20] Internet pornography websites were also filtered at a high rate, though China has only recently decided to concentrate on blocking these sites. The effort to filter out pornography has led to considerable "overblocking"—for example, sex education websites such as www.premaritalsex.info are inaccessible to Chinese users.[21]

In addition to filtering objectionable websites, the Chinese government also monitors all email and instant messaging, and it tries to regulate the burgeoning blogosphere. The government has shut down many blogs that have written about the Tiananmen Square incident or even more general topics, such as government corruption and the hardships of unemployed workers. In some cases it must rely on the Internet companies that host the blogs. In 2006 Microsoft closed down a popular Chinese-language blog hosted on MSN Spaces when the blog sharply criticized the government's firing of the editors at a progressive Beijing newspaper. Microsoft was criticized for taking this action, but defended itself with this statement: "MSN is committed to ensuring that products and services comply with global and local laws, norms, and industry practice in China."[22]

Finally, China forbids any access to global social media platforms, such as Facebook, Twitter, and Tumblr. In many countries these platforms have been used as organizing tools for protesters. But in China, Facebook and Twitter were permanently blocked in 2009 after riots in Xinjlang. These sites feed the natural impulse to share and disseminate information, not all of which is benign (at least from the Chinese government's perspective). YouTube was permanently blocked in 2008 after videos of unrest in Tibet created a stir in the country. Each one of these platforms host too much uncensored content about human rights, politics, and religion. There are social networking platforms like RenRen that substitute for Facebook, but they are carefully monitored by the Chinese censors.

China's great firewall has ramifications that go well beyond China. The country's "giant cage" has undoubtedly contributed to a more balkanized and fragmented Internet. Thanks to China and other authoritarian governments, the Internet is no longer a borderless global technology with few restrictions on information flows, but a collection of nation-state networks that heavily restrict content. While information may move more freely within a country there is far less mobility across cultural borders. This process of balkanization threatens to completely revolutionize the Internet, dismantling the social structures that once seemed beyond the government's control.²³

Cisco in China

The Chinese authorities could not build or sustain their "Great Firewall" without the technological assistance of giant high-tech Chinese companies like Huawei and ZTE. It has also had the assistance of some U.S. companies, which have helped China construct its Internet infrastructure. One company that has played a central role in this construction is Cisco. Cisco was founded in 1984, at the height of the personal computer revolution, when opportunities abounded for companies developing network technologies. Known for its customer service mentality and superior product line, Cisco took full advantage of the surge in private organizations which wanted Internet connectivity. Cisco also provided local area networks and many other network solutions to a wide variety of corporate clients.

The company's core products, including switching equipment and routers, are manufactured primarily for the telecommunications industry. Competitors in this segment of Cisco's business include Sweden's Ericsson, China's Huawei, and France's Alcatel-Lucent. The router is a synthesis of hardware and software that provides data-routing capability central to the Internet infrastructure. Routing is the process by which a path or route is selected for transmitting packets of data across the Internet in accordance with the TCP/IP protocols which break that data (such as an email message or website content) into packets. This flexible routing system is achieved through a "hopping" process whereby data is passed from one computer to another until it reaches its destination.²⁴ By 1999, Cisco had an 80 percent share of this dynamic global market for routers, and it remains a dominating industry leader. In later years Cisco has expanded into a whole range of application software in order to provide more seamless and comprehensive solutions to its customers.

Cisco, along with its three main competitors, is a principal supplier of routers and switching equipment to many foreign countries including China. How do its products factor into this country's technologies of control? There are eight large gateways coming into China from the global network that provides Internet access for Chinese citizens. The Chinese Government requires the Chinese telecom companies that control these gateways to configure their routers in order to screen and filter out objectionable content. The Chinese government controls these telecom companies (such as China Telcom), which use Cisco routers for the "backbone" of the Chinese network. After they are purchased from Cisco, these routers are equipped with packet filtering capability that enables the filtering-out of unwanted content. While the primary purpose of routers is to direct or "route" Internet traffic to its correct destination, they can also be easily configured to block content and thereby *prevent* information from getting to its destination. These specially modified gateway routers can block an entire website (such as taiwandemocracy.com) based on an access control list, or process web content through "deep packet inspection." With deep packet inspection software, the router can examine the specific content of data packets. Any message or "packet" of information that contains forbidden language will be blocked. The router itself, therefore, becomes the censor.[25]

Of course, these routers and filtering mechanisms, used for the purpose of censorship, are far from foolproof. Like all firewalls China's has a certain level of porosity. Circumvention technologies, like proxy servers located outside of China, can help sophisticated Internet users to bypass the firewall. There are also anti-censorship software tools. Yet the best estimate of researchers is that only one percent of Chinese Internet users take advantage of such tools to access forbidden content or social networks like Twitter and Facebook. This may be due to fear of getting caught, a lack of awareness that such tools exist, or perhaps a lack of interest in what lies beyond this formidable "firewall."[26]

Cisco has come under harsh criticism for supplying China with networking equipment, and also for selling the country surveillance software. There are two lawsuits, which accuse Cisco of helping the Chinese government censor the Internet. But is this criticism fair? In its defense, Cisco management has always made it quite clear that they do not equip those routers with any filtering software that allows for deep packet inspection. In Congressional Hearings in 2006 and 2008, called to investigate Cisco's activities, the company's senior vice-president, Mark Chandler, acknowledged that networking equipment has to include some limited filtering capabilities to restrict hackers and to block damaging materials. But he protested that Cisco sells the exact same standard, unmodified networking equipment to all countries seeking its services. Moreover, he added, Cisco "does not customize, or develop specialized or unique filtering capabilities in order to enable different regimes to block access to information."[27] Nonetheless, Cisco routers, specially configured by Chinese experts to stand guard over the virtual borders of China, have been transformed into a censorship tool. Should Cisco still sell to China its "unmodified" routing equipment, equipped with generic packet filtering capability, knowing in advance that they will become a principal component in the great China firewall? Should companies be held accountable for the misuse of their products by an authoritarian state?

A more embarrassing problem for Cisco has been allegations of its possible involvement in China's surveillance projects. China is building a sophisticated surveillance system, in the heavily populated city of Chongqing in southwestern China, that will include 500,000 cameras for video surveillance. The project is called "Peaceful Chongqing." Cisco was asked to supply networking equipment that is essential to operate this massive and complex surveillance system. These networks include servers, switches, and controllers that store, analyze, and distribute the videos captured by the surveillance cameras. Other Western companies, such as Intergraph and Hewlett Packard, are also involved in the project at some level. In response to critics, one Cisco executive told *The Wall Street Journal*, "We're just the technology platform," and it's the responsibility of buyers to "meet and adhere to laws and policies" of their jurisdictions.[28] With criticism mounting, however, Cisco ultimately declined to participate in the questionable "Peaceful Chongqing" project.

Before we discuss the experience of Yahoo and Google, it would be instructive to make a few remarks about Cisco's defense of its business transactions in China. In general, we set too high a standard if we expect companies to be fully responsible for how their products are used or misused. Cisco is selling to China unmodified routers, which are essential tools for the backbone of China's Internet. Despite the censorship, the Internet has undoubtedly created positive social and economic effects for the Chinese people. Once the Cisco routers are acquired, they are customized to block objectionable content. It seems unreasonable to hold this networking company responsible for everything its customers do with generic switching equipment and routing technologies. Cisco sells routers to China for the ethically suitable purpose of enabling Internet connectivity, and a side effect of that transaction is the modification of those routers by its customer with censoring architectures. Cisco does not share in China's intentions to block entire websites and filter web content. Any culpability Cisco might deserve as a cooperator in China's great firewall is strongly mitigated by the fact that Cisco does not use its resources to configure these gateway routers to restrict content. Moreover, forgoing the sale of router equipment to China would not prevent this wrongdoing, since other telecommunications manufacturers would be eager to take their place.

More problematic is the supply of networking equipment and servers as the foundation for a surveillance system, since this sale represents more direct involvement in China's censorship and surveillance regime. In this case, Cisco is more closely involved in China's questionable activities. While it may be acceptable to sell unmodified routers to China for the purpose of Internet connectivity, selling equipment which provides the connectivity infrastructure for a surveillance system to be constructed by a totalitarian government is exceedingly more difficult to justify. As companies like Cisco debate their role within China, a reasonable and morally prudent policy would generally allow the sale of neutral Internet technology products like routers for the benign purpose of Internet connectivity, while prohibiting the sale of hardware, software, and networking products whose sole purpose is to function as a platform for China's filtering and surveillance activities.

Google in China

Google, the ubiquitous U.S. Internet search engine company, was founded in 1998 by two Stanford graduate students, Sergey Brin and Larry Page. The company's original mission was "to organize the world's information, and make it universally acceptable and useful." Their specific goal was to create software that facilitated the searching of the Internet's expanding pools of information. Thanks to its PageRank algorithm, the Google search engine overcame the search spam problem, as it delivered more reliable search results than its rivals by giving priority to web pages that were referenced or "linked to" by other web pages. Google's simple and user-friendly home page also encouraged early adopters. Google monetized its technology by licensing its search engine and by paid listings, or "sponsored links," that appeared next to web search results. Both Yahoo and AOL licensed the Google search engine.

Google remains the most popular search engine on the Web and still powers the search technology of major portals and related sites. Google has about a 65 percent share of the global search engine market, with rival companies Yahoo and Microsoft falling way behind. After constructing their own search engines to compete with Google, neither company has been able to achieve any momentum in this competitive industry. Microsoft launched Bing in 2009 but has yet to take substantial market share away from Google. Google owns YouTube and has expanded in many directions with products such as Google Maps, Gmail, Google Docs, and a browser called Google Chrome. Google entered the cell phone market with its Android operating system that powers many mobile phones made by companies like HTC, Motorola, and Samsung. In 2012 Google purchased Motorola's cell phone business.

Google is well known in the computer industry for its strong principles, as expressed in three fundamental corporate values: (i) technology matters; (ii) we make our own rules; and (iii) "don't be evil." Google is committed to cutting edge, technological innovation and to sustaining a creative leadership role in the industry. The "don't be evil" principle is primarily actualized through the company's commitment not to compromise the integrity of its search results, and to allow ads to appear with those results only if they are relevant. Google has set high ethical expectations for itself and is often criticized when it deviates from its core values.

Google introduced a version of its search engine for the Chinese market in early 2006, google.cn.[29] Google's biggest rival in China is Baidu.com, Inc., which had an overwhelming 60 percent share of the Chinese Internet search engine market in 2007. Google had a

26 percent share at that time, followed by Yahoo China with 9.6 percent and Sougou with about 2 percent. Given the size of the market and its future potential, the company admitted that it was motivated to enter China because it was "strategically important" for its future.[30] However, Google faced a rare uphill battle in China's Internet search engine business. Baidu has dominated the home market since its founding, claiming that its success comes from its emphasis on service to its customers rather than on "innovation for innovation's sake."

Google's entry into China has not been without significant controversy. In order to comply with China's austere censorship laws as a condition of doing business there, Google agreed to purge its search engine results of any links to politically sensitive websites, disapproved of by the Chinese government. These included international websites like Human Rights Watch, or those supporting the Falun Gong cult, or the independence movement in Tibet. A search for "Tibetan independence," for example, would yield sanitized search results about that country excluding any websites of dissidents or human rights groups discussing Tibetan independence. As one reporter indicated:

> If you search for 'Tibet' or 'Falun Gong' [al]most anywhere in the world on google.com, you'll find thousands of blog entries, news items and chat rooms on Chinese repression. Do the same search inside China on google.cn and most, if not all, of these links will be gone. Google will have erased them completely.[31]

China's strategy in coopting companies like Google was to use these information intermediaries to make its censorship less transparent by erasing traces of censored websites so that people wouldn't even realize the specific websites or blogs were being blocked by the firewall. Even without this form of censorship, the "technical opacity" of search engines threatens the ideal of equal access to information, but Google makes things far worse by showing Chinese users only the links the government wants them to see.[32]

In order to avoid further complications, the company decided not to host user-generated content, such as blogs or email, on its computer servers in China for fear of the government's role in monitoring its users. Unlike its competitors, Google alerted users to censored material by putting a general disclaimer at the top of the search results indicating that certain links had been removed in accordance with Chinese law. Also, Chinese users could still access Google.com with its uncensored search results (though links to controversial sites would still not work thanks to the firewall).

Human rights groups met Google's cooperation with the Chinese government with great disappointment. These groups, and many other critics, accused Google of hypocrisy and of violating its high-minded corporate ethos. Shortly after Google introduced the censored version of its search engine to China, it was sharply criticized by the U.S. Congress: legislators asked how a company that strives to do no evil could "conspire" so blatantly with China's censorship regime. When asked how Google knew which sites to censor, the company's representative explained that Google studied and copied the filtering habits already in use by its competitors. A stunned congressman replied:

> So if this Congress wanted to know how to censor, we'd go to you—the company that should symbolize the greatest freedom of information in the history of man? This is a profound story that's being told.[33]

In its defense the company vigorously argued that its presence in China had a positive influence. Google expanded opportunities for Chinese citizens to have greater access to many forms of information. Most technical experts agreed that Baidu's search results were not nearly as comprehensive or accurate as Google's. Google simply had more experience with search engine technology and more sophisticated algorithms. According to a Google spokesperson, "While removing search results is inconsistent with Google's mission, providing no information (or a heavily degraded user experience that amounts to no information) is more inconsistent with our mission."[34] Google firmly believed that its presence in China contributed to the country's economic reform and modernization, and that this consideration must be balanced with the legal requirements imposed by the Chinese government.

The company itself was always ambivalent about its presence in China under these conditions. One of Google's founders, Mr. Brin, explained that the company was struggling with difficult questions and ethical challenges for which there was little precedent: "Sometimes the 'Don't be evil' policy leads to many discussions about what exactly is evil."[35] But in 2006 Google's pragmatic reasoning led it to the ethical conclusion that overall its policy was optimizing net expectable utility. Despite its censorship of some information sources, Google still provided Chinese citizens with an opportunity to learn about AIDS and other health-related issues, environmental concerns, the dynamics of global economic markets, and troublesome political developments in other parts of the world. Hence the benefits outweighed the harm.

However, after four years of complying with China's censorship regime, Google suddenly decided to reverse course. The catalyst for this decision was a cyber attack on Google.com that clearly targeted the Gmail accounts of human rights activists. As a result, on January 12, 2010 Google announced that it would no longer "self-censor" its China search engine. Google ceased offering Web searches on its main Chinese site and instead directed people to its servers based in Hong Kong. Google does not censor the Hong Kong site, though, thanks to the firewall, Chinese users will still be unable to access hundreds of thousands of websites censored by the government. It has been reported that Sergey Brin was the driving force behind this decision, while others, like CEO Eric Schmidt, believed that Google should persevere with its current China policy. Brin's change of heart came after the 2008 Summer Olympics in Beijing when the Chinese government began to intensify Web censoring and interference with Google's operations.[36]

Google must decide about the status of its future in China. Its share of the Web-search market fell to 17 percent in 2012, largely to the benefit of Baidu. However, Google has not completely abandoned the Chinese market, nor has it given up on the idea of a stronger presence there in the future. It hopes to capitalize on the growth of Android, the operating system that powers many of the mobile phones used in China. One of its tentative goals is to introduce Android Market, which offers thousands of apps for cell phones, into the Chinese market. It has also launched a product called Shihui, which allows people to search Chinese sites that offer discounts at local stores.[37] The problem is that Google's insubordination has upset many Chinese government officials and so its future success in this huge Chinese market is far from guaranteed.

Yahoo in China

Yahoo, founded in 1994 by David Filo and Jerry Yang, was originally developed as a guide to the Web and as a way to keep track of website addresses. This guide quickly evolved into a commercial website and a thriving business. In 1995 Yahoo took on an experienced executive, Tim Koogle, as its CEO. From the outset, Yahoo saw itself as a media company and not just a search engine or gateway to the Internet. During 1996 and 1997 Yahoo added considerable content and communication facilities as it evolved into a full-fledged Internet entrance point or portal. Yahoo's primary services were called "properties." These properties included navigational services, which help users find websites and other information more easily. It also includes "community properties," in order to help users communicate with one another. For example, users could access the Yahoo Address Book, which allowed them to look up addresses from any connected system. There were also e-commerce properties for shopping or making travel arrangements. Like eBay, Yahoo hosted user-based auction sites. Millions of users also flocked to Yahoo for its email services, instant messaging, scheduling, and personal Web pages.

When Terry Semel succeeded Koogle as CEO in 2001, Yahoo was using Google's search engine technology. After a failed effort to purchase Google, Yahoo set out to build its own search engine. The company purchased Inktomi for its search technology and Overture for its system of auctioning key words to advertisers in imitation of Google's advertising strategy. But its efforts to challenge Google have so far been in vain.

Like Google, Yahoo was guided by a core set of values since its inception in 1995. In 2006 the company reasserted those guiding values. The global Internet company believes that "information is power," and that citizens across the globe can benefit from its services to access the information they need. Among its key principles, Yahoo includes the following:

- We believe the Internet is built on openness, from information access to creative expression. We are committed to providing individuals with easy access to information and opportunities to openly communicate and exchange views and opinions.

- We are committed to maintaining our customers' trust. Hundreds of millions of consumers around the world have put their trust in Yahoo for more than a decade. We take our users' privacy very seriously and never forget users come to us by choice.[38]

Yahoo quickly expanded into overseas markets with localized content and overseas operations. During its early years, Yahoo had the biggest global reach of any Internet brand—it offered 23 local versions in 12 different languages. Foreign users accounted for over 40 percent of Yahoo's customer base by 2000. Yahoo had always prided itself on good relations with foreign governments. According to *Forbes*, Yahoo devoted much energy to "hitting the international conferences and meeting heads of state to talk Internet policy and plead Yahoo's local interests."[39] Semel emphasized the imperative for international growth with his strategy of "buy, build, and partner."[40]

But Yahoo was no stranger to foreign controversies. During the spring of 2000 two French anti-racist groups (the French Union of Jewish Students and the International League against Racism and Anti-Semitism) filed suit against Yahoo, demanding that they remove swastika flags and other Nazi memorabilia from their American auction website (Yahoo.com). Judge Jean-Jacques Gomez ruled in favor of these two groups, concluding that Yahoo had violated French law and offended the "collected memory" of France. He ordered Yahoo to make it impossible for French users to access any auction site that contained illegal Nazi memorabilia. After some initial resistance, Yahoo capitulated over concern about Judge Gomez's sanctions. The company removed all Nazi memorabilia from its websites, announcing that "it will no longer allow items that are associated with groups which promote or glorify hatred and violence, to be listed on any of Yahoo's commerce properties."[41] Some observers, however, questioned the ethical and legal proprieties of a French judge exercising such authority over a U.S. company for content on Yahoo.com (not Yahoo.fr) that was hosted on servers physically located within the United States.

Yahoo's experience in China, however, was far worse and, by some measures, even more disastrous than Google's. Yahoo entered the Chinese market in 1999. The company's presence grew rapidly thanks to a partnership with the Chinese portal, Sina, and other deals. Yahoo offered many services to its Chinese customers aside from a Chinese language portal, and that included its popular email service. As Google gained momentum in international markets, Semel was determined to capitalize on Yahoo's early mover status in China. But as a condition for market entry, Yahoo was forced to filter any information that was a threat to the government. Yahoo signed the Public Pledge on Self-Discipline for the Chinese Internet Industry, thereby committing itself to "refuse access to those Websites that disseminate harmful information to protect Internet users of China from adverse influences of the information."[42] Accordingly, like Google, Yahoo censored its search engine results, and conversations in its chat rooms were filtered to catch forbidden phrases like "Tibetan independence."[43]

Yahoo's problems in China came to a head in April 2004, the fifteenth anniversary of the Tiananmen Square protests. A Chinese reporter by the name of Shi Tao used Yahoo's email service to send a message to an NGO called Democracy Forum complaining that the Chinese government would not allow any memorials or anniversary marches. Several days after the email was sent, the police presented a document to managers at Yahoo's Beijing office demanding the identity of the Yahoo user who had sent this supposedly inflammatory message. The document was called a "Notice of Evidence Collection," requesting "email account registration for huoyan-1989@yahoo.com.cn, all login times, corresponding IP addresses, and relevant email content from February 2004 to the present."[44] The Beijing manager reluctantly supplied the information about Shi Tao without consulting corporate headquarters and without much internal deliberation on the ethically proper course of action. With the help of that information authorities located Shi Tao who was promptly arrested. The reporter was convicted of sending the text of internal Communist Party messages to foreign-based websites, and sentenced to 10 years in prison.

Reaction to Yahoo's decision was swift and angry. Reporters without Borders accused Yahoo of becoming a "police informant" and a "Chinese police auxiliary" in order to advance its corporate interests in China.[45] A Yahoo spokesperson responded by maintaining that Yahoo was obliged to follow the laws of each country in which it does business: "Just like any other global company, Yahoo must ensure that its local country sites must operate within the laws, regulations, and customs of the country in which they are based."[46] As criticism mounted from other sources, Semel and other Yahoo leaders continued to focus blame on China for Shi Tao's fate, deflecting any criticism of complicity.

Over the course of the next year human rights groups discovered three more cases where Yahoo had supplied information which led to the arrest of political dissidents. Among these individuals was Wang Xiaoning, whose family later sued the company. However, Yahoo continued to insist that it had done nothing wrong. While founder Jerry Yang admitted that Yahoo felt terrible about what had happened to these individuals, he claimed that their arrests were unavoidable: "if you want to do business there you have to comply with local law."[47] Few were convinced of Yahoo's arguments, however, and many human rights groups and political leaders accused the company of unethical behavior. Yahoo's behavior precipitated Congressional Hearings in 2007 where the company was rebuked for abusing the human rights of Shi Tao and other political dissidents. Congressman Thomas Lantos was particularly harsh in his assessment of Jerry Yang and Yahoo executives: "While technologically and financially you are giants, morally you are pygmies."[48]

The Yahoo case illustrates the danger of ignoring human rights and following host country law. How can companies like Yahoo operate effectively in countries with authoritarian regimes that do not acknowledge and respect basic human rights such as free speech? Is there any merit to Yahoo's consistent defense that it had to follow the laws of the host country? Or are Yahoo's actions hypocritical in light of its corporate values, which commit the company to freedom to convey and access information by means of its services? As we saw in the previous chapter, philosophers like Rawls do not consider free speech to be a universal right, which seems to imply more moral free space for China and more ethical latitude for Yahoo. Is free speech a universal right, as articulated in the U.N.'s Declaration, or is it contingent on culture and history? We turn to these philosophical questions in the next section.

The Right to Free Speech and Intellectual Freedom

A proper ethical analysis of the corporate behavior of Yahoo and Google must begin with whether or not China itself is doing anything morally improper when it engages in systematic suppression of dissenting political speech on the grounds that such speech is not socially beneficial. One argument put forth on the country's behalf centers on the cultural moral imperialism of its critics. They are accused of being intolerant of China's different standard for free speech. Accordingly, in response to calls for "Internet freedom," Chinese officials have accused the United States of "information imperialism." They have consistently maintained that China's Internet regulations are compatible with the country's nationalistic pride and its cultural traditions. In a White Paper released in 2010, China hailed the Internet as a "crystallization of human wisdom," but stated emphatically that China's "laws and regulations clearly prohibit the spread of information that contains contents subverting state power, undermining national unity, or infringing upon national honor and interests." China goes on to warn outsiders that "the Internet is under the jurisdiction of Chinese sovereignty."[49]

Many information technology ethicists like Hausmanniger have staunchly defended the ethical obligation to respect different moral belief systems, however discordant they are with traditional Western norms. Correlative with the turn to subjectivity is the post-Cartesian "turn to contingency" which gives primacy to difference and plurality, instead of cultural or social uniformity. As a logical consequence, there must be respect towards "the free actions that create difference and plurality."[50] Echoing Rawls, these philosophers have similarly argued that we must be more sensitive to the reality of ethical pluralism, which presumes that there are a broad range of ethical viewpoints that can be validly chosen by different communities. Pluralists may find some moral positions to be invalid but believe that cultures deserve copious moral free space and so their values must be presumptively authoritative.

Some cultural relativists take this argument a bit further and contend that the whole notion of universal human rights is antithetical to the recognition of cultural diversity. Samuel Huntington, for example, warns that the propagation of Western ideas such as human rights and individualism amounts to "human rights imperialism" that will only lead to a "reaffirmation of indigenous values."[51] Rights are a byproduct of the Enlightenment project's rationalism, and reflect the

Western ideology of "possessive individualism." Hence, the imposition of these rights on all cultures is imperialistic because it slights non-Western values such as those of Asian or Islamic cultures. Each society has a unique history and culture and therefore it makes perfect sense that every society will have distinctive ideas about entitlements.[52] Not every culture, for example, seeks to build the iconoclastic intellectual culture that is associated with Western society.

Along these lines, defenders of China's policy observe that it has a different conception of the person's role within the state. Like many non-Western societies, China values communities more than individuals, and therefore it promotes a more collectivist view of human rights, and this justifies its overall approach to censorship. The Chinese government respects in broad terms the value of free expression, but interprets that value differently than its counterparts in the West. The Confucian tradition sees the purpose of law as the protection of social harmony, which is inconsistent with the normative individualism of the Western liberal tradition. Confucianism embodies a social vision of family and society where "all key relationships were those of superior to inferior with a general duty of obedience owed by the inferior to the superior and a reciprocal duty of caring, support, and guidance owed by the superior to the inferior."[53] The regime provides durable political order resting on the rule of law, and in turn its citizens must be loyal to the state and obey that law. Thus, deference to authority and unwavering loyalty are traditional Confucian values that have shaped Chinese culture and provide some warrant for the country's constraints on defiant forms of political speech.

Since the days of Chairman Mao's cultural revolution, the country has sought to control knowledge and restrict expression in order to propagate the state's uniform message unencumbered by the dissonant voices of dissenters. This restriction is consistent with China's nationalism, which sees unequivocal support for the state as the only way for China to regain its long-lost greatness and avoid the humiliation the country has repeatedly suffered at the hands of the West. According to Vincent, "The fundamental rights and duties of citizens are to support the leadership of the Communist Party of China, support the Socialist system, and abide by the Constitution and the laws of the People's Republic of China."[54]

Given these cultural anomalies and different value structures, it is no surprise that China adopts a divergent view of intellectual freedom and free speech "rights," which are defined with such a narrow scope. The general norm of free expression is being interpreted according to a different set of particularities and cultural imperatives. The Chinese standard, which heavily limits intellectual freedom for the sake of the collective good, represents the concrete reality of ethical pluralism, which must be factored into moral decision-making by those doing business in China. In their defense of pluralism, Ess and Thorseth argue that: "As global citizens . . . we must learn and respect the values practices, beliefs, communication styles and language of the Other." Failure to do so, they contend, "makes us complicit in forms of computer-mediated imperialism and colonialism."[55]

This pluralistic understanding of ethics, which sees most conflicting ethical positions in different cultures as equally valid, is implied in the public responses of Google, Yahoo, and Microsoft to criticism about their policies. All three companies have argued at one point that their policies reflect the moral flexibility mandated by a moderately strong version of cultural moral relativism. According to Microsoft, "Like other global organizations we must abide by the laws, regulations, and norms of each country in which we operate."[56] Implicit in this argument, defending a "when in Rome" approach to morality, is the notion that ethical norms, like customs, have only local validity because they are prescriptive or action-guiding. The social norms and civil liberties in China and Iran are simply different from the norms and liberties enjoyed by U.S. citizens, and it's imperialistic to maintain that U.S. norms are superior. This moral perspective, if tenable, would seem to validate the questionable behavior of Internet gatekeepers like Google and Yahoo. In this context, despite the vociferousness of their critics, the companies are doing nothing morally wrong when they cooperate with China's extensive censorship and surveillance regime.

One problem with the application of the cultural diversity argument to human rights is that it presumes more cultural uniformity than is warranted. There is no single set of Asian or Islamic values. Asia is culturally diverse and many Asians support supposedly Western values such as the sanctity of life and the desire for liberty. The Chinese government may simply be appealing to "Asian values" and the dogma of Confucianism as a pretext to justify political repression in order to preserve the status quo. Debates about universal rights and cultural differences often fail to differentiate the traditions and beliefs within a culture from the sovereign state, which falls back on notions such as "Islamic values" to validate their restriction on rights.[57]

Instead of pluralism, we have defended the position of a moderate universalism, a comparatively thick set of universal human rights that limits the free moral space of every culture. In our discussion of rights in Chapter Four, we argued that there are intrinsic human goods valued for their own sake as constitutive aspects of human flourishing and that those goods entail an account of a common human nature. These substantive goods constitute the foundation of normativity and provide a secure grounding for moral judgments about justice and human rights. Where does free expression fit into this paradigm? Free expression is not a basic good, since it does not directly contribute to human flourishing. It is difficult to see how free speech would be valued in itself apart from the relational goods it supports. On its own, it doesn't really fulfill or perfect us, but it does allow us to pursue other forms of personal fulfillment. Thus, it is desired as a means to another end, that is, as instrumental to certain intrinsic goods that directly provide personal fulfillment. For example, speech or open communication is essential for the harmonious cooperation necessary to build community and create bonds of fellowship. Miscommunication or misunderstanding among people is common, but this reality means that communication efforts must be refined or revised, certainly not suppressed. Dissenting political speech often brings to light problems and conflicts that must be resolved if a political community is to overcome differences and evolve into a more authentic communion of persons based on the common good.[58] A persuasive case can be advanced that, because free speech fosters the intrinsic goods of social harmony and community it is an instrumental good, necessary in some ways for human flourishing. Hence there is a requirement imposed upon others not to interfere with a person's enjoyment of this form of good we call free speech, and this requirement can be expressed in terms of a right to free speech.

Speech is also essential to support and preserve the intrinsic goods of knowledge and reflective understanding. People cannot be coerced in matters of speech and communication in a way that interferes with their capacity to inform others of the truth. The acquisition of objective and true knowledge by people in a community is contingent on the ability of teachers and others within that community to disseminate that knowledge without fear of retribution or punishment. Censorship and suppression of certain information is typically motivated by a desire to keep the truth from citizens and to prevent them from overcoming ignorance and error. The restriction of free expression aims to achieve conformity of thought; it does not promote the intrinsically valuable good of knowledge.

From this analysis we can deduce that there is at least a moral presumption in favor of broad (but not absolute) free speech rights because free speech is an essential instrumental good. The rights promoting free speech protect a person's ability to participate in several intrinsic human goods that constitute the basis of human flourishing. These goods (objective knowledge and sociability) are not confined to the West or to liberal societies, but are sought by all rational persons as intrinsic to their personal fulfillment, and therefore it is plausible to argue for the universality of this right. Basic human rights are grounded in necessity, in what persons need and rationally desire "for the exercise and development of distinctive human powers."[59] The right to free expression, therefore, is necessary for the pursuit of several intrinsic goods common to all persons. All human beings, regardless of their cultural differences, need free expression to build authentic community and grow in fellowship and to advance in knowledge of the truth. Like most rights, the right to free speech must be limited in different ways that are consistent with the common good. Many sovereignties, such as the United States, do not protect perverted forms of speech such as obscenity nor hate speech that incites violence.

Further support for the universality and intrinsic value of this right to free expression is its endorsement by the United Nations in its Declaration of Human Rights: "Everyone has the right to freedom of opinion and expression; this right includes freedom to hold opinions without interference and to seek, receive and impart information and ideas through any media and regardless of frontiers."[60] The United Nations is certainly sensitive to cultural issues, but it also recognizes that some rights transcend cultural differences. As we have discussed, the U.N document clearly favors the universalism suggested by natural law theorists instead of the radical ethical pluralism of some contemporary philosophers. Implicit in its endorsement of these rights is the assumption that people possess them, not by some government's fiat or cultural consensus but as a matter of natural justice. This declaration also assumes that some cultures can be morally deficient and blind to the truth about particular rights, such as free speech.

If we assume that there is a natural, universal right to free speech, properly configured to protect morally justified privacy, secrecy, and security concerns, the Chinese government violates this right by prohibiting legitimate dissent, good faith disagreement with government policies, or attempts to correct the historical record so that future generations will know the truth about events such as Tiananmen Square. As we have seen, China relies on its cultural tradition and its history as an oppressed state as a rationalization in support of its nationalistic and authoritarian impulses. Loyalty and deference to authority have a grounding in Confucianism. However, there is a difference between the virtue of loyalty and blind loyalty to the state, or any authority. The Chinese state is not above committing injustice and when it does citizens must be free to call attention to that injustice and demand its correction. Yet China's laws and social structures do not allow for this type of critical political speech. China is guilty of a moral failing by not respecting this right to free political expression, which many of its citizens have demanded for decades. The natural impulse to speak openly about the state is seen in the immense popularity of microblogging, which is widely appreciated as a tool to speak candidly about matters such as school bus safety or the blunders of government authorities.

If this analysis is sound, the moral culpability of Google and Yahoo logically follows. Both multinational companies actively cooperated in depriving the Chinese people of their free speech rights, even though the government itself played the primary role in causing that deprivation. Thanks in part to Google, a Chinese dissident's pro-democracy website or a blogger's critique of the country's one-child policy becomes impossible to find. Companies have a duty to avoid depriving people of their rights, and rights deprivation can involve cooperative as well as direct actions. Instead of defying the Chinese government, both

Yahoo and Google assisted the government in perpetuating its censorship regime that deprives people of their free speech rights. If China is willfully violating free speech rights by blocking certain forms of speech and keeping important information from its people, the supportive actions of Yahoo and Google are unjust and immoral. Arguably, if Cisco were to provide the connectivity infrastructure for a surveillance and monitoring system, this company would be derelict in its duty to help protect the Chinese people from the deprivation of their rights.

The basic moral imperative at stake in these cases is that a moral agent should not cooperate in the wrongdoing or rights violations initiated by another. This simple moral principle seems axiomatic. If someone intentionally helps another individual carry out an objectively wrong choice, that person shares in the wrong intention and bad will of the person who is executing such a choice, and is guilty of formal cooperation. Google and Yahoo are culpable of formal cooperation, since they intentionally participated in the wrongdoing (human rights abuses) carried out by the Chinese government. Google did not share completely in the bad will of the Chinese censors since it disagrees with their ends. Nonetheless, it intended the chosen means of abetting those censors in order to have a presence in the world's second largest market. However reluctantly, Google intended to censor its search results and further the aims of China's censorship regime as a condition of doing business in China. Neither this ulterior motive nor any extenuating factors mitigate its responsibility. It makes no difference that Google disapproves of China's policy or that its reasons or motives for censoring search results do not coincide with the reasons of the Chinese government. It is blameworthy for formal cooperation by virtue of choosing the wrong means to achieve its valid business objectives.

To sum up: in the absence of clear international laws and conflicting host country standards, corporations like Google and Yahoo must rely on ethical self-regulation. We maintain that proper self-regulation should lead companies to preserve their core values by respect for universal rights and avoidance of formal cooperation with host governments willing to violate those rights. The tradition of Confucianism may mean that the Chinese do not need or want the same level of intellectual freedom found in the West, but there must be freedom to criticize the government when it is corrupt or unjust in order to strengthen political community. A strong but limited right to free speech is considered by business ethicists as a substantial hypernorm; it is endorsed by many international agencies, including the United Nations; and there is compelling evidence that it is a condition for full human flourishing.

Conclusions

The Internet's open architecture was once expected to help promote democracy and free expression in authoritarian countries like China. The state's withering power was supposed to have created new forms of governance and political control. But the opposite has occurred, and far from being a tool for liberation, Internet architectures have become another mechanism for exercising the state's authority. The Chinese government has discovered the potentially hegemonic nature of Internet protocols and exploited them to its advantage. To accomplish this task it has depended on domestic companies like Huawei, along with the assistance and technological expertise of Western multinationals. China has used these companies to help build and maintain its censorship regime centered around the Great Firewall and the Golden Shield. It relies on manufacturers like Cisco for the routers and networking equipment to build this infrastructure. At the same time, it co-opts information intermediaries like Google and Yahoo to conceal the existence of the objectionable material being censored. This raises a dilemma for Western companies, which must balance the risks against potential profits.

Cisco does not participate in the construction of China's censorship infrastructure, but only endures it as a side effect, foreseen but not intended, of its choice to sell routers to China for the purpose of Internet connectivity. On the other hand, the sale of networking equipment to be used solely as the foundation for an authoritarian regime's surveillance system is morally questionable, since this transaction more closely involves Cisco in China's wrongdoing. The moral accountability of the Internet intermediaries, Yahoo and Google, is more unambiguous. By censoring online content, both companies were directly involved in formally cooperating with the Chinese government to deprive its citizens of valid free speech rights. Google's self-censorship of its search engine results cannot be condoned, and the company itself eventually realized the error of its ways.

The conflicts faced by Internet companies like Google, Yahoo, and Twitter exemplify the tensions between respect for local law and culture and the protection of universal rights. While China is an extreme case where virtually all forms of dissenting political speech are subject to censorship, there are borderline cases in other countries, which restrict speech in more limited ways. Twitter has been criticized for handing over to French prosecutors information about its users who tweeted anti-Semitic messages. The company also blocks many tweets in Brazil due to the country's demanding anti-defamation laws.[61]

Some may argue that free expression is not a universal right but one that is culturally conditioned. Rawls did not believe that this right had any "urgency," and so presumably it could be marginalized based on cultural consensus. China's Confucian tradition might also support the country's collectivist view of human rights, which hollows out the essential meaning of the right to free political speech. But if an analysis of rights proceeds from an understanding of those intrinsically valuable human goods we all share in common, the necessity of a strong but limited right to free expression and intellectual freedom becomes readily apparent. Lending support to this viewpoint is the unequivocal affirmation of this universal right within the United Nations Declaration of Human Rights.

It is wrong to frame the free speech debate in terms of the clash between the collective good and the individual's rights, since the collectivity is made up of individuals and the good of each individual and of their community "involves, as an intrinsic factor, that he or she is treated with fairness."[62] The thinly veiled utility arguments advanced by the paternalistic Chinese Government for subduing online dissenting discourse are not convincing. The responsible multinational corporation, which is committed to honor and protect basic human rights, must tread very carefully in China where these rights have been truncated for the sake of the state's political ambitions and its nationalistic pride.

Notes

1 Steven Secklow, Farnaz Fassihi, and Loretta Chao, "Chinese Tech Giant Aids Iran," *The Wall Street Journal*, October 27, 2011, A16.
2 Steven Secklow and Paul Sonne, "Mideast Uses Western Tools to Battle the Skype Rebellion," *The Wall Street Journal*, June 1, 2011, A1, A16.
3 Rebecca MacKinnon, *Consent of the Networked* (New York: Basic Books, 2012), 60.
4 Eric Schmidt and Jared Cohen, *The New Digital Age* (New York: Knopf, 2013), 85–6.
5 Shira Ovide, "Free Speech a Test for Twitter," *The Wall Street Journal*, August 5, 2013, B1-2.
6 Bernard Williams, "Censorship," in *Encyclopedia of Applied Ethics*. ed. Ruth Chadwick (San Diego: Academic Press, 1998), 436.
7 Alexander Galloway, *Protocol* (Cambridge, MA: MIT Press, 2004), 42.
8 Larry Lessig, *Code and Other Laws of Cyberspace* (New York: Basic Books, 1999), 85–99. Winner's more seminal insight was his conception of technology not as an autonomous and apolitical force but as socially constructed. See Langdon Winner, *Autonomous Technology: Technics Out-of-Control as a Theme in Political Thought* (Cambridge, MA: MIT Press, 1978).
9 Pierre Bourdieu, *Practical Reason: On the Theory of Action* (Stanford, CA: Stanford University Press, 1998), 138–9.
10 Gilles Deleuze, "Control and Becoming," in *Negotiations* trans. Martin Joughin (New York: Columbia University Press, 1990), 175. According to Deleuze, "The old sovereign societies worked with simple machines, levers, pulleys, clocks, but recent disciplinary societies were equipped with thermodynamic machines [and] control societies operate with a third generation of machines, with information technology and computers." See "Postscript on Control Societies," in *Negotiations*, 180.
11 *Reno v. ACLU*, 521 U.S. 844 (1997).
12 Schmidt and Cohen, *The New Digital Age*, 137–42.
13 "Chinese Internet Use Surges Ahead," *BBC Online*, July 17, 2013.
14 China Internet Network Information Center (CNNIC), 17th Statistical Report on the Internet Development in China, July, 2012; available at http://www.cnnic.net.cn (accessed March 31, 2013).
15 Loretta Chao and Brian Spegele, "Beijing Tightens Cyber Controls," *The Wall Street Journal*, December 17, 2011, A11.
16 "A Giant Cage: China and the Internet," *The Economist*, April 6, 2013, 11.
17 Quoted in "The Party, the People and Power of Cyber-Talk," *The Economist*, April 29, 2006, p. 27.
18 "A Giant Cage," 5–7.
19 Open Net Initiative (ONI), "Internet Filtering in China 2004-2005: A Country Study," April 14, 2005, Berkman Center for Internet and Society, Harvard Law School.
20 ONI, "Internet Filtering in China," 24.

21 "China Moves Against Internet Porn," BBC News.com, August 1, 2004, available at: http://news.bbc.co.uk/2/hi/asia-pacific/3943445.stm (accessed November 11 2010).
22 Quoted in Kathy Chen, "Microsoft Defends Censoring a Dissident's Blog in China," *The Wall Street Journal*, January 6, 2006, A9.
23 Schmidt and Cohen, *The New Digital Age*, 85.
24 Galloway, *Protocol*, 44–5.
25 Jack Goldsmith and Tim Wu, *Who Controls the Internet* (Oxford: Oxford University Press, 2006), 93–4. See also Schmidt and Cohen, *The New Digital Age*, 84.
26 MacKinnon, *Consent of the Networked*, 35.
27 Mark Chandler, Cisco Testimony before House International Committee, February 16, 2006, available at: http://blogs.cisco.com/gov/cico_testimony_before_house_international_relations_subcommittee (accessed February 19, 2013).
28 Loretta Chao and Don Clark, "Cisco Poised to Help China Keep an Eye on its Citizens," *The Wall Street Journal*, July 5, 2011, A1, A12.
29 In 2000 Google began providing a Chinese language version of its search engine from the U.S., but it had to deal with sluggish performance thanks to the firewall along with occasional blockades by the Chinese government. By moving its servers to China, Google could provide faster service, since it wasn't subject to the firewall, but it would have to deal with China's censorship law.
30 Declared in a 2004 company presentation. Quoted in Jason Dean, "As Google Pushes into China, It Faces Clashes with Censors," *The Wall Street Journal*, December 16, 2005, A1, A12.
31 Clive Thompson, "China's Google Problem," *New York Times Magazine*, April 23, 2006, 51.
32 See MacKinnon, *Consent of the Networked*, 37–8. Also, for a discussion on the politics of search engines see Julie Cohen, *Configuring the Networked Self* (New Haven, CN: Yale University Press, 2011), 193–9.
33 Quoted in Tom Zeller, "Web Firms Questioned on Dealings in China," *The New York Times*, February 16, 2006, 4.
34 Quoted in "Google in China," *The Wall Street Journal*, January 30, 2006, A 18.
35 Dean, "As Google Pushes into China," A12.
36 Jessica Vascellaro, "Brin Drove Google's Pullback," *The Wall Street Journal*, March 25, 2010, A1, A18.
37 Amir Efrati and Loretta Chao, "Google Softens China Stance," *The Wall Street Journal*, January 12, 2012, B1, B2.
38 Yahoo Inc., "Yahoo: Our Beliefs as a Global Internet Company," February, 2006; http://yahoo.client.hsreholder.com/press/relaesedetail.cfm?Release ID=187401 (accessed February 19, 2013).
39 Quentin Hardy, "Yahoo: The Killer Ad Machine," *Forbes*, December 11, 2000, 174.
40 Kevin Delaney and Dennis Berman, "A Big Buy for Yahoo Isn't Likely – Company to Focus Spending Spree on Expanding Global Presence and Increasing its User Base," *The Wall Street Journal*, December 14, 2004, A1.

41 Quoted in Goldsmith and Wu, *Who Controls the Internet*, 8. See also *La Ligue Contre Racisme et L'Antisemitisme v. Yahoo Inc. and Yahoo France*, Interim Court Order, The County Court of Paris 6, May 22, 2000.
42 Quoted in Goldsmith and Wu, *Who Controls the Internet*, 9.
43 Goldsmith and Wu, *Who Controls the Internet*, 10.
44 "Beijing State Security Bureau: Notice of Evidence Collection," translated by Dui Hua Foundations, 2004; htttp://www.duihua.org/medi/nes/070725_ShiTaodpf (accessed April 16, 2009).
45 Reporters without Borders, "Living Dangerously on the Net: Censorship and Surveillance of Internet Forums," May 12, 2005; http://www.rst.org/article.php3?id_article=6793 (accessed April 18, 2009).
46 "Yahoo Helped Jail China Writer," BBC Online News, September 7, 2005.
47 Peter Goodman, "Yahoo Says It Gave China Internet Data," *The Washington Post*, September 11, 2005, 33.
48 Quoted in Mackinnon, *Consent of the Networked*, 134–5.
49 Quoted in Schmidt and Cohen, *The New Digital Age*, 86–7.
50 Thomas Hausmanninger, "Allowing for Difference: Some Preliminary Remarks concerning Intercultural Information Ethics," in *Localizing the Internet. Ethical Issues in Intercultural Perspective*, in *Schriftenreihe des ICIE*, Band 4. ed. Rafael Capurro, Johann Frühbauer, & Thomas Hausmanninger (Munich: Wilhelm Fink Verlag, 2007), 39–56.
51 Samuel Huntington, "The Clash of Civilizations," *Foreign Affairs*, 72 (1993), 56.
52 Michael Freeman, *Human Rights* (Cambridge: Polity, 2011), 120–4.
53 Daniel Chow, *The Legal System of the People's Republic of China in a Nutshell* (St. Paul, MN: West, 2009), 42–3.
54 R. J. Vincent, *Human Rights and International Relations* (New York: Cambridge University Press, 1998), 56.
55 Charles Ess and M. Thorseth, "Global Information and Computer Ethics," in *The Cambridge Handbook of Information and Computer Ethics* ed. Luciano Floridi (Cambridge: Cambridge University Press, 2010), 168.
56 BBC News, "Yahoo Helped Jail China Writer," *BBC Online*, Sept. 7, 2005; available at: http://www.news.bbc.co.uk/l/hi/world/4221538.stm (accessed June 2, 2007).
57 "A Survey on Human Rights Law," *The Economist*, December 5, 1998, 9–10.
58 Germain Grisez, *Living a Christian Life* (Chicago, IL: Franciscan Herald Press, 1993), 397–8.
59 H. L. Hart, *Essays in Jurisprudence and Philosophy* (Oxford: Oxford University Press, 1983), 17.
60 United Nations Charter, "The Universal Declaration of Human Rights," in *Moral Philosophy for Managers* 5th ed. Richard Spinello (New York: McGraw-Hill, 2008), 293–7.
61 Ovide, "Free Speech a Test for Twitter," B1-2.
62 John Finnis, "Human Rights and their Enforcement," in *Human Rights and Common Good: Collected Essays*, Volume III (Oxford: Oxford University Press, 2011), 33.

6

PATENTS, PATIENTS, AND MEDICINE

Big Pharma and Developing Countries

Introduction

The reputation of the pharmaceutical industry has been badly tarnished over the past two decades. There has been a surge of public disapproval over unsafe drugs, along with high prices and excessive profits. The industry's woeful image problems have not been helped by Hollywood. In the 2005 movie "The Constant Gardener," based on a John Le Carré novel, a rapacious multinational pharmaceutical company is conducting clinical trials of a dangerous drug in Kenya. Why Kenya? Human life in this African country is expendable and hefty payoffs keep local officials subdued. This is fiction, of course, but some audiences and movie reviewers believed that the movie accurately reflected the dark side of the pharmaceutical industry. One prominent reviewer praised the movie as a "timely indictment of Big Pharma." The fact is that many drug trials are conducted in Africa. But this is where certain diseases tend to spread rapidly, so drug companies can get a better understanding of the drug's safety and efficacy when the product is tested there.[1]

To be sure, the pharmaceutical industry is hobbled by crippling problems, that include the withdrawal from the market of several high-profile drugs. There have been highly publicized safety crises involving Vioxx and the popular diabetes drug Avandia. Avandia, which allegedly contributes to cardiovascular problems, has been called "the worst drug safety crisis in our lifetime."[2] Drug companies stand accused of concentrating on "me-too" drugs that provide little clinical benefit over existing medicine and of being too precipitous in bringing some drugs to market without adequate clinical testing.[3] Research and development costs continue to skyrocket. In addition, some of the industry's most profitable blockbuster drugs such as Lipitor, Zyprexa, Plavix, and Seroquel have recently lost patent protection, opening the door for generic products.

One of the chief controversies that engulfs Big Pharma is the high price of many life-preserving drugs. The crisis over affordability came to a climax in 2001, at the height of Africa's HIV/AIDS crisis. Major drug companies, such as Merck and Bristol-Myers, initially refused to lower their prices for AIDS therapies until they were shamed into doing so by the media and by generic manufacturers such as India's Cipla. A lawsuit by several pharmaceutical companies against the South African government did not help matters. Once prices were lowered, U.S. advocacy groups seized on the low price points to demonstrate how large a profit drug companies make on their products. "All you have to do is look at how much they're selling drugs for in other countries to see [how] high they're jacking up prices in the U.S.," remarked an agitated industry observer.[4]

Despite the drug industry's reluctant concession on AIDS drugs, problems of accessibility remain acute in developing countries. Pharmaceutical products to treat chronic diseases like tuberculosis, cancer, and heart ailments are priced beyond the means of populations in poor countries. The problem is compounded to some degree by Trade Related Aspects of Intellectual Property Rights (TRIPS), which symbolizes the globalization of intellectual property rights. This regulation mandates the enforcement of intellectual property rights, including 20-year patents for all member nations of the World Trade Organization (WTO). Most developing countries have signed on to TRIPS to preserve their standing in the WTO. While the purpose of TRIPS is to better balance property rights and obligations, critics claim that it undermines national sovereignty over the rules that regulate and stimulate innovation.

Places like Africa, Brazil, and India struggle to enhance the welfare of their citizens by making drugs affordable, safe, and effective. They must often deal with the proliferation of counterfeit drugs, such as the bogus malaria drugs that were introduced into Africa in 2012. These places also want to stimulate innovation and research for diseases like malaria and sleeping sickness that are not a high priority for Western drug companies. These two objectives are in tension, and patents are at the center of the conflict. But the story of drug patents is complex, full of paradoxes and conundrums.

A big part of that story is the ethical rationale for patents, the scope of patent protection, and the social justice issue of distributive equity. These inter-related issues are the main axis of discussion in this chapter. Life-preserving pharmaceutical products are a socially important good, but markets do not always ensure that the distribution of these goods is morally arbitrary. The key ethical question is to what extent pharmaceutical companies must try to resolve the inequitable distribution that comes about when people in developing countries cannot afford to buy life-preserving drugs because patents drive up the price. How much of this burden should fall on Big Pharma's shoulders, as opposed to local governments and international political institutions? The larger policy question is how to satisfy the distributional requirements of life-preserving drugs while not doing long-term damage to the prospects for innovation.

Big Pharma

The term "Big Pharma" refers to the major Western pharmaceutical companies such as Pfizer and Merck in the United States, GlaxoSmithKline in the UK, Novartis and Roche Holding Co. in Switzerland, Bayer in Germany, and Sanofi-Aventis in France. These companies have dominated this fragmented industry for quite some time. Pfizer is the largest global corporation, with revenues of almost $60 billion in 2012. Novartis and Roche Holding Co. follow close behind. Thanks to stronger patent laws and a rising urban middle class, the stage is set for the growth of firms in developing countries such as India, where Ranbaxy and several other companies may soon be poised to become major industry players.[5]

The industry has been consistently profitable during its long history, which dates back to the end of the nineteenth century, when "ethical" drugs of a fixed chemical constitution first appeared. The top drug companies typically earn high profits, with Return on Equity (ROE) usually running over 25 percent. These numbers are well in excess of other manufacturing companies, which do not compete within such a favorable industry structure. In 2012, global spending on prescription drugs approached $1 trillion, but growth has slowed over the last few years in Europe and the United States. The United States is the largest market, accounting for almost $350 billion in annual sales, followed by Europe and Japan. These countries account for 85 percent of the world pharmaceutical market. However, with growth stagnant, companies like Pfizer and Merck are looking to emerging markets. Pfizer has a joint venture with Zhejiang Hsui Pharmaceuticals in China to develop generic drugs because it sees huge opportunities in this untapped market.[6]

Pharmaceutical companies have usually depended on a few "blockbuster" drugs (those with over $1 billion in global annual sales) like Lipitor or Viagra to drive profits and revenues. In order to control costs and prevent holdup, they have tended to be vertically integrated, performing all value chain activities in-house from research and development to manufacturing and marketing. This trend has begun to change in recent years, however, as companies now outsource some of their manufacturing and sales operations.

Most pharmaceutical companies still spend vast sums of money on Research and Development (R&D). Merck, for example, spends in excess of $8 billion a year on R&D, excluding special charges. Pfizer was the industry leader in R&D expenditures, spending over $9 billion in 2011. But recognizing that much of its R&D was not cost effective, Pfizer reduced its spending to $6.5 billion in 2012. Instead of expensive R&D laboratories, Pfizer now favors greater dependence on smaller biotech companies and academia.[7] Investment in research can pay off handsomely if it leads to the development of a blockbuster drug. Once it enters the market, a patent-protected drug is highly profitable, with typical gross margins of 90–5 percent. When patents expire (after 20 years) generic manufacturers usually sell the off-patent product at a price that comes close to the marginal cost of production.[8] However, the number of new drugs introduced into the market has fallen off dramatically. Pharmaceutical companies have employed many questionable techniques to extend the life of a patent, but regulations have made it easier for generic companies to enter the market as soon as the patent on the branded product expires.[9]

The biggest threat to Big Pharma continues to be the formidable challenge of dealing with generic products. Many blockbuster drugs have had their patents and market share challenged by cheaper generic rival products. As a result, drug company sales, which grew by 10–15 percent throughout the decade of the 1990s, have slowed down to single-digit growth.[10] As companies like Pfizer face generic competition, its sales have declined. With fewer drugs in the pipeline, there is minimal opportunity to offset patent losses. Although billions have been spent on research, only a few blockbuster drugs have successfully come to market within the last decade. Safety concerns have also complicated the industry's research efforts. Despite the fact that drug prices are under close scrutiny, these pressures have led to higher prices as companies try to squeeze as much revenue as possible out of their existing product base. In addition, generic manufacturers in developing countries are successfully contesting legitimate patented drugs and winning approval to introduce their own versions into foreign markets.[11]

To deal with these threats and a changing marketplace, the pharmaceutical industry consolidates and becomes more concentrated. Pharmaceutical companies continue to spend billions to buy biotech companies, which focus on specialized areas of medicine. This consolidation has caused many significant adjustments in the value chain and given companies a greater stake in generic drugs. France's Sanofi-Aventis has acquired generic manufacturers in Brazil, Mexico, and the Czech Republic. It also recently purchased the Cambridge biotech company, Genzyme, which specializes in drugs for rare diseases, as a base for its early drug research. Through the expensive Genzyme purchase, Sanofi hopes to strengthen its R&D capabilities and concentrate more on developing its knowledge of the biology of different diseases.

This research-based industry is heavily regulated in virtually every country where drugs are developed, manufactured, and sold. The United States system has come to represent a regulatory paradigm for the industry that has been imitated and refined by other countries. The first regulation on the books in America was the 1906 Wiley Act, which prohibited the mislabeling or misbranding of drugs by means of false or misleading information. Subsequent regulations have mandated safety and efficacy tests for all products before they can be released to the public. After preclinical tests there must be extensive clinical trials to verify safety, determine the right dosage, evaluate the drug's efficacy, and uncover side effects that might result from short or long-term usage. The Food and Drug Administration (FDA) reviews these findings and gives final approval before a drug can be marketed and sold to the public.[12] It usually takes 12 or 13 years for drugs to go through the cycle of testing and FDA approval, with an estimated total development cost of $1 billion.[13] Thanks to heightened safety concerns, raised by drugs like Avandia, drug trials are longer and larger, and hence they are more expensive. This higher economic risk makes a pharmaceutical company reluctant to start down the road of safety tests and clinical trials unless it is reasonably assured of success.[14]

Patents and the WTO's TRIPS Accord

Innovations are the lifeblood of the pharmaceutical industry, and innovations depend on patents. Patents create barriers to entry and allow companies to fully exploit their first mover advantages. As a result, they have contributed enormously to the industry's profitability. But are these profits too high, and are patents in the public interest, not just in the interest of Big Pharma? Are there other ways to encourage innovation besides the patent system? It is fair to question both the logic and ethical propriety of patents, especially in light of the industry's recent overzealousness in the assertion of its exclusive patent rights during the African AIDS crisis.

Many economists concede that patents are economically sensible because they are necessary to promote research investment for the development of innovative industrial products. This is especially true for the pharmaceutical industry where the cost of research and development is so high.[15] Since most innovations are creations of information they are public goods that can be easily copied. Patents give inventors a property right in their innovation so that they can exclude others from that invention and thereby appropriate the added value without interference from free riders. Without patents, those free riders would enter the market and, unburdened by any of their own research costs, force the price down to the marginal cost of production, making it exceedingly difficult for the innovator to recover his investment. Thus, the patent system prevents others "from reaping where they have not sown."[16]

While it is generally admitted that patents enhance aggregate social welfare by encouraging ingenuity and investments in new technologies, there are costs or secondary economic problems associated with the patent system. These problems include impediments to cumulative innovation along with foregone consumer surplus associated with economic rents. Patents can also encourage rent-seeking, which can entail social harm if companies dissipate scarce resources in their quest for "buried treasure," such as a big research breakthrough and a blockbuster drug.[17] Finally, there is the social cost associated with administering the patent system. The high cost of defending and litigating patents is a waste from a social welfare perspective. The objective of policy makers should be a balanced patent policy that rewards technological innovation while also minimizing the secondary costs of patents by ensuring that they are awarded prudently and only when necessary.

According to the U.S. Patent Act, a patent is to be awarded to "whoever invents or discovers any new and useful process, machine, manufacture or composition of matter, or any new and useful improvement thereof."[18] Thus, a patent-eligible invention must satisfy the criteria of novelty and utility, and it must fall under the category of a process, machine, manufacture, or composition of matter. Patents last 20 years from the date a patent is filed. Since drugs are clearly compositions of matter, they are patentable; both the production method and the actual substance are protected. Over the past few decades the scope of patent protection has been expanding to include computer software, surgical procedures, research tools, and business methods. Even living organisms are now patentable subject matter under certain conditions. In *Diamond v. Chakrabarty* the U.S. Supreme Court opined that the patent statute should cover "anything under the sun that is made by man."[19] The Court ruled that genetically altered life forms such as plants and animals are eligible for patents. There are, however, still exceptions to patentable subject matter, most notably, laws of nature, physical phenomena, mental steps, formulas, and abstract ideas. Existing material elements, along with plants and animals cannot be patented since they are discovered rather than invented. Such discoveries are "manifestations of . . . nature, free to all men and reserved exclusively to none."[20]

Patents are controversial, particularly in the health sector, because they are limited monopolies that generate economic rents, higher prices, and lower output. In the case of pharmaceutical products, lower output and high prices often means that life-preserving drugs will not be available to everyone who needs them. From a policy perspective, the goal of the patent system's exclusionary, output-restricting monopolies is to maximize the creation of applied inventions and innovations, including pharmaceutical products. The presumption is that "thick" property protection will give the innovator the incentive to invent, and provide a favorable environment for the acquisition of the complementary assets, capital, manufacturing, marketing and sales support, which are necessary in order to bring that invention to the marketplace.[21] Despite excesses in current patent law and its application, patents create value for patent holders and for society, which benefits from this stream of innovations.

Western society's highly positive vision of thick and durable patents for pharmaceutical products is not in harmony with the experience of most developing countries, which have been quite skeptical of this policy tool. After India was given its independence from the British Empire, it conducted a review of the patent system it had inherited from the British and concluded that this system had failed "to stimulate inventions among Indians and to encourage the development and exploitation of new inventions."[22] Many other countries, including Brazil, Mexico, and Argentina, came to the same conclusion. Like India, they weakened their patent laws to make drugs more affordable and accessible. India's reconfigured patent system, passed in 1970, limited patent length to 5–7 years and allowed for the patenting of manufacturing processes, but not the substance itself. The new patent law did not permit patents on imports—only locally manufactured products were patent-eligible. At the same time, it instituted a Drug Price Control Order (DPCO) that put a cap on prices for life-saving and essential drugs.

Big Pharma was dismayed over these developments, and so was the U.S. government. At its insistence, intellectual property rights became a chief concern during the negotiations for the establishment of the World Trade Organization (WTO). In an effort to harmonize patent protection, the World Trade Organization introduced its Agreement on Trade Related Aspects of Intellectual Property Rights (TRIPS). The TRIPS accord is ostensibly designed to reduce distortions in international trade that often occur when property rights conflict between two trading nations. TRIPS consists of provisions protecting copyrights, trademarks, geographical indications, industrial designs, patents, and trade secrets. Since TRIPS went into effect in January 1995, some of the most controversial provisions of TRIPS have been those regarding patent protection. A central provision of this multilateral regulation requires that products and manufacturing processes be patentable for 20 years in all countries belonging to the WTO. According to Article 27, "patent rights shall be enjoyable without discrimination ... whether the products are imported or locally produced." Article 31 of TRIPS authorizes compulsory licensing under certain conditions. This means that with government approval a third party can copy a patented product without the consent of the patent holder. The conditions include cases of national emergency or "extreme urgency."[23]

TRIPS may be beneficial for the United States and Europe, but is it beneficial for countries like India and Brazil? Prior to TRIPS many developing countries had exempted pharmaceutical products from patentability, or, like India, offered only weak patent protection. Putting in place this "one-size-fits-all" system seems to make little sense since these countries are at different stages of economic development. Many argue that the case for a global intellectual property system is thin. As Drahos points out, there is a certain hypocrisy involved in obliging both the United States and Rwanda, the least-developed member of the WTO, to have the same patent protection for pharmaceutical products when Rwanda doesn't even have a research-based pharmaceutical industry.[24] In addition, countries cannot follow the model of Switzerland, which had no patent laws for a long time. The Swiss were able to copy foreign inventions and only when it had developed an indigenous base of innovation and research did it put patent laws into place. Yet, thanks to TRIPS, developing countries cannot take the same path as these developed economies, since they cannot take advantage of loose protections that speed the dissemination and assimilation of knowledge.[25] TRIPS raises many questions, but perhaps the most pressing is whether or not developing countries must be able to exclude life-preserving and essential medicines from patentability for the welfare of their citizens.

Some countries, such as India, seem quite ambivalent about their commitment to these globalized intellectual property rights. In 2005 the Indian Parliament ratified The Patents Amendment Act, which put the country's patent system in compliance with TRIPS. Little noticed at the time was a provision that sets a higher bar for the approval of patents because it stipulates that patents will only be granted when products are more efficacious. The law wants to ensure that the innovation is "significant." Thus, the Indian patent office has denied patents for products that are accepted in most other countries. For example, Novartis' application for Glivec was denied on grounds that the company did not demonstrate improved efficacy over earlier versions of this medicine.[26] Moreover, a number of patent rulings in India have backed generic producers. In 2012, Germany's Bayer was ordered to issue a license to the Indian drug company Cipla to copy its patented cancer drug, Nexavar. The case seemed to be decided simply on the basis of Cipla's arguments that the Indian population needed access to cheaper cancer drugs. These rulings underscore the lingering suspicions about TRIPS, along with the obstacles multinationals still face in penetrating India's fast-growing market with their patented products.[27]

Normative Justifications for Patents and Intellectual Property Rights

How can pharmaceutical patents and other intellectual property rights (such as copyrights or trademarks) be defended on purely normative grounds? The nub of this defense is that these rights, like all property rights, are essential for a fair and just society. There is a strong rationale for rewarding innovative and creative work with substantive legal rights, which converts that work into a useful economic asset. At the same time, these exclusionary rights are permeated with limits and constraints. These limits mean that intellectual property rights, like patents, are subject to redistributive policies that correct any injustice caused by the granting of these exclusive rights.[28]

There are several normative theories suitable for the justification of intellectual property rights, but we will consider here only the two most prominent theoretical frameworks. First, according to the utilitarian paradigm, intellectual property rights are justified on the basis of the fact that they yield net gains in aggregate social welfare by providing an incentive for innovation.[29] This utilitarian or instrumental argument for intellectual property proceeds as follows: those rights are necessary in order to maximize the production of innovative products and literary expression by providing authors, inventors, and other creators with the reward of an exclusive property right for their work. Without such a reward, which takes the form of the owner's right to exclude others from the use of the subject matter of that right, there will be fewer such creations or inventions. Absent this intellectual property protection, people will be more inclined to copy what has already been created rather than investing in the creation of new ideas or products.[30]

This version of utilitarianism, known as "incentive theory," represents a classic *ex ante* justification of property rights that parallels the economic rationale for these rights. It has been articulated in many works, including those of Nordhaus, who sought to demonstrate that an increase in the longevity or robustness of patents would stimulate more innovations.[31] Moreover, the disclosure of an invention once it becomes patented offers great benefits for society, since others will be able to develop incremental innovations based on the original invention.[32] This incentive or reward justification for thick, exclusive property rights takes precedence over other normative justifications, at least in American jurisprudence. U.S. patent law seems to be based primarily on the conceptual foundation of utilitarian reasoning. According to one U.S. Supreme Court opinion, "the patent monopoly was not designated to secure to the inventor his natural right in his discoveries. Rather, it was a reward, an inducement to bring forth new knowledge."[33] The persistence of this incentive paradigm can also be attributed to the language of the U.S. Constitution, which suggests a causal relationship between an "exclusive Right" for an inventor's discoveries and the promotion of "the Progress of Science and the useful Arts."[34]

The philosopher, John Locke, on the other hand, claimed that property is a natural right and not a matter of economic pragmatism. A Lockean analysis, therefore, justifies intellectual property rights, including patents and copyrights, on purely non-economic grounds. Supreme Court opinions notwithstanding, it is our opinion that Locke's theory is superior to utilitarianism, which suffers from an indeterminacy due to its inability to definitively prove a correlation between ratcheted up property rights and more innovation.[35] According to the Lockean perspective, a person has a property right: that is, the right to exclude others, in his person, in his actions and labor, and in the products of that labor. Thus, Locke relies on a labor theory, justified by this thesis of self-ownership, to demonstrate why property rights are warranted when someone adds his or her labor to what is held in common. As Locke explains:

> Man has a Property in his own person. This no Body has any right to but himself. The Labor of his Body and the Work of his Hands we may say are properly his ... Whatsoever then he removes out of the State that Nature had provided ... he hath mixed his Labor with and joined to it something that is his own, and makes it his Property (II: § 27).[36]

There have been many commentaries on Locke's theory demonstrating how it applies both to physical and intellectual property, since production of the latter also involves creative effort and labor. As Easterbrook points out, "intellectual property is no less the fruit of one's labor than is physical property."[37]

It should now be evident that labor allows for the privatization and appropriation of what was formerly public or held in common, since labor puts a distinction between an appropriated object and the common by its transformation of that object. For example, if someone takes a piece of common, unusable land and, through the sweat of his brow, cultivates that land and converts it into something valuable and useful, that person has appropriated this land through his labor and deserves exclusive ownership. According to Locke, "As much land as a man tills, plants, improves, cultivates, and can use the product of, so much is his property. He, by his labor does, as it were, *enclose it from the common*" (II: § 27; my emphasis). Private property, therefore, is a fusion of labor mingled with pre-existing resources. According to

Waldron, the "acquisitive action ... is the act of laboring on the resource," by transforming it or improving it in some way to make it new and useful.[38]

Locke's analysis recognizes that it would be unjust not to let people possess the benefits of their industry, which they take such pains to procure. Implicit in Locke's theory is the notion that property is deserved as a just return for the laborer's efforts, and taking the product of that labor would be an unjust enrichment. As Locke stipulates, one who takes the laborer's property desires the benefits of another's hard work, to which he has no right. While this notion of dessert for one's efforts is reflected in Locke's general theory, it is important to underscore that a person is entitled to what he or she has worked on, primarily because labor belongs to that person. The foundation of property is within the person. I am justly entitled to the fruits of my labor because my labor has been "annexed" to those transformed common resources, and only secondarily because that labor is often difficult, time-consuming, and onerous (§ 32).

However, people should only appropriate property sufficient for their needs. For Locke, there are moral limits on what man can acquire through labor. This restriction is known as the Lockean proviso. Locke formulates this proviso as follows: "Labor being the unquestionable Property of the Laborer, no man but he can have a right to what that is once joined to, *at least where there is enough and as good left in common for others*" (II: § 27). Thus, an intellectual property right is by no means absolute, and cannot be compared with that subset of natural rights (such as the right to life or the right not to be tortured) which are absolute. On the contrary, property rights are subject to several limitations, implied by the proviso, to appropriate property while leaving "enough and as good for others." As long as this proviso is satisfied, then the appropriation "does as good as take nothing at all" (II: § 33).

While Locke's scheme limits what can be appropriated through labor, his philosophy allows for broad or expansive property rights so long as they do not interfere with the rights of others. This has engendered sharp reproaches of Locke for his "possessive individualism," and general failure to give enough attention to the common good.[39] In contrast to Locke, some philosophers, like John Rawls, give less emphasis to individual property rights and more to the fair and equitable distribution of assets. Rawls has argued that a just society will ensure that each citizen will "have an equal right to the most extensive system of basic liberties compatible with a similar system of liberty for all." Such a society will also arrange social and economic inequalities so that they work "to the greatest benefit of the least advantaged."[40] However, a broad property right is not among these basic liberties. Those liberties include the right to possess certain items of "private personal property," but not the right of "private property in productive assets."[41] According to Merges, "Rawls starts with egalitarian fairness and adjusts for property rights, in contrast to Locke . . ., who (roughly speaking) begins with property and then adjusts for collective fairness."[42] Unlike Locke, Rawls does not regard thick but limited property rights as essential for a just and fair society.

In summary, Locke's philosophy is a reminder that private property is a means to human well-being and that the person, as laborer or entrepreneur, has a right to exclude others from the unowned resources he has transformed through work and thereby appropriated. Of course, he also has a duty to the community to be prudent in what he appropriates and respects the needs of others. Despite the moral logic of limited property rights, they are frequently condemned as the source of injustice and inequities. In addition to the moderate criticism of philosophers like Rawls, they have been subject to more substantial critiques by Marxists critics. For the sake of balance, this critique deserves some consideration.

According to a Marxist-inspired perspective, intellectual property rights are a new form of feudalism, which foster relationships of great inequality. "Information feudalism" represents a transfer of "knowledge assets from the intellectual commons into private hands," with the effect of raising "private monopolistic power to dangerous global heights."[43] Just as capitalism has given capitalist owners property rights over labor so does information feudalism give private companies, monopolies and "biogopolies," control over intellectual objects.[44] Patents have come to symbolize the capitalist ideology, with its tendency to commodify all of nature, even the human genome itself. Patents and copyrights are pillars of capitalist economies, but these "rights" only represent a means for exploiting creative, intellectual labor. Capitalist owners, rather than workers, end up owning most of the intellectual property that is produced within a capitalist economy. These intellectual property rights are yet another means by which one class organizes and controls the production undertaken by another class. These rights are also suspect because they ignore the social and collaborative dimensions of labor, since they reward only the person or company that files for the patent, but not those who contributed to his or her innovation.

Intellectual property law, therefore, performs a disservice by commodifying the vast majority of intellectual objects, which are then integrated into the capitalist structure. According to this line of reasoning, society would be better off with a system that avoided the commodification of intellectual and creative works, so that they are not alienated from their actual creators and openly available to anyone. This system would encourage and reward the sharing of information and the advancement of scientific knowledge to the benefit of developing countries. This sort of information socialism would foster more creativity, along with "greater political and economic equality."[45]

The Marxist critique also claims, with some warrant, that intellectual property rights help to exacerbate inequalities between rich and poor nations. Developing countries, such as those in Africa, account for only a very small percentage of world research and development, and as a result they are heavily dependent on the transfer of proprietary knowledge and technology from developed countries. Exclusive intellectual property rights, which drive up prices, often impede the transfer of that technology and other intellectual resources, which are desperately needed in many nations in sub-Saharan Africa, Asia, and Latin America. These patents, which are primarily the domain of Western multinationals, also damage local competition and divert research and development funds away from the needs of poor countries.[46]

There is no doubt that strong copyrights and patents can sometimes hurt developing countries, especially when those countries are quite destitute and have no intellectual property to protect. Forcing such countries to adopt strong patents is the biggest defect of TRIPS. But, for other developing countries that are making some economic progress, such as Brazil or India, the story is a bit different. Over time, these countries can become more self-sufficient through stronger intellectual property protection. Without the support of these exclusive rights, the level of innovation will always be suboptimal. Prior to the introduction of broader intellectual property protection in 2005, Indian biotech entrepreneurs who developed innovative products were typically unsuccessful at commercialization and so abandoned their research. The weak Indian patent law enacted in 1970 did not adequately cover innovations such as pharmaceutical products, so the results of their costly research were impossible to protect from free riders. The system of incentives provided by a strong patent, however, is a major stimulus to local research. Ethiopian coffee-growers have claimed trademark protection for their authentic Ethiopian-grown coffee beans, as a way of differentiating themselves from imitators in other countries. Finally, in Mexico young musicians had a hard time signing contracts with major record companies because two-thirds of the CDs sold in that country were pirated, but stronger copyrights for their indigenous-influenced music solve the problem. Thus, at least in some developing countries, intellectual property protection can encourage domestic industry, economic development, and even the affirmation of cultural autonomy.[47]

The thrust of this section is that limited intellectual property rights, especially when seen in the light of Locke's justification, are both fair and just. A just society rewards innovators and creators with an exclusive property right as a matter of fairness, but it also limits those rights for the sake of distributive equity. The problem with the pharmaceutical industry has been a systemic failure to perceive the moral limits on its patents, even if those limits are not recognized by patent laws and policies.

AIDS in Africa

Opponents to thick and durable patents point to the AIDS crisis as an illustration of how damaging such exclusionary property rights can be. The Acquired Immune Deficiency Syndrome, known as AIDS, ravaged segments of the United States population in the 1980s. AIDS was a mystery, but after considerable research scientists linked AIDS to a deadly virus that was to be called the human immunodeficiency virus (HIV). Once the invading virus enters the bloodstream it slowly destroys white blood cells, which play a major role in the body's immune system. This virus is not spread through casual contact but requires the direct interaction of bodily fluids. Burroughs Wellcome, an American subsidiary of the British pharmaceutical company Wellcome plc, pioneered the first treatment for AIDS, an antiviral medication known as AZT. The drug was approved by the FDA in 1987 and sold for $8,200 an annual dose. The high price sparked outrage and the company was immediately put on the defensive. "It would be theoretically possible," declared a Burroughs Wellcome executive, "for us to give away all our drugs. Everyone would get it for a while and then we'd go bankrupt."[48] Several years later, researchers developed protease inhibitors that halted the infected cells from spreading the virus. Thanks to these drugs, and other preventative measures, the AIDS epidemic began to subside in the United States.

However, just as the AIDS epidemic was being brought under some measure of control in the West, it spread to sub-Saharan Africa with particular virulence and ferocity. According to the World Health Organization (WHO), 25 million Africans were infected with AIDS by 2001, with the number growing steadily each day. In South Africa, 4.2 million people suffered from this syndrome, which had become the leading cause of death. AIDS also swept through the vulnerable populations of Botswana and Zimbabwe.[49] There were ominous predictions about Africa's bleak future as it fought this losing battle with AIDS.

Although treatments for AIDS were becoming more efficacious, they were also quite expensive. The drugs on the market didn't cure AIDS, but kept the disease under control and prolonged the patient's life for many years. Major companies marketed an effective drug cocktail of protease inhibitors. Merck sold a drug called Crixivan, and Glaxo Wellcome plc marketed Combivir, a mixture of AZT and two other drugs that formed the core of its AIDS therapy. An annual dose of Combivir sold for over $10,000 in the United States. Most African nations were too poor to afford this medicine even at much lower prices. Also, making the drug accessible was not just a matter of lowering prices. Africa lacked the necessary health care infrastructure to deliver and administer the drugs, monitor their use, and educate people about how to use them.

Most countries in Sub-Saharan Africa had no resources to buy these drugs from Western companies in order to treat their afflicted citizens, and they did not have the funds to invest in manufacturing plants to make generic drugs. These countries were too poor to afford much funding for any sort of health care. Without follow-up systems and medical assistance the drugs could easily be misused. Thus, the problem of AIDS in Africa did not lend itself to easy solution, even if drugs were available.[50] Nevertheless, Doctors without Borders, along with several NGOs, were determined to remedy this crisis, and the first step was to acquire enough antiviral medication to treat as many afflicted Africans as possible.

However, in spite of pleas from AIDS activists and the World Health Organization (WHO), companies like Merck, Glaxo, and Bristol Myers refused to lower the price of their antiviral drug cocktails. When the United Nations and the WHO set up a pilot program to provide AIDS drugs at low prices, U.S. companies initially refused to participate. Discounts are always a delicate matter for the drug industry, which worries about threats to its patents along with pressure to lower the prices of their other life-saving drugs.

In desperation, the South African government passed the Medicine and Related Substances Control Act. The law permitted "parallel importing," so that South Africa could import pharmaceuticals from any source, including generic manufacturers, without the patent holder's permission. But Western drug companies quickly filed a lawsuit, claiming that the law infringed on their patents, by allowing the importation and manufacture of generic drugs supplied by drug manufacturers like India's Cipla. Cipla's president, Yusef Hamied, offered to make low cost generic drugs available to South Africans by breaking patents if necessary. Cipla had re-engineered patented AIDS drugs to make its own cocktail, and the company asked the South African government for a compulsory license to start selling its generic version of the drug. The company was prepared to sell its three-drug cocktail for $350 a year.

With Cipla's offer pending and public pressure intensifying, the pharmaceutical companies were forced to drop their contentious lawsuit. These companies were vanquished by a powerful coalition of American advocates for AIDS patients, European doctors, African officials, and aggressive lawyers.[51] The industry's swift retreat was accompanied by steep drops in AIDS medicine prices. Cipla's actions had set off a price war for supplying these antiviral drugs to Africa. Initially, in 2000 the Western drug companies had struck a deal to sell AIDS drugs with an 80 percent price cut but insisted that countries had to demonstrate they had an adequate infrastructure before getting the price break. But a year later, with no conditions attached, Merck agreed to sell Crixivan for $600 a year per patient, and Stocrin for $500; both are critical components of its cocktail therapy. These figures, Merck claimed, represented "no profit" for the company. The total wholesale price of Crixivan and Stocrin was $11,700. Glaxo offered to sell an annual dose of the Combivir cocktail for $1,330, well below its $10,880 price tag in the United States. Merck President Raymond Gilmartin spoke at the time about his company's "evolving stance:" a refusal to discount prices, initial price reductions with strings attached, and then steeper price reductions. This is all part of "gaining experience" for how to handle such complex issues.[52]

These bold and dramatic price reductions, however, failed to bring the crisis to closure or to mute the criticisms of activists and African country officials. Observers complained that the drug manufacturers were still making money. Cipla had revealed, for example, that the active ingredients for making an annual dose of Combivir could be purchased on the international generic market for only $240.[53] Also, despite the apparent magnanimity of providing these "break-even" prices, many Africans still could not afford the product. AIDS activists continued to demand lower prices, but over time a concerted world effort had begun to address the African AIDS crisis more comprehensively. In the wake of the AIDS crisis, the "Doha Declaration" was signed by WTO signatories in 2001, limiting the rights granted under TRIPS. The Declaration clarified the TRIPS provision on compulsory licensing. "The TRIPS agreement does not and should not prevent members from taking measures to protect public health. We affirm ... WTO members' right to protect public health, and, in particular, to promote access to medicine for all."[54] In cases of national emergency, countries have the latitude to manufacture their own generic version of medicine or import generic copies from other countries.

The story of the fight against AIDS has not been one of the more inspiring chapters in the history of Big Pharma. The industry gets high marks for developing efficacious and safe therapies like AZT and Crixivan so quickly, but low marks for how they handled the AIDS catastrophe in Africa. Companies finally did what was right, but only in response to intense public pressure. The industry was squeezed by an indignant public and generic companies like Cipla, which were perceived as heroic for their willingness to break patents and supply generic versions of AZT and Crixivan. The industry itself concedes that mistakes were made. One Bristol Myers executive attributes the failure to bureaucracy: "The challenge in the big company is to do the right thing more quickly than inertia and momentum and bureaucracy allows."[55]

But this story is not just about inertia or corporate bureaucracy. The pharmaceutical industry is always worried about the slippery slope, and whether or not giving in to demands for compulsory licensing or discounting will affect other products, leading to a calamitous "rippling effect" throughout the whole industry. This fear is not completely unfounded, and it underscores the complexity of these issues for a responsible company seeking to find a compromise between preserving patents and taking care of poor AIDS patients. We review the ethical implications of Big Pharma's behavior in the final section of this chapter.

The Case For and Against Pharmaceutical Patents

In *Against Intellectual Monopoly*, two economists, Michele Boldrin and David Levine, offer a strident polemic against the doctrine of intellectual property rights. Their basic contention is that intellectual property rights do not adequately resolve the market failure of the underproduction of public goods (i.e., goods that are non-excludable and can be easily copied) because they do not optimize social welfare. These rights lead to excessive monopoly rents and distributional inequities that should not be tolerated in a just society. In their view, an intellectual monopoly cannot be justified on the grounds of an economic calculus since benefits do not exceed the costs. The authors give many examples of how the patent and copyright systems have been abused and why the costs are too excessive to warrant their continuation. Boldrin and Levine endorse a radical curtailment and eventual elimination of all IP rights: "to secure our prosperity and freedom, we must abolish intellectual monopoly . . . entirely."[56]

The authors single out the pharmaceutical industry for special scorn. They disagree that the products of this industry warrant patent protection, despite the high R&D costs involved in bringing new drugs to market. Boldrin and Levine maintain that the case for pharmaceutical patents is much thinner than we have been led to believe. They point out that many drugs are discovered by government-sponsored research, especially the National Institute for Health (NIH), and that "Big Pharma" is more focused on redundant research that yields trivial rather than substantive innovation. How can we be so sure, they inquire, that valuable medicine would no longer be invented if patents were abolished? They conclude that "far from encouraging great new health and life-saving products, the system instead produces too much innovation . . . of the wrong kind—me-too drugs to get around the other guy's patents and get a share of a lucrative monopoly."[57]

Marcia Angell makes a similar case for radical reform in her book called *The Truth about the Drug Companies*. She describes the industry as parasitical for the way it depends on the NIH and the way it profits so abundantly from drugs developed from publicly supported research. She and other critics contend that big innovations are rarely developed by the single company that is awarded a patent, but by a network of institutions including government agencies and academia. Despite the occasional blockbuster drug, this industry, "corrupted by easy profit and greed," consistently fails to develop innovative products at affordable prices.[58] Her solution is tighter regulations, including price controls.

There are abuses in this industry, but the debate over the validity of patents does not always get a fair hearing in these books, or in other critiques of intellectual property rights. There is convincing empirical evidence that this industry, perhaps more than any other, needs patents for its survival, since there is a positive correlation between patents and research investment.[59] Consider the case of India. After its weak 1970 patent law went into effect, R&D budgets fell to 0.2 percent of sales, compared to 17 percent for Western companies. Indian drug companies had little incentive to conduct expensive research on malaria or other diseases that afflicted the Indian population. The case of India and other developing countries indicates that, without thick patents, research and development will be appreciably reduced and so will the volume of new medicines.

In addition, a recent study of 35 profitable "blockbuster" drugs showed that while NIH sponsored research played a role in development, private sector research geared to applied science and commercialization was indispensable. Zycher and DiMasi, who authored the study, conclude that "without the scientific advances yielded by private-sector research, most drugs would not be developed." Hence public policies (such as those affecting patents) that lead to a reduction in private pharmaceutical research and development will reduce the economic benefits of NIH research along with "the immense medical benefits derived from the continuous development of new and improved medicines."[60] Even if the discovery of a new chemical compound that can impede a disease takes place at a research university, a pharmaceutical company still has to finance the long testing process and decipher how to manufacture that drug in a safe and effective way that will benefit patients.

On the other hand, it seems beyond dispute that the pharmaceutical industry was at fault for the mishandling of the AIDS crisis in sub-Saharan Africa. In its zeal to protect its patents, companies failed to consider the scope of their social responsibility when a medical crisis is precipitated by the inaccessibility of patented pharmaceuticals. The crisis was a challenge to the fairness of the intellectual property rights system, and even to liberal capitalism, which gives priority to private economic freedoms over distributive equity and social justice. In this chapter we have argued that the most promising normative justification for intellectual property rights can be found within John Locke's political philosophy. But is there a way to reconcile Locke's paradigm with a more ethically responsive approach to the African AIDS epidemic? As we have observed, Locke's exclusionary rights are permeated with limits and boundaries. While Locke's theory sanctions strong property rights based on self-ownership, labor, and effort, those rights are constrained by the sufficiency proviso, which mandates that everyone leave "enough and as good for others," after they have appropriated what they need. But there is another limitation, stipulated by Locke, that is not so well known: the charity proviso which we briefly discussed in Chapter Two. According to Locke:

> And therefore no Man could ever have a just Power over the life of another, by right of property in Land or Possessions, since 'twould always be a Sin in any Man of Estate, to let his Brother perish for want of affording him Relief out of his Plenty. As Justice gives every Man a Title to the product of his honest industry, and the fair Acquisitions of his Ancestors descended to him; so Charity gives every man a Title to so much out of another's Plenty, as will keep him from extreme want, where he has no means to subsist otherwise . . . (I: §42).[61]

Locke is insisting that people in "extreme want" have a right, or a "Title," to another's presumptive property in order to ensure their subsistence or survival when there are no other means available.

The charity proviso clearly implies that Locke would take quite seriously the distributive inequity that besets the problem of a socially important product like life-saving drugs. The proviso implies that, as a last resort, there should be an attenuation of patent rights over these life-preserving pharmaceuticals in order to ensure their optimal distribution, so that the destitute have access. In these situations of dire need, pharmaceutical companies are morally required to accept a lower reward for the work and efforts that led to their innovation.[62]

We have been arguing throughout this book that multinationals have a minimal obligation to avoid depriving people of their rights and sometimes to help protect people from the deprivation of their rights. People have a right not to be deprived of the intrinsic goods of life, health and bodily integrity by acts contrary to those goods. It follows that they also have a right not to be deprived of essential health care and life-saving medicines, which are instrumental goods necessary for preserving life and sound health. Given their importance for human flourishing, the provision of these goods is required of others in justice, and hence it is a right.

The state and local political community have the joint obligation to ensure that the conditions are met for sustaining the health and well-being of citizens, who need access to doctors and hospitals, along with safe and effective therapies to treat their illnesses. But sometimes a sovereign state is too poor to provide the conditions for adequate health care. It must then seek out the help of the international community, which has a moral duty to provide that assistance, within reason, based on every person's right to the means to preserve his or her health. Delivering such aid and medicine, however, can sometimes be a complicated business (as we saw in the AIDS crisis), and it requires the goodwill and cooperation of many parties. When life-preserving drugs are needed in these situations, pharmaceutical companies have a duty to cooperate. More specifically, they have a duty to protect this right to essential medicines from deprivation, when that deprivation is occurring primarily because of the enforcement of their patents. Thanks to insurance coverage, price controls, and consumer wealth, patents under normal conditions do not typically interfere with a person's access to life-preserving medicine. But in situations like the AIDS crisis, where patents block fair access to these medicines, patent rights must be waived. Under these exigent conditions of "extreme want," pharmaceutical companies fail to protect from deprivation a person's right to life-preserving medicine unless they are willing to compromise or surrender their own *bona fide* property rights and cooperate with other institutions in order to ensure equitable access. The application of Locke's charity proviso leads to the same conclusion, and it also helps us to appreciate how human rights are limited by each other and by the common good.[63]

We must tread carefully, however, because a pharmaceutical company is not a charity. It has an economic mission and its primary obligation is to create value for society by developing, manufacturing, and selling pharmaceutical products. A large part of its value-creating activities involves bringing new innovations to market. In determining the specifics of how far these companies should go in their obligations to make medicine accessible, there are a number of key considerations. Overriding patents will have some detrimental effects on other stakeholders. Given the nature and complexity of pharmaceutical research, one stakeholder group that cannot be neglected is that which will suffer from potentially treatable or curable diseases in the future. If overriding patents will diminish investment for innovations aimed at those diseases, this group will be potentially disadvantaged by Big Pharma's generosity. In calling for the relinquishing or loosening of patent rights, we cannot neglect this critical dimension of intergenerational justice. How will attenuating patent rights today affect future generations of disease sufferers? Will weakening of patents for some segments of the world population lead to less R&D because of diminished revenue streams and lower profits? These are very difficult questions to answer, thanks to the lack of empirical data. Nevertheless, the salient issue of intergenerational equity must be taken into account when resolving the problem of providing fair access to patented pharmaceutical products for those who cannot afford them. Charity today must be balanced with concern for the benefits research and innovation will yield for tomorrow.[64]

One implication of these intergenerational justice concerns is that the burden of providing affordable medicine to the disenfranchised should not fall disproportionately on the pharmaceutical industry. NGOs, charitable foundations (such as the Gates Foundation), local governments, and multilateral institutions like the WHO and the United Nations, should collaborate to ensure an adequate supply of life-saving drugs to those in need. A moral attitude of solidarity, which has not been evident in the rhetoric or actions of pharmaceutical companies, is necessary for a long-term solution to the problem of access to basic medicines. Countries which are the beneficiaries of this largesse might make their own contribution by enforcing TRIPS in the case of illegal generics for patented drugs that treat non-life threatening diseases (such as Viagra or Cialis).

Conclusions

In spite of its notable success in developing cures and treatments for many diseases, as well as HIV/AIDS, Big Pharma no longer seems to enjoy much public approbation. Industry criticism is often laced with hyperbole, but some of this disparagement is justified. Particularly disturbing is the industry's overzealous protection of its patents, even in the face of calamities such as the African AIDS crisis. Pharmaceutical companies have been exceedingly apprehensive that overriding patents would push the industry down a slippery slope, with more and more countries breaking patents to provide drugs for their indigent citizens. Perhaps this is why pharmaceutical industry leaders looked upon the whole AIDS incident as an "economic war."[65]

Patents are limited monopolies that allow the patent-holder to reap monopoly rents as a reward for the risk and expense of developing innovations. The pharmaceutical industry, where new drugs cost about $1 billion and take on average 12.8 years to come to market, depends on patents to protect itself from free riders so it can appropriate the value it has created. But patents create secondary economic problems, such as rent seeking expenditures, excessive economic rents that reduce consumer surplus, higher prices, and lower output. As a result, affordability becomes a serious problem for those who lack the resources to purchase these expensive patented products.

Yet patent laws have been strengthened throughout the world. Thanks to TRIPS, all countries belonging to the WTO have agreed to 20-year patents for pharmaceutical products. While countries like India have signed on to TRIPS they have repeatedly violated the spirit of this international law. Critics of TRIPS claim that it makes little sense to prescribe the same patent ground rules for each country when so many developing countries have no intellectual property to protect. However, TRIPS, coupled with the Doha Declaration, give countries considerable latitude in the case of national emergencies.

Although pharmaceutical patents generate market distortions, they still create value for the patent holder and society. We have argued that patents are theoretically justified as an incentive to encourage innovation, but most especially on non-economic grounds as a just appropriation of the fruit of one's labor and investment. This Lockean argument is predicated on the thesis of self-ownership: a man has exclusive property in his embodied personhood, his actions, and his labor, and hence is entitled to pre-existing common resources transformed by that labor. But property rights, unlike certain other rights, are not absolute. Locke recognized their intrinsic limitations, which were expressed in terms of the sufficiency and charity provisos.

Critics of the patent system claim that these limited monopolies interfere with achieving distributional equity, since the destitute, who need medicine, are deprived because they cannot afford it. They cite the African AIDS crisis as a prime example of the enormous human toll of this flawed patent system. Lack of access to essential patent-protected medicines, especially for life-threatening diseases like malaria and tuberculosis, persists as a major challenge for the governments and the global health care industry. However, in cases of "extreme want," destitute people have a right to life-preserving medicine, even if they are protected by a patent. If we accept Locke's balanced approach to property rights, there is a duty on the part of pharmaceutical companies to protect against the deprivation of this right to life-preserving medicines by relinquishing patent rights when those rights block fair access to that medicine and when there is no other recourse. This moral obligation to assist the poor in this way, however, must be balanced by a commitment to future research for the sake of intergenerational justice.

Notes

1 Roger Bate, "The Companies Everyone Loves to Hate," *The Wall Street Journal*, September 16, 2005, W13.
2 Andrew Jack, "Perils for Pill Pushers," *Financial Times*, September 22, 2010, 9.
3 "An Overdose of Bad News – The Drug Industry," *The Economist*, March 19, 2005, 89.
4 Gardiner Harris, "AIDS Gaffes in Africa Come Back to Haunt Drug Industry at Home," *The Wall Street Journal*, March 7, 2001, A1, A14.
5 Tracy Stanton, "Top Pharma Companies by 2012 Revenues," http://www.fiercebiotch.com/top-pharma-companies-2012 (accessed August 31, 2013).
6 Stanton, "Top Pharma Companies by 2012 Revenues."
7 Andrew Jack, "Supply Running Low," *Financial Times*, February 10, 2011, 9.
8 Barbara Martinez and Jacob Goldstein, "Big Pharma Faces Grim Prognosis," *The Wall Street Journal*, December 6, 2007, A1, A14.
9 See Feldman's discussion of the Hatch-Waxman Act in Robin Feldman, *Rethinking Patent Law* (Cambridge, MA: Harvard University Press, 2012), 159–62.
10 "Prescription for Change – A Survey of Pharmaceuticals," *The Economist*, June 18, 2005, 3–5.
11 Martinez and Goldstein, "Big Pharma Faces Grim Prognosis," A14.
12 For a more thorough review of these regulations see Peter Termin, *Taking Your Medicine: Drug Regulation in the United States* (Cambridge, MA: Harvard University Press, 1980).
13 This is a disputed figure but it is often cited by the industry. The last serious independent study, by Joseph DiMasi at Tufts, puts the figure at $802

million: $400 million in out-of-pocket expenses and the remainder represents the discounted cost of capital. See "Prescription for Change – A Survey of Pharmaceuticals." See also Joseph DiMasi, Ronald Hansen, and Henry Grabowski, "The Price of Innovation: New Estimates of Drug Development Costs," *Journal of Health Economics*, 22 (2003), 151–85.
14 Jack, "Perils for Pill Pushers," 9.
15 One study, for example, found that intellectual property rights played a definite role in spurring innovation in the chemical and pharmaceutical industries. See Richard Levin, *Appropriating the Returns from Industrial Research and Development* in *Brookings Papers on Economic Activities*, vol. 3. (Washington, D.C.: Brookings Institute, 1987).
16 Kenneth Dam, "The Economic Underpinnings of Patent Law," *Journal of Legal Studies*, 23 (1994): 247–71. I have relied on Dam's analysis in this discussion on the economic justification for patents.
17 Dam, "The Economic Underpinnings of Patent Law," 251–2.
18 U.S.C., § 35, par. 101 (2006).
19 *Chakrabarty v. Diamond* (1980) 447 U.S. 303.
20 *Funk Brothers v. Kalo Inoculant Co.* (1948) 333 U.S. 127.
21 F. S. Kieff, "Property Rights and Property Rules for Commercializing Inventions," *Minnesota Law Review*, 85 (2000): 697. See also Feldman, *Rethinking Patent Law*, 77.
22 S. Vedaraman, "The New Indian Patent Law," *International Review of Industrial Property and Copyright Law*, 3 (1972), 39. See also Peter Drahos, "Negotiating Intellectual Property Rights: Between Coercion and Dialogue," in *Global Intellectual Property Rights* ed. Peter Drahos and Ruth Mayne (New York: Palgrave Macmillan, 2002), 165.
23 Carlos Correa, "Pro-competitive Measures under TRIPS to Promote Technology Diffusion in Developing Countries," in *Global Intellectual Property Rights*, 49–50.
24 Peter Drahos, "Introduction," to *Global Intellectual Property Rights*, 1–9.
25 Martin Khor, "Rethinking Intellectual Property Rights and TRIPS," in *Global Intellectual Property Rights*, 205–206.
26 Geeta Anand, "Drug Makers Decry Indian Patent Law," *The Wall Street Journal*, February 12, 2010, B1–2.
27 R. Jai Krishna and Jeanne Whalen, "A Bumpy Road in India," *The Wall Street Journal*, April 2, 2013, A1–2.
28 Robert Merges, *Justifying Intellectual Property* (Cambridge, MA: Harvard University Press, 2011), 12–26. I have relied on Merges' discussion on foundations of intellectual property law found in the Introduction of his book.
29 Social welfare is understood as the maximization of aggregate wealth society gets from its scarce resources.
30 Edmund Kitch, "Taking Stock: The Law and Economics of Intellectual Property Rights," *Vanderbilt Law Review*, 53 (2000), 1727.
31 W. D. Nordhaus, *Invention, Growth and Welfare: A Theoretical Treatment of Technological Change* (Cambridge: MIT Press, 1969).

32 See *Universal Oil Products v. Globe Oil Co.* (1944): "As a reward for inventions and to encourage their disclosure, the United States offers a seventeen-year monopoly to an inventor who refrains from keeping his invention a trade secret," 484. Critics of incentive theory point out that intellectual property rights such as patents can actually deter cumulative innovation on a patented work and therefore they can be counterproductive.
33 *Graham v. John Deere of Kan. City* 383 U.S. 9 (1966).
34 U. S. Constitution, art 1, § 8, cl. 8.
35 For a more substantial presentation on the problems of utilitarianism from which some of this analysis was adapted, see Richard A. Spinello and Maria Bottis, *A Defense of Intellectual Property Rights* (Cheltenham, UK: Edward Elgar, 2009), 177–204.
36 John Locke, *Second Treatise of Government* ed. P. Laslett (Cambridge: Cambridge University Press, 1988). References in the text are to paragraph numbers in this edition.
37 Frank Easterbrook, "Intellectual Property is still Property," in *Information Ethics* ed. Adam Moore (Seattle, WA: University of Washington Press, 2005), 113–22.
38 Jeremy Waldron, *The Right to Private Property* (Oxford: Oxford University Press, 1988), 263–4.
39 C. B. Macpherson, *The Political Theory of Possessive Individualism* (Oxford: Oxford University Press, 1962), 3. In Locke's philosophy, explains one philosopher, "the individual, the ego, had become the center and origin of the moral world, since man – as distinguished from man's end – had become that center or origin." Leo Strauss, *Natural Right and History* (Chicago, IL: University of Chicago Press, 1950), 248.
40 John Rawls, *A Theory of Justice* (Cambridge, MA: Harvard University Press, 1971), 302. According to Rawls' theory of "justice as fairness" the first principle of equal liberties has "lexical priority" over the second principle, which stipulates that social and economic inequalities are justified only if they are to everyone's advantage. The latter principle cannot be satisfied at the expense of abrogating basic rights.
41 John Rawls, *Justice as Fairness: A Restatement* (Cambridge, MA: Harvard University Press, 2001), 138.
42 Merges, *Justifying Intellectual Property*, 107.
43 Peter Drahos and John Braithwaite, *Information Feudalism: Who Owns the Knowledge Economy?* (New York: The New Press, 2002), 2–3.
44 Drahos and Braithwaite, *Information Feudalism*, 150–68.
45 Brian Martin, *Information Liberation* (London: Freedom Press, 1998), 7.
46 "Patents and the Poor: The Right to Good Ideas," *The Economist*, 2001, 21–3.
47 Merges, *Justifying Intellectual Property*, 49. See also "Patents and the Poor," 21.
48 Marilyn Chase, "Burroughs Wellcome Reaps Profits, Outrage from its AIDS Drug," *The Wall Street Journal*, September 15, 1989, A1.

49 Sheryl Stolberg, "Africa's AIDS War," *New York Times*, March 10, 2001, A1, A4.
50 Patricia Werhane and Michael Gorman, "Intellectual Property Rights, Moral Imagination, and Access to Life-Enhancing Drugs," *Business Ethics Quarterly* 15 (4) (2005), 604–5.
51 Andrew Pollack, "Drug Companies Drop Suit over their AIDS Medicines," *New York Times*, April 20, 2001, A6.
52 Mark Schoops and Michael Waldholz, "AIDS Drug Price War Breaks Out in Africa, Goaded by Generics," *The Wall Street Journal*, March 7, 2001, A1, A14.
53 Melody Petersen, "Lifting the Curtain on the Real Costs of Making AIDS Drugs," *The New York Times*, April 24, 2001, C1, C10.
54 World Trade Organization, "Declaration on the TRIPS Agreement and Public Health," Doha Ministerial Declaration, November 20, 2001, www.wto.org. In later years clauses have been added to TRIPS that clarify even further the steps to be taken by a country to issue a compulsory license and, if necessary, to obtain generic drugs if the country is unable to manufacture that drug on its own. See Arthur Daemmrich, "Stalemate at the WTO: TRIPS, Agricultural Subsidies, and the Doha Round," (Boston, MA: Harvard Business School Publications, 2012).
55 Schoops and Michael Waldholz, "AIDS Drug Price War Breaks Out," A1.
56 Michele Boldrin and David Levine, *Against Intellectual Monopoly* (Cambridge: Cambridge University Press, 2008), 223.
57 Boldrin and Levine, *Against Intellectual Monopoly*, 238.
58 Marcia Angell, *The Truth about the Drug Companies* (New York: Random House, 2004), 33.
59 See, for example, J. H. Stuart Graham, Robert Merges, and Pamela Samuelson, "High Technology Entrepreneurs and the Patent System: Results of the 208 Berkeley Patent Survey," 24 *Berkeley Law Journal*, 1256 (2010). This survey determined that patents were much more important in the biotechnology industry than in other industries such as computer software. See also Merges, *Justifying Intellectual Property*, 281–2.
60 B. Zycher, and DiMasi, J. (2006), "The Truth about Drug Innovation," Manhattan Institute for Policy Research; available at http://www.manhattan-institute.org/html/mpr_06.htm (accessed July 8, 2012).
61 Elsewhere Locke writes, "common Charity teaches, that those should be taken care of by the Law, who are least capable of taking care for themselves." John Locke, "Some Considerations of the Consequences of the Lowering of Interest and the Raising the Value of Money;" at http://socserv.mcmaster.ca/econ/ugcm/3113/locke/consid.txt (accessed April 30, 2013). This text was quoted in John Tomasi, *Free Market Fairness (*Princeton: Princeton University Press, 2012), 128.
62 St. Thomas Aquinas holds a similar position on the moral limits of property rights. He endorses such personal property rights as essential for the proper management and distribution of resources. But in exigent circumstances when people are in dire need, "all resources become common resources."

Scriptum super Libros Sententiarum Petri Lombard (Commentary on the Sentences of Peter Lombard), IV, d. 15, q. 2, a. 1 sol.4 ad 2. in Latin ed: *Sancti Thomae Aquinatis Doctoris Angelici, Opera Omnia* vols, VII–XI, eds. S.E. Frette and P. Mare (Paris: L. Vives, 1889–90).

63 See Richard DeGeorge, "Intellectual Property and Pharmaceutical Drugs: An Ethical Analysis," *Business Ethics Quarterly*, 15(4) (2005), 549–76. Following DeGeorge, these arguments apply to drugs that are essential for the preservation of life (life-preserving drugs) but not necessarily life-enhancing drugs like Viagra. Also, others such as Merges have used the charity proviso in this context. See *Justifying Intellectual Property*, 270–87.

64 Merges, *Justifying Intellectual Property*, 281–6. According to Merges, we must "weigh the intergenerational effects against the immediate benefits of expanded access," 282.

65 "Jean Pierre Garnier, Head of Glaxo, Will Drop the Price of his Drugs to the Poorest Countries," *The Guardian*, February 18, 2003, 1.

7

Corporate Environmental Responsibility and the Petroleum Industry

Introduction

There has been much fanfare about the "greening" of global business, a more acute awareness of the natural environment's fragility and the urgent need for its protection. Despite this heightened consciousness about the dangers of environmental degradation, some multinational corporations have not always been sufficiently assiduous in their handling of environmental issues. They have been remiss in assuming their stewardship obligations, and they have failed to invest the necessary funds in order to protect environmental integrity. While improvements have been made, there is an extensive history of irresponsibility, negligence, and a lack of adequate concern for the welfare of future generations.

The global oil industry, dominated by multinationals like British Petroleum (BP), Royal Dutch Shell, Exxon Mobil, and Chevron, has a mixed record on environmental issues. There have been problems in developed economies like the United States, such as the Exxon Valdez oil spill in Alaska. More recently, BP's Deepwater Horizon accident has caused great damage to the Gulf region's ecosystem and generated severe economic losses for many Gulf-area businesses and individuals. Whether BP was guilty of gross negligence, as some allege, is a matter of debate. There have been persistent allegations of safety compromises on BP's part, though some of the blame clearly falls on the suppliers of drilling equipment. Fortunately, thanks to regulatory oversight, BP was compelled to establish a $20 billion fund in order to compensate victims for their losses related to the oil spill.

There is also a long and troubling history of problems in developing economies where, unlike in the United States or Western Europe, regulations are feeble and enforcement virtually nonexistent. In these more remote locations, where the rule of law is so casual, victims often have a difficult time vindicating their rights.

Consider the dreadful behavior of Texaco (now ChevronTexaco) in the Latin American country of Ecuador. Ecuador has long sought to overcome its poverty by unlocking its underground wealth of gold, silver, copper and oil. Some of that wealth lies in the Ecuadorean Amazon, home to indigenous Indian populations and many rare species, such as squirrel monkeys, scarlet macaws, and freshwater pink dolphins. The Indians hunt the land and fish its rivers and lakes for their livelihood. When oil was first discovered in the Ecuadorian Amazon, it was seen as a way of helping the country pay off its $12 billion foreign debt obligations.[1]

Multinational oil companies, led by Texaco, rapidly seized on the opportunity to invest in this impoverished country. Texaco entered into a partnership with the state oil company, Petroecuador. Although Texaco only owned 37.5 percent of this joint venture, it was given full operational control. After a short period of exploration, Texaco began drilling for crude oil in a number of different locations. Four hundred drilling sites were constructed along with necessary infrastructure, such as roads and pipelines. Texaco's wells, scattered about the Amazon, were productive but exacted a high social cost. There have been reasonable estimates that the primary pipeline has spilled over 17 million gallons of oil over a 20-year period. In addition, over four million gallons of toxic waste has allegedly been dumped into unlined pits, so that it eventually found its way into rivers and streams. Some of the oil spills have flowed down into neighboring regions of Peru. The waste pits were burned to treat toxic chemicals, but those chemicals returned in the form of "black rain," causing even more pollution. Experts believe that Texaco's antiquated equipment and generally low environmental standards were to blame for this ongoing ecological disaster. For example, strict environmental standards call for the re-injection of waste deep into the ground rather than the use of unlined pits.[2]

The company has always vaguely insisted that it abided by "international standards," and that most of the oil spills were the result of natural disasters rather than corporate negligence. But that claim is little consolation for those who have contracted cancer and other ailments thanks to Texaco's behavior. Experts claim that there have been over 1,400 cancer deaths in this segment of the Amazon jungle. Geological reports show an excessively high level of toxins in the soil and water in the vicinity of the Texaco production sites.[3]

Under concerted pressure from environmentalists and the Ecuadorean government, Texaco embarked on an extensive cleanup operation from 1995–8, at a cost of $40 million. In 2001 Texaco merged with Chevron to create ChevronTexaco, and this new corporate entity has been dealing with the fallout from its Ecuador investment for many years. A lawsuit was filed against Petroecuador and Texaco, claiming that these companies caused serious environmental harm as a direct result of their oil and drilling operations.[4] The court case, whose venue was shifted from New York to Ecuador, has dragged on for over a decade and still causes adverse publicity for ChevronTexaco. Ecuador's populist president Rafael Correa, elected in 2007, has accused Texaco of "savage exploitation," that has "killed and poisoned people." He also claimed that Texaco's cleanup was a "charade" and a sham.[5] In 2011, the Ecuadorean court found for the plaintiffs and awarded them a staggering $18 billion in damages. The money has yet to be paid, however, since Chevron has initiated arbitration proceedings against Ecuador at the Permanent Court of Arbitration in the Hague.

Texaco's appalling carelessness in this region, which seems beyond dispute, reflects an indifference to environmental concerns that has plagued the oil industry for many decades, especially in developing economies where proper regulatory oversight is often lacking. Many companies have improved standards and no longer blatantly sacrifice safety and environmental integrity to keep costs down. But the recent BP oil spill and other incidents suggest that there is still much room for improvement.

This chapter explores these complicated environmental issues, which confront multinationals and often require difficult tradeoffs. Perhaps the most difficult is between economic development and the integrity of public goods. Many companies, like ChevronTexaco and BP, produce private goods while preserving public goods. This leads to a fundamental tension, because corporations are compensated for the private goods (oil) they produce, but not for the public goods (a sound ecosystem) they might strive to protect.[6] Complicating the issue for multinational corporations is the matter of regulatory arbitrage: these companies (like Texaco) are subject to loose regulations and low standards in their host economies that differ from the higher standards in their home economies. To what extent can companies take advantage of this discrepancy? While we consider such issues, the major portion of this chapter is devoted to a consideration of the ethical basis for environmental protection and some treatment of how companies can balance responsible stewardship with economic efficiency. But we begin with a brief overview of the types of environmental damage that continue to cause persistent pressures on the ecology. Included in this overview is a discussion on the difficulties developing nations have had in dealing with the problem of global pollution.

Environmental Degradation

In the past, corporations throughout the world were able to largely ignore environmental issues. The reason for this indifference is that water, air, and the earth are free goods or public goods. The physical environment was conceived as a common good or common property that no one owns. Hence, this "property" can be used with impunity to emit waste or air pollutants without taking into account the damage that might be done. A DuPont plant in West Virginia, for example, dumped 10,000 tons of waste into the Gulf of Mexico until it was finally stopped in 1974.[7] In the 1980s it was discovered that the Pine River in Michigan had been heavily polluted by poisonous chemicals dumped into the river by the Michigan Chemical Company. And in 1969 the Cuyahoga River in Ohio became so polluted with industrial waste that it caught on fire. The list of such environmental abuses is virtually endless. These are classic cases of market failure, where a negative externality imposes costs on those powerless to effect the outcome.

This ethically naïve view of the environment as a "free" good came to an abrupt halt when the cumulative effects of all this pollution and environmental pillaging became obvious. Constant air pollution, along with the careless dumping of toxic wastes by so many companies, was slowly creating a "tragedy of the commons."[8] As a result, governments, businesses, and other institutions became more attentive to environmental externalities. This tragedy of the commons came into more discrete focus with the intellectual help of environmentalists like Aldo Leopold, who passionately argued that ethics rather than economic self-interest must be the guiding norm for the use of environmental resources. According to Leopold, "A thing is right when it tends to preserve the integrity, stability, and beauty of the biotic community; it is wrong when it tends otherwise."[9]

Leopold's principle may be an oversimplification of complicated issues, but it captures the importance of taking into account ecological integrity when investment and production decisions are made. The environmental question must be addressed as a moral issue, not just an economic one, and risks to the environment must be prudently managed. Taking this moral imperative seriously, however, does not necessarily imply an incompatibility between economic development and environmental integrity. It does mean that economic growth should not come at the expense of environmental quality, especially when alternatives are available to use fewer resources and emit less pollution. Some of those alternatives may even create opportunities for corporations to increase profits by enhancing their environmental performance.

Thanks to the work of Leopold, and other environmentalists such as Rachel Carson, improvements have been made and the physical environment is in far better shape than it was several decades ago. In the United States, legislation such as the Clean Air Act and the Clean Water Act has begun to reverse years of damage caused by the careless pollution practices of corporations. However, the decline in pollution and other forms of environmental destruction, that has taken place in advanced economies during this period, has not been matched in developing economies. Millions of children still die each year because of adulterated drinking water. Similarly, urban smog, which has receded in major Western cities, continues to be a serious problem in urban areas in developing economies. Part of the problem is that these countries cannot afford pollution abatement or other mechanisms. As these economies mature, there is hope that there will be more substantial investments in environmental controls.[10] In some of these countries, like Mexico, sound environmental restrictions are in place, but in the past enforcement has been suboptimal.

In China, accelerated economic growth, linked with a laissez-faire attitude to environmental performance, has taken a heavy toll on the environment. Studies released in 2013 blame heavy air pollution caused by coal combustion for reducing life expectancy by five years in parts of the country. Toxic and rancid smog, contaminated soil, and heavily polluted waterways are among the country's biggest problems. The primary cause for all of this pollution is the voracious need for material resources, required by China's expanding economy. While China accounts for only 16 percent of the world's output, it consumes between 40–50 percent of the world's coal, copper, steel, aluminum, and zinc. Beijing's fatal smog attack in 2013, and the discovery of rice tainted with a poison called cadmium, have finally stirred Chinese government officials from their complacency about environmental issues. China has committed to spending $275 billion over a five-year period to clean up its polluted air. The country has also promised to reduce carbon emissions by 30 percent by the end of 2017, but experts are skeptical that this is a realistic target. The Chinese government's commitment is commendable, but the environment remains a "second tier" concern, even with the public, which is more fixated on income inequality and the high cost of housing.[11]

The ongoing environmental degradation in China demonstrates that there are still pressures on the world's fragile ecological systems and threats to human welfare. Among the most severe and troubling global environmental problems are the following: ozone depletion, global warming, continuing water and air pollution, and toxic waste disposal into the earth. Wetlands and coastal erosion is also a prime concern. Many of these problems may seem to be localized but actually have a broad reach—failure to contain air pollution in a small city affects not just the citizens of that city, but neighboring communities and at some level the whole ecological system. Pollution in the border areas of Mexico, for example, will have an impact on southwestern areas of the U.S.

Some of these environmental problems are exacerbated by deforestation trends. Denuded forests erode more easily and allow for more sediment to flow into waterways. Forests and wetlands filter and purify water and they act as reservoirs to capture rain and melting snow. Forests also act as "sinks" for carbon dioxide gases. Hence the degradation of these areas disrupts the ecosystem. The lumber industry along with the extractive industries, such as oil and coal, are responsible for a significant portion of the deforestation that has taken place over the last century.

According to most environmentalists, the gravest of these environmental dangers is global warming. Certain gases, such as carbon dioxide (CO_2) and nitrous oxide (NO_2), trap solar heat in the earth's atmosphere, preventing it from radiating back into space. This trapping of energy insulates the earth's surface and thereby causes the earth's temperature to rise. Since these gases trap heat, they are known as "greenhouse gases" and the rising temperature is known as the "greenhouse effect." Carbon dioxide, which is emitted by burning gas and other fossil fuels, is the chief greenhouse gas. Scientists estimate that about 26 billion metric tons of this gas are emitted annually into the atmosphere, with 80 percent of this amount resulting from the burning of fossil fuels.[12]

There is no doubt that atmospheric carbon dioxide has risen over the years as a result of intensified industrial activity and deforestation. There is also no doubt that global average temperatures have increased over the past two centuries. The Intergovernmental Panel on Climate Change (IPCC) predicts that the global mean surface air temperature will rise 2°C by the year 2100. This is an appreciable increase, but it is much less than the rise in global average temperature that was predicted by earlier computer models.[13] The unreliability of these unrefined computer models, that predicted increases as high as 5°C, underscores the fallibility of our knowledge about the climate and the earth's ecosystem. Nonetheless, the IPCC cautioned that "the average rate of warming would probably be greater than any seen in the last 10,000 years."[14]

Despite the downward revision of these estimates, many scientists remain convinced that global warming trends, if left unchecked, will have cataclysmic effects on the surface of the planet. The biggest fear is that global warming will cause polar ice caps to melt. That melting, combined with thermal expansion of the oceans, will lead to a rise in sea levels that will cause flooding in coastal areas. The best estimate of the IPCC is an inordinate 50 cm increase in average sea level by 2100.[15] Some scientists are persuaded of this dire prognosis while others argue that warming of the earth's atmosphere by 2° or so will be insufficient to cause such a drastic chain of events.[16] Other effects of global warming include more severe storms and weather events (such as floods or extended droughts), disruptions to agriculture, and an increase in tropical disease. Current climate models, however, cannot accurately confirm the likelihood of these events. The uncertainty of the science behind global warming and the difficulty of establishing causal connections have clouded the policy debates over this issue. One thing is certain, however: if this massive public goods problem is to be dealt with effectively it will require a high level of global cooperation. It will also require that multinational corporations be more conscientious about integrating environmental concerns into their corporate strategies and policies.

Perhaps what complicates environmental issues more than any other problem is the inevitable tradeoff between economic development and conservation of the environment. Policy makers and multinationals must come to terms with what level of economic cost is acceptable for preserving environmental assets. At what point does conservation and environmental become too costly? Should Champion International, for example, forego harvesting forests in the Northwest United States at great cost to its employees and other stakeholders for the sake of protecting the northern spotted owl's habitat?

When considering the tradeoff issue at a country level, the objective of sustainability is critically important. But is it sufficient to frame that issue primarily in terms of economics? From this perspective, sustainability is achieved so long as the resource profits from cutting trees or extracting for oils and minerals are reinvested in productive assets so that the country's total capital stock is increasing. While such a development trajectory may make sense at a national level, what will it mean for the global ecosystem?[17]

International Environmental Policy

The global nature of environmental problems demands global solutions. The global push to protect the environment was given a big boost thanks to the international community's engagement over the issue of chlorofluorocarbons (CFCs). This refrigerant, used in air conditioners and refrigerators, emits chlorine when it is released into the air, which assaults the ozone layer that protects the earth's surface from harmful solar radiation.

In a rare gesture of international cooperation, industrialized nations agreed to a ban on this ozone-depleting substance. These nations reached consensus on this ban in the Montreal Protocol on Substances that Deplete the Ozone Layer, signed in 1987. DuPont, the world's largest producer, initially opposed the ban but eventually relented when the scientific picture about CFC damage became clearer. The company refrained from exporting its technology to developing countries, even during the period when they were permitted to do so according to the terms of the Protocol. Recognizing the negative environmental impact of the continued use of CFCs, DuPont correctly exercised corporate leadership to drop CFCs, despite the economic cost, and to search for a replacement. CFCs have been replaced by hydrofluorocarbons (HCFCs), which also contain ozone-depleting chlorine but at a much lower level than CFCs. Environmentalists continue to press for the adoption of a viable alternative to HCFCs.[18]

Global warming is a far more serious long-term problem. While conceding the greenhouse effect, skeptics have repeatedly questioned the causes of climate change. Is it the result of natural factors, such as volcanic eruptions or significant fluctuations in solar radiation, or is it due primarily to human actions, specifically, the release of greenhouse gases like carbon dioxide into the atmosphere? If the former is the primary cause of global warming, human intervention will be ineffectual. There is still some uncertainty around the primary causes of global change, but scientists have assembled reasonable evidence to show that man-made forces are having a serious impact.[19]

All of this mounting evidence made government officials across the globe apprehensive enough to take concerted action. A global treaty on global warming seemed to be the most sensible way to deal with this pressing environmental problem. The 1992 Earth Summit, in Rio de Janeiro, laid the groundwork by affirming the notion of "common but differentiated" responsibilities so that the burden of dealing with these problems falls on rich countries rather than poor ones.[20]

Subsequent to the Rio treaty, the Kyoto Protocol was signed by the industrialized nations in 1997. By signing this Protocol 150 nations agreed to reduce their emissions of greenhouse gases. The Protocol required industrialized nations to reduce carbon dioxide emissions during the first commitment period by an average of 5.2 percent below 1990 levels. The United States agreed to reduce its emissions to 7 percent below 1990 levels. Developing countries, like India and China, were not required to cut their emissions during this period. In keeping with the Rio treaty rich countries agreed to take the lead and act first.[21]

All of the signatories accepted some measure of flexibility by means of market mechanisms. Countries could trade emissions permits among themselves. Although the technical details were never worked out, this international market in emissions credits was designed to make it less burdensome for countries like the United States to meet their obligations under the treaty. Countries could also get credit for "sinks" such as forests, which absorb carbon from the atmosphere. However, there was considerable ambiguity in the definition of such carbon sinks.[22]

Despite this flexibility, the United States never signed the treaty, thanks to the opposition of the Bush Administration. The Kyoto Protocol was a source of contention in the United States as soon as it was signed. Supporters of Kyoto argued that the consequences of global warming were too severe to ignore, while opponents focused on the unpredictable costs of dealing with climate change this way. The Administration cited the uncertainties of climate science and the prohibitively high economic cost of reducing greenhouse gas consumption. The IPCC had determined that the treaty would likely reduce global GDP by 1.1 percent by 2010. In spite of general agreement on the need for flexibility and the use of market mechanisms, there was also disagreement between Europe and America on the parameters of emission trading and the definition of carbon sinks. The United States sought unrestricted trading and broad definitions of sinks, but these features were opposed by the European Union. It is fair to say that the Europeans were adopting a more "moralistic stance," insisting that a larger proportion of the reduction in greenhouse gases come from emissions cuts in each country.[23] Although emissions trading may be politically sensible, buying the right to pollute the environment seems ethically suspect, since the purchasers avoid assuming their fair share of the burden to curtail energy growth.

The treaty was finally ratified in 2004, but its efficacy is quite questionable, given the absence of the United States, the major source of the world's carbon emissions. A treaty to correct global warming that lacks the support of the country with the biggest emissions is undoubtedly doomed to failure. But the problem of global warming is not about to disappear, so the need for global action remains acute. As developing economies like Brazil, India, and China continue to ramp up their economies, global environmental problems will only get worse. Since 2000, China itself has accounted for two-thirds of worldwide growth in carbon dioxide emissions. According to the Stockholm Environment Institute, the world must restrict these emissions to 700 billion tons per year between now and 2050 in order to prevent a rise in global temperatures no greater than the predicted 2°C. Yet, if China continues on its current economic growth trajectory it will emit two-thirds of that amount (450 billion tons) within the next decade.[24] New international negotiations got underway in 2009, but it remains to be seen if the international community is willing to cooperate in developing a flexible and adaptable long-term framework.

For multinational corporations, especially those responsible for producing fossil fuels that emit carbon dioxide, a new treaty would likely pose a difficult dilemma. Most multinationals stayed on the sidelines during the Kyoto debates. But some companies in the oil industry voiced their opposition to Kyoto, and even demanded compensation for lost sales if the treaty was passed. Kenneth Derr, the CEO of Chevron, criticized the marketing of climate change as "an urgent need to shift fossil fuel use from 'overdrive' into 'reverse.'"[25] This recalcitrant attitude does not augur well for the future if a new multilateral treaty is agreed upon.

While many companies were sympathetic with the general goal of reducing CO_2, they were not sympathetic with the specific requirements of Kyoto. But should corporations that expect to bear a substantial share of the cost of emission reductions support this multilateral regulation for the sake of the common good? Or should they lobby against it in order to safeguard their own vested interests? How unambiguous does the science have to be before you take action? And when does the common environmental good trump corporate self-interest? Some corporations probably believe that if a new Kyoto-like protocol were on the horizon, it would be in their enlightened self-interest to support this protocol, perhaps by taking steps to reduce harmful emissions before mandates were handed down from Washington legislators. These companies might fare better than opponents of such an international protocol since some of their stakeholders, especially employees and customers, would respond positively to their proactive stance.[26]

The general question is the scope of a multinational corporation's obligation to sustainability and to environmental integrity. Is it enough to follow current legal guidelines, especially in democratic societies where those guidelines really reflect the will of the people? Or is it imperative to exercise corporate leadership by proactively investing in more environmental quality protections than what is required by law? Should companies follow the example of DuPont's progressive environmental strategy, even in a climate of scientific uncertainty? The next section reviews some of these challenging questions.

Ethics and the Environment

Many corporate executives are more aware than ever before of the urgent need for sound environmental policies. They are cognizant of the severe pressure points that still exist in the environment, such as excessive carbon dioxide emissions. They sense the need for energy conservation and for better internal regulation of environmental externalities. This shift in perspective from the laissez-faire attitude of the 1950s and 1960s is driven in part by stakeholders who demand environmental improvement. Responsible companies focused initially on pollution prevention but then shifted their concentration to the adoption of "clean" technologies and the use of renewable energy whenever possible. The goal is to help society achieve a sustainable development path where the resource needs of the present do not undermine the needs of future generations.

Some multinational companies which have adopted sustainability practices, seek to use the environment as a lever to achieve competitive advantage. Improving environmental performance becomes a source of strategic opportunity, rather than a costly burden. For example, a corporation which enhances its environmental performance might then seek to recover the cost increase by differentiating that product by highlighting its environmental quality. The Heinz Corporation's StarKist subsidiary raised prices once it had implemented its plans for "dolphin-safe" tuna, which became a means of differentiating StarKist from other tunas. Environmental product differentiation is not always feasible. As a result, some companies search for "innovation offsets" or private cost savings that can be realized through waste reduction, or more efficient manufacturing processes that utilize fewer resources. Other companies invest in environmental conservation as a means of managing risks better than their competitors. DuPont, for example, dramatically exited the CFC market in 1988 before it was necessary in order to both reduce regulatory risk and put pressure on its competitors, who were way behind in the development of more environmentally suitable substitute compounds.[27]

Environmental concern as a source of strategic opportunity, however, may obscure the ethical issues at stake in these debates, along with the need to sometimes subordinate economic objectives to environmental goals. While the sustainable use of natural resources, protecting the biosphere, and risk reduction are undoubtedly sound business practices, is there an ethical basis for pursuing such policies and, if so, how is it justified?

An ethical appreciation of environmental issues should begin with a proper understanding of the role of the natural environment in human affairs. In the past, there has been an unfortunate tendency to commodify nature and to regard it as material for human exploitation. This attitude assumes that sub-personal realities are devoid of intelligibility and natural beauty, and are merely at humanity's disposal. Technology becomes a vehicle to serve humanity's insatiable desires, no matter how extravagant or excessive they may be. There are no limits on such exploitation except self-interest. This reckless view of nature, if taken to its extreme, can easily lead to irreversible changes in the ecosystem and a steady depletion of the world's natural resources.[28]

This tendency toward the objectification and exploitation of nature has its roots in the same philosophical soil that has nurtured the Cartesian tradition of subjectivism, which conceived all extended matter as objects to be controlled by the thinking subject. The natural world is thereby stripped of its marvelous depth, beauty, and complexity, and it comes to be seen merely as an instrument for technological manipulation. As Spengler observed, "One no longer sees a waterfall without transforming it into the thought of electric power."[29]

According to Heidegger, this form of subjectivism comes to manifest itself in modernity's dominating attitude of *technicity* (*die Technik*). Heidegger's term expresses how all beings, even the person and his or her body, are raw material for humanity's use and disposal. All natural beings are submitted to man's tight control, objectified by his calculations, planning, and cultivation. Everything in the world is a pawn, an "empty shell" devoid of any independent value, that man can manipulate the way he might manipulate scientific experiments.[30] Within this worldview, that drives modern technology, it is not surprising that the value of nature is reduced to its economic usefulness for the purpose of scientific progress.[31]

Any sound view of the environment must overcome this pernicious attitude of technicity, which regards the earth as a collection of raw materials for exploitation and conquest. Influenced by this mindset, those who dwell on the earth submit nature to their own dispositions rather than "tend to" nature as a "watchman" or "shepherd."[32] On the contrary, humanity must safeguard and preserve sub-personal things, in accordance with their true value, rather than dominate and exploit them. We can use these sub-personal entities when necessary to promote our own human flourishing, but we cannot misuse them.

Once we can appreciate the inauthenticity of the attitude of *Technik*, we are in a better position to address the limits of technology, which is blind to personal and environmental concerns. We can also isolate the fundamental moral obligations of corporations and other moral agents whose actions have an impact on the environment. Given the environment's natural beauty and value, and especially its importance for human flourishing, human action and technological intervention needs to take into account three fundamental ecological considerations: each thing's essential nature and its place within the cosmos, the limits and non-renewability of natural resources, and the impact of economic development on the quality of human life, especially in industrialized areas. A good faith regard for these three factors represents an ethically responsive, rather than exploitative, approach to nature, which calls for using natural things reasonably and with restraint.[33]

With these general standards in mind, we can articulate several concrete and specific moral norms for multinational corporations and other international moral agents. First, nature should be respected and left undisturbed whenever possible, out of respect for the value immanent in nature and because contemplation of natural beauty fulfills the human person. This principle implies that people and corporations should not disrupt natural things except to serve some human good, and they should deal with nature to serve their needs only as their valid human purpose demands. Humanity needs sources of energy to provide a means for transportation and protection from the cold. There is nothing wrong with developing those sources of energy found within the earth, so long as one always does so in a reasonable and restrained manner that deploys resources prudently in order to prevent waste and minimize any environmental degradation.[34]

A correlative principle of this norm is the ethical imperative to respect indigenous rights by consulting and compensating the inhabitants of tribal territories before exploiting resources on their land. Respect for native rights cannot be segregated from environmental issues, since indigenous people are rightly worried about the social problems generated by the "westernization" of their lands. Brazil's otherwise commendable hydroelectric project called Belo Monte is marred by the legal challenge of Amerindian tribes who claim that they have not been properly consulted.[35]

Second, a multinational corporation must not unfairly accept bad side effects to other persons' health through its neglect of environmental concerns, even if the law of a certain country allows it to do so. According to Frederick and Hoffman, solutions to environmental challenges must be economically and technically feasible, environmentally manageable (i.e., not cause irreversible environmental harm), and ethically responsible. A decision is ethically responsible if it "poses no unreasonable threat to human life or health" and does not unjustifiably violate human rights.[36] An oil company's use of inferior equipment, which significantly increases the risk of oil spills or environmental contamination that would adversely affect the health and welfare of people in the area of its pipelines and drilling sites, is a flagrant instance of moral irresponsibility because it unjustly accepts the possibility of these harmful side effects. This is especially true if the risk of health hazards can be reduced by the use of state of the art technology. Similarly, pollution of waterways with hazardous material can never be condoned because it fails to avoid unreasonable risk to human health. As we saw in Chapter Four, health and life are fundamental human goods. Hence intentional acts contrary to health are always wrong, along with the unreasonable acceptance of side effects harmful to others' health due to negligence or moral indifference. The goods of life and health are protected by rights that cannot be set aside merely for utilitarian purposes. Multinational corporations have a duty to protect those rights from deprivation by taking all necessary and reasonable environmental precautions to ensure that any risk to human health is minimized.[37]

Third, in accommodating the real human needs of the present, multinational enterprises must strive to avoid long-term and incremental environmental damage or resource depletion that will be detrimental to the quality of life for future generations. Multinationals must commit to an unequivocal sustainability strategy that gives priority to the use of renewable resources (such as solar energy or hydro-electric power), minimizes waste, and limits the use of non-renewable resources, such as fossil fuels, whenever possible. This commitment is a matter of intergenerational equity and reflects an attitude of stewardship rather than technicity.

In summary, respect for the values immanent in nature, the avoidance of unreasonable threats to human health and welfare by minimizing risk, and the sustainable use of natural resources, are matters of justice that reflect a proper respect for the rights and esthetic interests of human persons.[38]

But what about the claims of the deep ecologists, who argue that even this level of moral commitment is inadequate? They contend that the environment must be preserved and "tended to" for its own sake, not just because mistreatment of the environment, or environmentally unfriendly policies, harm humanity in some way. What sort of moral standing do subhuman beings have? In my view, this is an extremely difficult question to assess, aside from looking at nature from a religious or metaphysical perspective. God's creation, by virtue of its very existence, has an ontological goodness that deserves some measure of acknowledgement and respect. This perspective falls short of the biocentric viewpoint suggested by the deep ecologists, that comes close to deifying nature and often calls for radical proposals that impede some legitimate uses of natural resources.[39]

The deep ecologist typically sees the cause of the environmental crisis as the anthropocentric character of Western culture. Environmental ethics has been heavily influenced by Lynn White's highly influential 1967 essay that traces our environmental problems to the anthropocentric perspective of the Genesis creation story, which segregates man from the rest of creation and authorizes his dominion over nature.[40] The only answer for this "arrogance" is "biocentric egalitarianism," that would drastically limit humanity's ability to meet its material needs.[41] This is a far more radical solution to the problem than we have proposed, and many will be uncomfortable with its practical implications. Contrary to White's thesis, the Judeo-Christian tradition insists that nature is not just raw material for our exploitation but a gift of the Creator, to be conserved wisely and used prudently. According to Pope John Paul II, "The dominion granted to man is not an absolute power, nor can one speak of a freedom to 'use and misuse,' or to dispose of things as one pleases."[42]

This ongoing debate about deep ecology is far too complicated to be discussed in these pages. Rather than defend a secular view of deep ecology or the more moderate religious view, we might simply note that most environmental damage has an adverse impact on people in some way, either directly or indirectly. The integrity of the environment is vital for future generations, and by protecting the wilderness and its wildlife from plunder or careless development, we protect ourselves. As Hoffman observes, "in most cases, what is in the best interests of human beings may also be in the best interest of the rest of nature."[43] If multinational enterprises concentrate on protecting their present and future human stakeholders from environmental harm, they will go a long way in living up to their responsibilities to the natural environment itself.

Royal Dutch Shell in Nigeria

Before concluding this chapter, it would be instructive to revisit the problems multinational oil companies have had in developing countries because of their moral laxity about environmental degradation. Royal Dutch Shell's unfortunate experience in Nigeria in the 1990s epitomizes the ethical and social challenges that oil companies face in developing countries. Royal Dutch, founded in 1890, merged with the United Kingdom company, Shell Transport and Trading, in 1907. Royal Dutch was responsible for activities upstream in the value chain, such as oil exploration, drilling and refining, while Shell handled downstream activities, such as the sale of petroleum products.

Royal Dutch Shell's involvement in Nigeria traces all the way back to 1937, when Nigeria was still a British colony. At that time, the Anglo-Dutch oil company, in partnership with British Petroleum (BP), was given an exclusive right to explore and drill for oil. When oil was discovered in 1956 in the Niger River delta Royal Dutch Shell was the first of the major oil companies to begin drilling for oil. In the early 1970s, Royal Dutch Shell and BP entered into a joint venture with the Nigerian Natural Petroleum Corporation (NNPC), owned by the Nigerian government. After a while, the NNPC bought out BP's stake and sold minority holdings to two European companies, Elf and Agip. By 1995, this joint venture controlled about 60 percent of Nigeria's discovered oil reserves. With over 5,000 employees, it produced 930,000 barrels of oil a day from oil wells scattered around the fertile Niger delta.[44]

Nigeria has always been a terribly poor country, rife with crime, corruption and social discord. Little of the country's oil revenue is used to update the country's infrastructure or help its destitute citizens. Poverty breeds crime and criminal activities can make things difficult for the oil industry. Building and securing Royal Dutch Shell's extensive network of pipelines and oil fields in the Niger Delta area presented a formidable challenge. Most oil companies operating in Nigeria relied heavily on elite members of the Nigerian military and police force for protection. These police, known as supernumeraries, were frequently accused of committing acts of brutality in their eagerness to protect Royal Dutch Shell's property. Shell's involvement with the Nigerian military appears to be deeper than the company first admitted. Documents released in 2011 revealed that Shell paid these police to stop peaceful protests against pollution that were taking place in the area.[45]

Ninety-six of Shell's oil wells were concentrated in a region of the Niger River Delta called Ogoniland, home to a relatively small Nigerian tribe known as the Ogoni. Under the leadership of Saro-Wiwa, the Ogonis conducted a campaign against Shell. Saro-Wiwa demanded a "fair proportion" of oil revenues and more investment in environmental quality. Among the Ogoni's most prominent complaints was Shell's systematic mistreatment of the environment and the Niger Delta's fragile ecology. The Ogoni activists cited many environmental abuses beginning with the pipeline network that blighted the landscape. Those pipelines periodically leaked oil that ruined the land and obstructed farming and fishing activities. There were 111 oil spills over a nine-year period. Some of these spills were due to sabotage, but others were caused by natural disasters or equipment breakdowns. In addition, the Ogoni people were forced to contend with natural gas flaring—the burning of natural gas that is a byproduct of oil production. Flares from tall vents constantly lit the sky and polluted the air.[46]

In his speeches, aimed primarily at Shell, Saro-Wiwa described a "deadly ecological war" where "people die all the time." According to the Ogoni leader, "Men, women, and children are at risk; plants, wildlife and fish are destroyed, the air and water are poisoned, and finally the land dies."[47] Saro-Wiwa's dramatic message resonated with environmentalists. But, as more objective observers have pointed out, there were many other factors such as population growth, low environmental standards of Nigerian firms in the region, and local corruption that contributed to the negative environmental impact described in these speeches. Litvin claims that Shell came to symbolize the worst problems of the Ogonis, along with the lack of control of the oil under their land.[48]

Ogoniland was not the only area polluted in the Niger River Delta, where Shell shares operations with four other multinational oil companies. There have also been substantial oil spills at Oruma, Goi, and Ikot Ada Udo between 2004 and 2007. The five oil companies that operate in the Delta produce about two million barrels of oil per day. According to a 2001 study of the area, oil spills have dumped over 2.5 million gallons of oil into the delta region from 1986 to 1996. This is ten times the amount of oil spilled in the Exxon Valdez disaster. Hence it is no surprise that the delta has been called an "environmental basket case" by environmental groups. A World Bank environmental study of the region described how frequently oil leaks into the delta waters, indicating "poor or no treatment of effluents."[49]

Shell has claimed that much of this negative publicity is exaggerated, but it has conceded that its environmental standards in Nigeria were inferior to its standards in Europe and the United States. Part of the problem is that the Nigerian government, the lead partner in its joint venture, refused to pay its share for environmental upgrades, and Shell has been reluctant to unilaterally bear the burden for these costly protections. Shell has also had a difficult time controlling the sabotage of its pipelines, which accounts for a major proportion of the oil spills.

After decades of drilling, and despite constant complaints about pollution, Shell had never done an environmental impact study of the region, which could have become the basis for improving environmental performance. A study was finally commissioned in 1996 in light of the negative publicity of the events in Ogoniland. In an interview at the time Shell's CEO, Mr. Moody-Stuart, admitted that this was a huge oversight: "What I regret is that we did not launch our Niger River Delta Environmental Survey six or seven years ago."[50]

Shell itself has admitted to a lack of responsibility in the way it handled its Nigerian operations. Its poor environmental record also created a public relations disaster for Shell. Even some shareholders turned against the company, demanding it issue a report on its environmental and corporate responsibility policies. But Shell always insisted on their mitigated accountability, claiming that they had been victims of sabotage and that their majority partner, the Nigerian government, did not pull its weight in addressing the Niger River Delta's environmental problems.

How do we assess Shell's corporate policies and behavior from a moral point of view in light of our framework for reviewing the ethical implications of environmental issues? To be sure, there are some complexities that complicate such an assessment. However, it is questionable whether there was any need to drill for oil in this region, where the production activities would be so disruptive both to the environment and to the vulnerable population of the Delta area. Oil pollution exacerbated the pollution already plaguing this area due to its overpopulation. Pipelines in such close proximity to Ogoni villages are quite dangerous. There is a valid human need for oil, especially until alternative energy sources are cultivated, but arguably there are more reasonable places to explore for oil and engage in oil production. There may be conditions where oil production operations in the Delta region would be acceptable, such as a large share of revenues returned to the Ogoni people so they could escape the shackles of poverty, and a high priority given to environmental quality, but those conditions were not met in this case. Also, the Ogoni people were not consulted, and their interests were never properly taken into account.

The second problem stems from Royal Dutch Shell's partnership with the Nigerian government, which was a condition of doing business in Nigeria. Perhaps Shell should not have invested in Nigeria under these conditions, given the history and past behavior of the government. But, notwithstanding that decision, should Shell pay for environmental upgrades when its major partner in the joint venture (the NNPC) flatly refuses to pay its share? Also, since a number of the oil spills were due to sabotage, should the company still pay compensation to the victims? Shell routinely refused to make such payments, when sabotage was suspected, because it said that payments would be an incentive for additional acts of sabotage by those looking for the opportunity of a quick pay-off.

Shell's arguments, however, cannot be defended from an ethical point of view. As we have argued in this book, the fundamental moral obligation of all international moral agents is to do no harm by upholding and protecting basic human rights. Also, common moral sense demands that in the event of unexpected or unintended harm, the injury must be corrected and compensation must be provided. It makes no difference whether an oil spill is an accident or the result of sabotage. In either case, there are innocent Nigerians victimized by broken pipelines that wind their way through villages. They should not be expected to bear the costs of these oil spills with no prospect of relief and remuneration. Shell chooses to drill for oil in the Niger Delta and it must address the negative externalities and unintended consequences that occur as a side effect of its actions. The company must find a way to secure the pipeline against sabotage. If it cannot provide such security, it must assume responsibility of sabotage that comes with an unsecured pipeline. Fairness requires that

Shell cannot refuse to compensate innocent victims even when sabotage occurs.

Shell also has an obligation to operate by the highest environmental standards, no matter where it produces oil. But Shell "was reluctant to sacrifice profits for costly environmental protection."[51] Shell's refusal to upgrade its equipment and adopt state of the art technology is ethically irresponsible. As we have argued, any solution to an environmental risk problem must be economically and technically feasible, but it must also be ethically responsible. A decision is ethically responsible if, and only if, it does not pose an unreasonable threat to the quality of human life and health. But using inferior and marginally safe equipment does pose such an unreasonable threat to health and safety for those who live in the Niger Delta. The use of such second-rate equipment unfairly accepts risks and bad side effects to others' health and welfare. Hence, by failing to take necessary precautions, Shell did not adequately protect the right to health of the people in this region from being deprived. An ethically responsible decision also gives proper consideration to the values, interests, and rights of those affected by that decision. There is no evidence that the Nigerian people's right to a safe environment was given the weight which it deserved. There are certain limits to what state-of-the-art technology can achieve. It cannot stop sabotage and acts of vandalism, but it can prevent those oil spills that happen due to accidents caused by shoddy, antiquated equipment.

Moreover, Shell cannot fall back on the argument that it could not afford to make these investments without the help of its major partner, the Nigerian government. Royal Dutch Shell is a company with vast economic wealth, and its behavior is not excused by the Nigerian government's insensitivity to environmental concerns. Every company must behave in an ethically responsible manner even if it has unwilling and uncooperative partners. Either Shell must invest in the proper equipment without the government's help and help protect the rights of the Nigerian people, or exit the country if it concludes that it cannot make a profit there by operating in a responsible way.

Shell's apparent complicity in human rights abuses also compounds its irresponsible behavior. Aside from Shell's disputed role in the conviction and execution of Ken Saro-Wiwa, Shell sought to forcibly stifle peaceful protests against pollution in the delta by hiring Nigerian military police.⁵² As we argued in Chapter Four, free expression and political participation are the basic human rights that corporations are always bound to uphold and protect. In this case, Shell allegedly deprived people of these basic rights, and such actions cannot be morally justified.

The Shell case has led to countless trials and lawsuits. To settle one case in 2009, Shell paid out $15.5 million to the family of Saro-Wiwa. The family alleged that Shell was complicit in the death of Saro-Wiwa and other activists. Shell denied any such complicity but agreed to settle to avoid the costs of further appeals and litigation. This lawsuit was filed under the auspices of the United States' Alien Torts Criminal Act (ATCA), but such suits will likely end thanks to the Supreme Court's ruling in *Kiobel v. Royal Dutch Petroleum*. In that case, Nigerian refugees alleged that Shell aided the government in a repressive campaign in the Ogoni region, but the U.S. Supreme Court dismissed the lawsuit, claiming that it was a misuse of the ATCA.⁵³ But in 2012, in a British court, Shell admitted liability for two oil spills around Bodo in the Niger Delta, and it faces three lawsuits in a Netherlands court. After the harsh publicity surrounding the Saro-Wiwa execution, Shell revised its business principles, with new policies on health, safety, and environmental standards. The company also committed itself to sustainable development and enhanced corporate responsibility efforts.⁵⁴

Conclusions

Environmental issues such as polluted waterways, deforestation, and global warming remain a paramount concern. While the West has made progress, developing countries like China have sacrificed ecological integrity for the sake of economic growth. Despite the scientific uncertainty about the cause of global warming, there is reason for grave concern and the need for global action. The international community has had a mixed record in its cooperative efforts to deal with environmental problems that have a global impact. Although it was successful in curbing CFCs, it has not been so successful in reducing the carbon dioxide emissions that cause global warming. Signatories to the Kyoto Protocol differed sharply over the degree of flexibility to be allowed in meeting quotas, along with the use of market mechanisms such as emissions trading.

Social demands for improving environmental quality have put considerable pressure on multinational enterprises to be more environmentally responsible. Some seek to profit from environmentalism by differentiating their products, by discovering offsetting cost savings, or by managing regulatory risks better than the competition. But sometimes addressing environmental contamination will conflict with economic objectives. Nonetheless, companies must acknowledge their ethical obligation to the environment even if it means lower returns to shareholders. The apposite ethical paradigm for thinking about the environment begins with the right mindset that overcomes the guise of technicity. The earth does not exist for our own aggrandizement. Nature's resources must be extracted from the earth to satisfy valid human needs but this must be done in a reasonable way and always with suitable restraint. In order to demonstrate respect for nature's immanent value along with basic human goods, companies must take into account as judiciously as possible every natural being's place within the cosmos, the limits and non-renewability of natural resources, and the impact of economic development on the quality of human life.

We can translate these high-level principles into several key specific norms. First, nature should be left undisturbed whenever possible, disrupted only for valid human purposes. Second, corporations cannot unjustly accept the bad side effects to others' health by failing to take necessary environmental precautions. This means that technical solutions bearing on the environment should always avoid unreasonable risks and be sensitive to human rights like health and safety. Using cheap or inferior technologies externalizes costs that society should not be forced to absorb. Third, all corporations should commit themselves to the goal of sustainable development.

Multinational corporations in the extractive industries, such as oil, must be particularly ethically proactive and progressive about their environmental policies, particularly in developing countries. They cannot take advantage of countries with dysfunctional governments or weak institutions to adopt lower safety standards or employ second-rate equipment. A good rule of thumb is the one followed by DuPont in its overseas plants: "If our safety standards are higher, we use ours, if the other country's are higher we use theirs."[55] Oil companies should recognize that there must be uniformly high safety standards rather than lower standards designed for countries with weaker regulations, so that the risk of oil spills and other ecological disasters is minimized. These companies must also correct and compensate for the social injuries they cause. The sorry track record of the oil industry, exemplified in the cases of Royal Dutch Shell in Nigeria and Texaco in Ecuador, reveals a pattern of injustice in managing its environmental impacts in developing countries that must be rectified.

Notes

1 Denis Arnold, "Texaco in the Ecuadorean Amazon," in *Case Studies in Business Ethics* 5th ed. Al Gini (Upper Saddle River, NJ: Prentice-Hall, 2005), 113–5.
2 Eyal Press, "Texaco on Trial," *The Nation*, May 31, 1999, 22–5.
3 Juan Forero, "In Ecuador, High Stakes against Chevron," *The Washington Post*, April 28, 2009, A12.
4 See *Aguinda v. Texaco, Inc.* 142F. Supp. 2d 534 (S.D.N.Y.) (2001).
5 Forero, "In Ecuador, High Stakes against Chevron."
6 See Forest Reinhardt, "Conceptual Overview: Business and the Environment," (Boston, MA: Harvard Business School Publications, 1999), 3.
7 Manuel Velasquez, *Business Ethics: Concepts and Cases* (Englewood Cliffs, NJ: Prentice-Hall, 1982), 187.
8 Garrit Hardin, "The Tragedy of the Commons," *Science*, 162 (3859) (1968), 1243–8.
9 Aldo Leopold, *A Sand Country Almanac* (New York: Oxford University Press, 1949), 88. Some have relied on Leopold's insights to support a biocentric view of these issues rather than an anthropocentric one. We're generally agnostic on this issue, but our concern is primarily with the ill effects of pollution on the welfare of human persons.
10 Jay Richards, *Environmental Stewardship* (Grand Rapids, MI: Acton Institute, 2007), 80–4.
11 "China and the Environment," *The Economist*, August 10, 2013, 18–21. See also Richard Silk, "China Weighs Environmental Costs," *The Wall Street Journal*, July 2, 2013, A7.
12 World Resource Institute, *World Resources: A Guide to the Environment* (New York: Oxford University Press, 1996), 316.
13 Intergovernmental Panel on Climate Change (IPCC), *Climate Change 1995: IPCC Second Assessment Report* (New York: Cambridge University Press, 1996), Part I, 6. See also Roy Spencer, "How do We Know the Temperature of the Earth? Global Warming and Global Temperatures," in

Earth Report 2000: Revisiting the True State of the Planet ed. R. Bailey (New York: McGraw-Hill, 2000), 20–31.
14 IPCC, *Climate Change*, Part I, 25.
15 IPCC, *Climate Change*, Part II, 13. At this rate of increase, 40–50 million people worldwide could be affected by flooding due to storm surges.
16 Singer, for example, presents data to show that while the global sea level has undergone a rising trend for the past century, its cause is unrelated to climate change. See Frederick Singer, Presentation at 1997 Meeting of the American Geophysical Union; www.sepp.org/scirsrch/slr-agu.html (accessed February 10, 2009). See also Richards, *Environmental Stewardship*, 90.
17 Reinhardt, "Conceptual Overview: Business and the Environment," 6–9.
18 John Holusha, "Ozone Issue: Economics of a Ban," *The New York Times*, January 11, 1990, D1, D6.
19 "Global Warming: Hotting Up in the Hague," *The Economist*, November 18, 2001, 81–3.
20 "Global Warming: Oh No, Kyoto," *The Economist*, April 7, 2001, 73–5.
21 "Global Warming: Oh No, Kyoto," 74. See also Kimberly Packard and Forest Reinhardt, "Global Climate Change," (Boston, MA: Harvard Business School Publications, 1999), 1–7.
22 "Global Warming: Hotting Up in the Hague," 83.
23 "What to do about Global Warming," *The Economist*, November 18, 2000, 22.
24 "China and the Environment," 21.
25 Kenneth Derr, "On the Threshold of Growth: Competitive Imperatives and Critical Challenges for the Global Oil Industry," World Petroleum Congress, Beijing, China, October 16, 1997.
26 See Packard and Reinhardt, "Global Climate Change," 8–9.
27 Forest L. Reinhardt, "Bringing the Environment Down to Earth," *Harvard Business Review*, July–August (1999), 149–57.
28 Germain Grisez, *Living a Christian Life* (Quincy, IL: Franciscan University, 1993), 771–2.
29 Oswald Spengler, *The Decline of the West* trans. Charles Atkinson (New York: Alfred A. Knopf, 1928), 178.
30 Martin Heidegger, *Holzwege* (Frankfurt: Klostermann, 1950), 237. See also William J. Richardson, "The Place of the Unconscious in Heidegger," *Review of Existential Psychology and Psychiatry*, 5 (1965), 281–2.
31 For Heidegger's more thorough treatment of these issues see *The Question Concerning Technology* trans. William Lovitt (New York: Harper Colophon, 1977). Deep ecologists who probe the deeper and more elusive meaning of the ecological crisis would be most sympathetic with a Heideggerian analysis of this sort. See Michael Zimmerman, "Implications of Heidegger's Thought for Deep Ecology," *Modern Schoolman*, 44 (4) (1986), 19–43.
32 Martin Heidegger, *Vorträge und Aufsätze* (Pfullingen: Neske, 1954), 179.
33 Grisez, *Living a Christian Life*, 775–6. See also Pope John Paul II, *Sollicitudo Rei Socialis* (Boston: Pauline Books and Media), §34. The Pope explains, for example, that using natural resources "as if they were inexhaustible, with

absolute dominion, seriously endangers their availability not only for the present generation but above all for generations to come."
34 Grisez, *Living a Christian Life*, 780–1.
35 "Dams in the Amazon: The Rights and Wrongs of Belo Monte," *The Economist*, May 4, 2013, 37–9.
36 Robert Frederick and W. Michael Hoffman, "Environmental Risk Problems and the Language of Ethics," *Business Ethics Quarterly*, 5 (1995), 705. See also W. Michael Hoffman, "Business and Environmental Ethics," *Business Ethics Quarterly*, 1 (1991), 169–84.
37 Grisez, *Living a Christian Life*, 532–3.
38 These moral norms are also expressed in the "Valdez Principles" (named after the Valdez oil spill in Alaska) which were published in 1989 by CERES (Coalition for Environmentally Responsible Economies).
39 Some philosophers propose a more radical approach to ecology than biocentrism. Luciano Floridi advocates what he calls an onto-centric, ecological macroethics. The biocentrists maintain that we should not needlessly destroy or harm any living being. The ontocentrist, on the other hand, declares that no being or informational object should be damaged or destroyed without sufficient reason. All beings have the Spinozian right to persist in being and a "constructionist right to flourish." Luciano Floridi, "Foundations of Information Ethics," in *The Handbook of Information and Computer Ethics* eds. Ken Himma and Herman Tavani (Hoboken, NJ: Wiley, 2008), 10–11.
40 Lynn White, "The Historic Roots of our Ecologic Crisis," in *The Environmental Ethics and Policy Book* (Belmont, CA: Wadsworth Publishing, 1994), 43–51.
41 Michael Zimmerman, *Heidegger's Confrontation with Modernity* (Bloomington, IN: Indiana University Press, 1990), 242–3.
42 Pope John Paul II, *Sollicitudo Rei Socialis*, 34.
43 Hoffman, "Business and Environmental Ethics," 838.
44 Lynn Sharp Paine, *Value Shift* (Boston, MA: Harvard Business School Press, 2003). See also Milan Moldoveanu and Lynn Sharp Paine, "Royal Dutch Shell in Nigeria," (Boston: Harvard Business School Publications, 1999), 1–6.
45 John Vidal, "Shell Oil Paid Nigerian Military," *The Guardian*, October 3, 2011, 1; http://www.guardian.co.uk/world/2011/oct/03/shell-oil-paid-nigerian-military (accessed August 22, 2013).
46 Douglas Farah, "Nigeria's Oil Exploitation Leaves Delta Poisoned, Poor," *The Washington Post*, March 18, 2001, A22.
47 Ken Saro-Wiwa, *Ogoni: Moment of Truth* (Port Harcourt, Nigeria: Saros International Publishers, 1994), 14–15.
48 Daniel Litvin, *Empires of Profit* (New York: Texere, 2003), 263.
49 Farah, "Nigeria's Oil Exploitation Leaves Delta Poisoned, Poor," A22.
50 Ken Pollard, "Nigeria's Deadly Oil War: Beleaguered Shell Defends its Record," *The New York Times*, February 13, 1996, A10.
51 Pollard, "Nigeria's Deadly Oil War," A10.

52 For more about the Saro-Wiwa case and related human rights issues see Joshua Hammer, "Nigeria Crude," *Harper's Magazine*, June 1996, 56–73.
53 *Kiobel v. Royal Dutch Petroleum Co.* 133 U.S. 1659 (2013).
54 Paine, *Value Shift*, 23.
55 Quoted in Thomas Donaldson and Thomas Dunfee, *Ties that Bind* (Boston, MA: Harvard Business School Press, 1999), 175.

8

POLITICAL ACTIVISM AND DISINVESTMENT

Introduction

Not far from Thomas Watson's hotel room, crowds of Germans were mesmerized by the intoxicating spectacle of SS troops marching briskly in lockstep at a customary Berlin party rally. The IBM CEO was in Berlin in 1935 to celebrate the accomplishments of IBM's successful German subsidiary, known as Dehomag. After enjoying a lavish dinner at the ornate Hotel Adoni, Watson consulted with his German staff about how corporate headquarters in New York could further help its prosperous German operations. Watson often boasted of IBM's great success abroad:

> Our trade abroad is improving, as shown by the fact that for the first ten months of 1934 our exports increased 35 percent over the corresponding period of 1933. One of the main factors contributing to industrial recovery may be found in the constantly increasing cooperation among political, industrial, and financial leaders.[1]

He was especially proud of Dehomag and his cooperative relationship with Germany's charismatic *Führer*, Adolph Hitler.

This German subsidiary, which became tightly linked with the Nazi regime, was almost as old as the IBM corporation itself. IBM began as the Tabulating Machines Company (TMC) in 1896. The company was invented by Herman Hollerith, who developed a machine that tabulated census data using punch-cards. Hollerith's versatile machines were used in the 1890 U.S. census with great results. Hollerith was a shrewd businessman and he sensed the global value of his technology. He soon assumed the risks of licensing that technology to foreign entrepreneurs. One of those entrepreneurs was Willy

Heidinger who established *Deutsche Hollerith Machinen Gesellschaft*, which became known as Dehomag. Heidinger paid a royalty to TMC based on the revenues generated from the machines imported from the U.S. TMC was sold to the Computer-Tabulating-Recording Company where the young Tom Watson was employed as the general manager. In 1924 Watson changed the name of CTR to IBM, or International Business Machines Corporation.[2] He built up a strong corporate culture and spoke often of the "IBM Family."

Shortly after Watson became CEO of IBM, he set his sights on the acquisition of Dehomag. Due to Germany's monetary crisis, IBM's German subsidiary was vulnerable because it could not afford to liquidate its substantial debts and make royalty payments. The company owed $104,000 and there was no way it could raise these funds. Consequently, Dehomag had two options: either bankruptcy or sell out to the parent company. Dehomag chose the latter option as IBM acquired 90 percent of the stock. But Watson left Heidinger in control. The German executive was particularly adept in promoting and selling the Hollerith technology.

In April 1933, after Hitler came to power, the Third Reich announced that a new census would take place for all Germans. The regime sought basic demographic data for the 41 million Germans living in Prussia. To expedite this arduous process, the government turned to Dehomag, which secured the 1.35 million Reichsmark contract to conduct the Prussian census. The company customized its technology to meet the requirements of the census. It discarded the 45-column cards and produced a 60-column card to accommodate the demographic information sought in the census (each column represented a biographical characteristic). With the help of these cards, the census tracked the following data: county, community, gender, age, religion, mother tongue, current occupation, and so forth.[3]

The company's simple punch-card technology was sold to many other customers besides the Third Reich. Among Dehomag's major clients were the German Post Office and the Ministry of Defense. Private sector customers included Siemens, Opel, and the elite automobile manufacturer, Daimler-Benz. Heidinger and IBM engineers had developed multiple applications for these machines, including inventory management and production scheduling. But the German government's census contracts offered the biggest financial bonanza for Dehomag. Sensing the potential for growth, Watson authorized additional investments in 1935 for printing presses that produced the punch-cards.

As the Nazi party became more entrenched under Hitler's dominating leadership, things became increasingly tenuous for Jews living in Germany. There were reports of atrocities at the hands of the Nazis, along with a concerted effort to dismiss those with "Jewish extraction" from government jobs.[4] Jewish businesses were routinely boycotted. It also became virtually intolerable for foreign businesses to retain Jewish workers. There was immense pressure to remove Jews from any management positions. With Watson's blessing, IBM followed this trend. In response to criticism over this policy, Watson said in an interview, "I am an internationalist. I cooperate with all forms of government, regardless of whether I can subscribe to all their principles or not."[5]

Watson returned to Berlin in 1937 after he was elected President of the International Chamber of Commerce (ICC). As the leader of this organization, created by the League of Nations to promote world trade and investment, Watson encouraged his colleagues to maintain a "business as usual" status with the German Reich, despite Hitler's bellicose declarations about world domination. During his visit, Watson met with Hitler, who assured him that he had no intentions of starting another war. Watson was also awarded the Merit Cross of the German Eagle for meritorious service by a businessman for the sake of the German Reich. Upon his return to the United States, Watson sent Hitler a personal note of thanks. Watson wrote, "Valuing fully the spirit of friendship which underlay this honor, I assure you that in the future as in the past, I will endeavor to do all in my power to create more intimate bonds between our great nations."[6]

IBM never divested its holdings in Germany or disassociated itself from Dehomag in the years leading up to World War II. On the contrary, it increased its investment and entered into a strong commercial alliance with the government and several of its agencies. Watson authorized the construction of a new factory in Berlin to produce the Dehomag machines, and in 1935 additional investments were made for specialized printing presses, which allowed Dehomag to print its own punch-cards. By 1937, 59 presses, shipped from Europe and the United States, were installed throughout Germany. In May 1938, after Germany's annexation of Austria, known as the *Anschluss*, Watson visited the country again and approved Dehomag's extension into Austria. And in June, with a new census on the horizon, Watson approved the purchase of more machinery for its assembly factories.

Was IBM morally lax in putting its technology at the disposal of the Nazi party for the purpose of the 1933 Prussian census? Perhaps it is expecting too much for IBM to have foreseen that one purpose of that census was the identification and tracking of the Jews who were so despised by the regime. However, IBM's willingness to increase investment in Dehomag operations throughout the 1930s is another matter. During the early years of the Nazi regime, Hitler's evil intentions to exterminate the Jewish race were not yet known. However, as early as 1933 there were portentous manifestations and hints of the malicious intentions of this racist regime. Hitler's anti-Semitic ravings in his autobiography, *Mein Kampf*, were common knowledge. Countless headlines in newspapers like *The New York Times* reported on the growing persecution of the Jews. In April 1933, the paper reported that 10,000 Jews had already fled Germany in the face of persecution, home invasions, and even torture at the hands of the Brown Shirts.[7] On April 1, 1933 Hitler ordered a national boycott of Jewish shops. He declared that "Jews were not Germans," and issued laws that banned them from public service, the universities and schools, journalism, farming, theater, and films. In 1934 they were summarily expelled from Germany's stock exchanges, and soon after they could no longer openly practice law or medicine. In September 1935 the Nuremberg Laws were passed, depriving the Jewish people of citizenship and forbidding marriage between Jews and Aryans. By the summer of 1936, when Germany hosted the Olympic Games, historian William Shirer estimates that over one half of the Jewish population was without any means of livelihood.[8]

Ethically sensitive and alert managers should have been able to perceive the depth and virulence of the anti-Semitism infecting Germany during the Nazification of its culture in the 1930s. That anti-Semitism was invading the workplace and every aspect of German social life. Surely, by 1938, the time frame for the second German census authorized to help implement the Nuremberg Laws, IBM should have realized the moral problems involved in their complicity with this regime. Many American and European businesses faced the same question Watson did between 1933 and Hitler's declaration of war: suspend doing business with this totalitarian state and forego the expected pecuniary rewards, or conduct business as usual and face the risk of disapprobation at home.

This brief account of IBM's experience in Nazi Germany evokes the primary theme of this chapter: are there countries so politically corrupt or morally offensive that the only viable ethical strategy is disinvestment? No country or state has ever achieved moral perfection. Each one is guilty of certain injustices, but when does the injustice become so extreme that it is no longer tolerable to do business in that country? A related issue to be considered in this context is the question of political activism by corporations. The issue of disinvestment suggests the intimate connection between politics and economics. When a business like IBM invests abroad it enters into a cooperative relationship with the host government. This calls for skill in understanding the political and social environment and in managing political issues. A weak political strategy often negatively affects economic performance. A multinational has every prerogative to protect its interests and property abroad, but sometimes it overreaches and intrudes too deeply into a host country's internal political affairs. We begin our discussion with several examples of such excessive political activism.

Political Involvement and Corporate Activism

Foreign investment is always a risky venture. Aside from wars and regional conflict, a multinational's property can be threatened by a wave of nationalist sentiment or by the election of socialist-leaning government. Multinationals are obliged to protect their assets and promote their interests, especially when they are convinced that their interests align with the common good of the host country. But what are the moral parameters of this sort of political involvement? We consider this question in this section by focusing on three multinationals, which used their power in ways that were ethically problematic and ultimately self-defeating.

In Chapter One we alluded to United Fruit Company's (UFC) misguided political activism in Guatemala. Recall UFC's ambitious but inappropriate plans to subvert the Arbenz regime because of its socialist leanings. UFC started out as the Boston Fruit Company in 1885 when a young entrepreneur began importing bananas from Jamaica. In 1908 Boston Fruit merged with another enterprise to form United Fruit Company. With more capital and resources, the newly formed corporation expanded into Central America to meet the rising demand for bananas in the United States. By the late 1920s, United Fruit was worth well over $100 million. It had 67,000 employees, owned 1.6 million acres of land, and had business interests in 32 countries.[9]

UFC had built up extensive operations in Central America and it soon became the largest employer in Guatemala. In most Central and South American countries where it operated UFC exercised considerable economic control. Its CEO was so powerful that he became known as "the uncrowned king of Central America."[10] Nonetheless, periodic labor disputes ruffled feathers at UFC's corporate headquarters in Boston and even at the U.S. State Department, which wanted to keep the region secure for American business. UFC saw itself as a benign and paternalistic employer, but many Guatemalans perceived their country as a captive of this giant United States corporation.[11]

From the United States' perspective, the political environment in Guatemala began to deteriorate when Jacobo Arbenz Guzmán was elected president. Arbenz has been described as a nationalist seeking to reform an "oligarchic society." He assumed the presidency in March 1951 and immediately set about the task of land reform. In 1950, the annual per capita income of agricultural workers was a meager $87. Moreover, 2.2 percent of landowners owned 70 percent of the country's land, but less than a quarter of that land was in use.[12]

Arbenz's goal of transforming his country into a modern capitalist state clashed with the economic interests of UFC. By now, United Fruit was the largest property owner in the country, with 550,000 acres on both coasts. But 85 percent of the land was uncultivated. As part of his agrarian reform and land redistribution program, Jacobo Arbenz sought to purchase some of UFC's unused land. In March

1953, 209,842 acres of UFC's uncultivated land was appropriated by the Arbenz government for a payment of $627,572. UFC claimed that the land was worth about $16 million, but the government believed that it had offered a fair price. UFC paid $1.48 an acre for this land and the government's offer amounted to $2.99 an acre.

Negotiations with the Arbenz regime were futile, so UFC turned to more sinister tactics. The company sought to promote the expulsion of the popular socialist leader by propagating propaganda that would convince Washington lawmakers of Arbenz's Communist sympathies. UFC hired a shrewd public relations expert to plant stories in the press favorable to UFC and to hype the story of Soviet Communism's role in Guatemala. United Fruit also funded the printing of a book called *Report on Guatemala—1952* that presumably documented this alleged "Moscow-directed Communist conspiracy" taking place in Guatemala. The book was sent to every member of the U.S. Congress and a long list of "decision makers." There were hardcore Marxists working in the Arbenz administration, but there was no evidence of any formal or informal links to the Soviet Union. Nonetheless, the thesis of Soviet influence in Guatemala fell on sympathetic ears in Washington. All of UFC's subversive efforts succeeded in creating a climate of deep suspicion about the Arbenz government.[13]

Thanks in part to UFC's public relations campaign and its aggressive lobbying, the Eisenhower Administration approved a plan, hatched by the Central Intelligence Agency, to overthrow Arbenz. A group of rebels, funded and supported by the United States, was organized to "liberate" Guatemala from communist influence. The hand-picked leader of the rebel army was Colonel Carlos Castillo. When the coup began, many of Arbenz's supporters (like the revolutionary leader Che Guevara) initially refused to back down, but they were no match for Castillo's well-armed militia. After 15 short days the rebel armies prevailed, and Arbenz was forced into exile. Castillo became the country's new president. The former Guatemalan president was rightly convinced that American corporations were instrumental in his demise:

> The United Fruit Company, in collaboration with the governing circles of the United States, is responsible for what is happening to us ...

In whose name have they carried out these barbaric acts? What is their banner? We know very well. They have used the pretext of anti-Communism. The truth is very different. The truth is to be found in the financial interests of the fruit company and the other U.S. monopolies which have invested great amounts of money in Latin America and fear that the example of Guatemala would be followed by other Latin countries...[14]

UFC's meddling represents an egregious ethical transgression because it helped to undermine a basic right of the Guatemalan people. As we observed in Chapter Four, a person or group of persons has the right to political participation, which implies the right to national self-determination. The Guatemalan people deserve the freedom and moral space to have their own internal debate about Arbenz's policies without unreasonable outside interference. Yet by helping to subvert a democratically elected government, UFC cooperated in depriving people of this right to national self-determination. This unfortunate case highlights the potential vulnerability of this right, especially in unstable developing countries, but it must be respected, even if a company is being treated unfairly by the host government. It is not surprising that this coup led to anti-American demonstrations throughout Latin America. The overthrow of the Arbenz regime remains a focal point in Guatemala's unsettled history and still casts a shadow over U.S. investment in Central and South America.

Not too long after these events, Union Minière, a Belgian mining company, found itself enmeshed in a political quagmire in the Congo. Union Minière mined the abundant resources of the Katanga province in the southern part of the Congo. Its mining operations included copper, cobalt, and uranium. The mining company employed over 20,000 workers, most of whom lived in a company town called Elizabethville. Like UFC, Union Minière regarded itself as a benevolent and paternalistic employer that provided jobs, security, and benefits for their workers.

In June 1960 the Congo was granted independence from Belgium. The charismatic Patrice Lumumba was elected prime minister. He was committed to a vision of a unified Congo functioning as a centralized state. But the president of the Katanga province, Moise

Tshombe, disagreed and declared the province's secession several weeks after Lumumba's election. Tshombe was more sympathetic to Union Minière, which worried about the anti-colonialist tone of Lumumba's speeches. As a result Union Minière enthusiastically supported the secession. The company paid its substantial taxes and duties (1.2 billion Belgian Francs) to the Katanga regime. Union Minière's monetary and political support for Tshombe gave that regime instant credibility. Union Minière also provided funding for a Katanga delegation in Belgium to enhance the fledgling regime's status, and even made some efforts to fund and support the military forces of Katanga. The company always insisted, however, that it was not meddling in the internal affairs of the Congo.[15]

Thanks to the financial support of Union Minière, the Katanga secession posed a major problem for Lumumba, who found himself without enough resources to quash this rebellion. He sought the help of the United Nations and even the Soviet Union. But in January 1961 Lumumba was assassinated. While Union Minière was not involved in these events there is some evidence that the Belgium government helped behind the scenes to orchestrate the assassination plot. The secession attempt ended after Lumumba's death, but when Mobutu seized power in 1965 he nationalized Union Minière's properties as part of a strategy to consolidate his power by reducing the risk of another secession in this region, which contained the huge asset of this Belgian company's mining empire.[16]

While Union Minière's interference is perhaps less egregious than UFC's, there is little doubt that the multinational went too far in protecting its vulnerable assets in this volatile region of the Congo. Yet Union Minière had little acumen or experience in dealing with this unstable political environment and ultimately its efforts backfired.

The third case involves the International Telephone and Telegraph Corporation (ITT) conspiracy to overthrow the Allende regime in Chile. ITT, which began operating in 1920, quickly became a major international provider of telephone switching equipment and telecommunications services during the pre-war years. Like IBM, ITT apparently saw no ethical problems in doing business with the Nazi regime. It supplied communications equipment to the German armies through its subsidiary, Focke-Wulf, and did so even for a short time after the United States entered the war.[17] From 1960 to 1977, under the leadership of Harold Geneen, ITT became a diversified conglomerate, acquiring more than 350 companies. The portfolio of businesses included Sheraton hotels, Avis Rent-a-Car, Hartford Insurance. Under Geneen's aggressive management, ITT grew into a powerful global corporation, with $17 billion in sales.

One of ITT's many foreign-owned properties was Chitelco, the Chilean Telephone Company. ITT had a 70 percent interest in this company; the remaining 30 percent was held by the Chilean Development Corporation. The estimated value of ITT's investment was about $153 million. When Marxist candidate, Salvador Allende Gossens, was elected president of Chile in October 1970, ITT knew that its property was in danger. Allende had campaigned on a platform calling for the expropriation of American businesses. In September 1971 Allende, true to his word, took possession of Chitelco. Like UFC, ITT sought to use its political influence to protect itself against Allende.

Prior to Allende's election, ITT offered over $1 million to the CIA to support opposition candidates such as the conservative leader, Jorge Alessandri. The CIA rejected ITT's offer. ITT also supported a right-wing newspaper known as *El Mercurio* by means of increased advertising and the circulation of its anti-Allende editorials throughout Latin America. In 1970, Geneen and others at ITT considered a plan proposed by the CIA to create "economic chaos" in Chile, but rejected that plan as unworkable. After ITT's property was expropriated, William Merriam, head of ITT's Washington Office, proposed another plan to U.S. officials on behalf of the company to "accelerate economic chaos" in Chile, with the hope of destabilizing the Allende regime. The plan, which proposed specific measures—such as, loan restrictions, delaying purchases, using American copper instead of buying from Chile—was never implemented.[18]

Declassified documents, released by the CIA in 2000, reveal that the company was even more deeply involved in efforts to overthrow Allende than had been previously suspected. After its property was expropriated, ITT provided financial assistance to the opponents of the Allende government so they could launch a military coup. ITT also relentlessly lobbied the CIA to provide assistance to these opposition groups. The company's hope was that the CIA would orchestrate a coup similar to the one that overthrew Arbenz in Guatemala. In general, ITT sought to persuade the U.S. government and the CIA to manipulate the outcome of the Chilean election, both before and after that election took place.[19]

All of these unfortunate cases exemplify the worst apprehensions and suspicions about the abuse of power by large multinational corporations, which are willing to go to great lengths to retain their assets within a host country. The multinational corporation, as a political actor on the global stage, suddenly became a frightening prospect for those who were already nervous about the excesses of corporate power.[20] Even more frightening was the likelihood of an umbilical connection between multinationals and the U.S. federal government. The rogue political activities of ITT and UFC, which were aimed at overthrowing democratically elected governments, cannot be morally justified, because they erode the sovereignty of these weaker nations and interfere with the will of the people, who have freely chosen their own form of governance.

The key lesson is that multinationals should avoid such overt involvement in political affairs and they should not attempt to shape the political environment to their economic advantage without consideration of a country's common good. A company like Union Minière has every right to protect its property by vigorously petitioning the local government or seeking the help of its home government. But it cannot use immoral means, such as clandestine support for a rebellion, to achieve this end. It is far from clear that secession would serve the Congo's common good, and no company should support political machinations that impair a country's common good.

In general, multinationals should not attempt to resolve complex political or social problems. Private companies are not custodians of the public interest. They lack the moral authority and democratic credentials to provide social goods, deal with the demands of social justice, or determine collective priorities to advance the public good. Nor do they possess the capacity to rectify human right abuses committed by the state even when they are the victims of that abuse.[21]

In response to the intrusive political engagement of Union Minière, UFC and ITT, companies began to move to the polar extreme, professing the need for political neutrality: a principle of strict "non-involvement" in a country's social or political affairs. A non-interference principle appeared in U.N. documents and other international codes of conduct, warning multinationals against the dangers of political interference, such as promoting regime change.[22] Companies vowed to respect national political sovereignty and not to meddle in internal politics. Royal Dutch Shell, for example, adopted "non-involvement" as one of its core values, and relied on this principle to defend some of its actions in Nigeria. To some extent, these multinationals took the advice of Milton Friedman, who urges corporations to eschew the realm of politics, where they have no competence.

However, depending upon its interpretation, a philosophy of unconditional political neutrality can also be awkward for a corporation. First, no corporation can conduct business in any country in a purely apolitical manner. It must submit to established government regulations and interact with government and local officials. It has a right to lobby policy makers in good faith on behalf of its own legitimate economic interests. Second, a stance of neutrality on moral and social issues has negative ethical implications, especially if it becomes a means of deflecting one's moral obligations. As we have contended, multinational corporations have two fundamental duties: they should never deprive people of their rights and in some situations they must be held accountable for safeguarding those rights when threatened by others. The former obligation also means that they must not cooperate in the deprivation of basic rights, which can occur just by being a loyal corporate citizen which follows unjust local laws.

The moral duty to respect and protect rights implies a certain degree of "political involvement." Sometimes the deprivation of rights is the result of the host government's laws and policies, but corporations are still obliged not to go along, despite the adverse consequences. Any aspiration to political neutrality cannot interfere with the moral duty to honor and protect human goods and rights rather than passively trade them off for the sake of "non-involvement" or neutrality. The critical question is how to determine the correct balance between too much or too little activism, and how to decide which forms of activism are morally and politically appropriate. Activism oriented toward the protection of rights for the common good is morally acceptable, but, absent the most exigent circumstances, activism that aims to change the state's identity from one form of government to another, or to tendentiously take sides in internal political conflict is unacceptable.

Disinvestment Decisions

One of the most difficult political decisions a corporation must make sometimes involves disinvestment in a host country when that country is involved in human rights violations or other reprehensible actions. The disinvestment decision raises a larger question: what should multinationals do when the culture and moral norms of a host country differ substantially from those found in a multinational's home country? Should multinationals accommodate themselves to local culture and to different political structures, attempt to engage the cultural and its political differences, or simply disengage? For example, should companies like IBM and ITT have exited Germany, given the racism and escalating human rights violations of the Nazi regime? Or is constructive engagement an acceptable alternative?

Sometimes foreign governments take action against a country when it is particularly repressive and unresponsive to promptings for moderation. In 2011, the United States government imposed economic sanctions on Syria that banned investment in Syria by U.S. companies. This was in response to the brutal and repressive tactics deployed by Syrian President Bashar al-Assad to remain in power, and his alleged stockpiling of weapons of mass destruction. Given the nature of the Assad regime, it could be argued that companies doing business in Syria should not have waited for direction from their home government before taking action. Rather, they should have voluntarily divested their holding in Syria as a way of communicating their unwillingness to cooperate in any way with the Assad regime. Yet even after the sanctions were imposed some companies were slow to respond, apparently preferring to remain in Syria rather than to exert economic pressures on the Assad government. NCR Corporation, which makes Automated Teller Machines or ATMs, was accused of violating the embargo by continuing to operate a Syrian subsidiary.[23] The presumption of sanctions is that the loss of foreign investment will eventually lead to changes in a country's behavior. However, coercion of this sort is not always effective and it can sometimes lead to the prolonged suffering of innocent citizens.

In the majority of cases *ex post* sanctions are not imposed and multinationals are left to make their own decisions about the ethical propriety of disinvestment. What are the rational and moral criteria for resolving such a dilemma? According to the conventional wisdom of business ethicists, responses to this moral dilemma will range along a continuum: from those which follow the "rule of relativism"—which calls for accommodation to local cultural norms, to those which abide by the "rule of absolutism." According to the latter rule multinationals should abide by whatever absolute moral standards apply in any given situation, regardless of the cultural context. In between these polarities falls the middle ground of a more pluralistic approach, which recognizes the legitimacy of any given society's norms, and therefore permits reasonable adjustments to local customs and lifestyles.[24] The philosophy of moderate universalism proposed in this book also occupies this middle ground (leaning closer to the "rule of absolutism"), since it recognizes respect for cultural and normative diversity up to the point where basic human rights are unjustly violated.

According to Schermerhorn, companies have three broad options for making disinvestment decisions. The first is unrestricted engagement in countries, even where there are human rights violations and oppressive policies. This policy option is supported by cultural relativism and an ethical stance of individualism that emphasizes the need for a corporation to follow its economic self-interest without violating the rules of law. Second, a multinational could opt for a strategy of constructive engagement. This solution is usually justified by utilitarian reasoning that emphasizes how continued investment will optimize consequences for all parties involved and further social development for the country in question. Critics of this solution have underscored the ambiguity of "constructive engagement." Is it enough for companies to dialogue over questionable practices and perhaps coordinate industry support to oppose rights abuses? Or should this "engagement" also include a substantial contribution to social development in order to offset some of the rights-abuses? Despite these legitimate questions, there may be merit in some circumstances to a strategy based on engagement of political and cultural diversity.

The final option is principled non-engagement. In this case a company is probably guided by core values that it refuses to compromise in any foreign situation. Levi Strauss & Co., a dominant player in the U.S. jeans market, reluctantly came to the conclusion that it had to leave China because remaining there was inconsistent with the company's global sourcing guidelines and code of ethics, both of which articulated high human rights standards. Levi Strauss had been sourcing its goods from China since 1986, and was looking to expand its presence in China. But in 1991 it abruptly abandoned a joint venture to open a manufacturing plant after realizing that it would have to help enforce China's one-child-per-family policy. Several years later the company decided to withdraw from all of its sourcing relationships in China. This decision is a prime example of principled non-engagement for the sake of consistency with a multinational's corporate value structure. Levi Strauss believed that "pervasive violations of basic human rights" were evident in China, so the country had to be abandoned as a sourcing and manufacturing option.[25] Rather than individualism or utilitarianism, the ethical orientation for such a strategy of voluntary withdrawal and deferment of direct investment is an uncompromising commitment to a set of universally binding moral norms that could be expressed as natural rights or as hypernorms. Principled non-engagement comes closest to following the "rule of absolutism." However, rigid absolution is unacceptable, since companies should strive to be tolerant of cultural diversity without obliging injustice.

Endorsing moderate universalism, which favors a fairly thick set of rights, should imply that disinvestment must become a serious option when these rights are consistently and blatantly abused by a host government. Multinationals cannot leave every country where rights are violated, and accordingly we propose a more precise guideline for withdrawal in the next section. Perhaps the real debate, for those who argue for minimal moral standards in terms of rights, is the set of rights which deserve universal validity. When is it possible to elevate cultural identity over our universal identity as people? The answer to that question will determine which rights can be dismissed altogether or be subjected to substantial cultural interpretation. As we have seen, philosophers like Rawls argue for a thin set of universal rights, a "special class of urgent rights," that omits some civil liberties endorsed in the United Nations Declaration on Human Rights.[26] Natural law theorists, on the other hand, are more inclined to support a thicker set of rights, more in line with the UN Declaration. According to that viewpoint, for example, the right to free speech must be properly specified but it cannot be radically reinterpreted or discarded by any government. Companies which accept the validity of free speech as a universal right will have a difficult time doing business in a totalitarian cultural environment that rejects this right especially if they are required to be complicit in enforcing the host country's standard. However, according to a Rawlsian perspective, which does not regard freedom of expression as a universal right, companies like Microsoft and Yahoo could more convincingly justify unrestricted or constructive engagement in China, even if they were forced to aid the Chinese government in censoring Internet communications.

Should companies follow Levi Strauss' lead and terminate foreign investments in the face of injustice or should they opt for constructive engagement and work for change from within? Before we specifically delineate the circumstances that should warrant withdrawal, we consider the case of foreign investment in Burma.

Unocal, Total and Investment in Burma

The American oil and gas company, Unocal, was founded in California in 1890. After decades of steady growth the company ran into financial problems in the 1980s, barely surviving a hostile takeover attempt. In its effort to rebuild oil and gas reserves, Unocal expanded its global presence. The company had just begun to focus its attention on Southeast Asia when it faced a major divestment decision. The decision involved the country of Burma, also known as Myanmar, located in Southeast Asia. In the mid-1990s Unocal entered into a joint venture with the state-owned Myanmar Oil and Gas Enterprise (MOGE). Also included in this venture was the French energy company, Total, and PTT, the energy company of Thailand. Unocal's stake was 28 percent. Their objective was to extract natural gas from the Yadana gas field located off the coast of Thailand. The low-risk project was estimated to generate $400 million of revenues per year.

Burma, which gained its independence from the United Kingdom in 1948, occupies a vital geostrategic position, which should have made it a prosperous country. However, Burma has never been able to live up to its economic potential. There has been sporadic civil unrest since 1948, and the country's commitment to socialism, known as the "Burmese Way to Socialism" was a complete failure. From 1988, Burma was run by a military junta, known as the State Law and Order Restoration Council (SLORC). The SLORC had taken firm control of the country, nullifying the democratic elections held in 1990. The leader of the opposition party, Aung San Suu Kyi, was placed under house arrest. The SLORC ruled with an iron hand, closing down universities and forbidding any public gatherings for the sake of securing public order. The country's economic prospects were dim as the government's four-year socialist plan had yielded little in the way of economic growth.

This poor economic performance accounts for the importance of Yadana, described as "the one project that really matters to the military junta."[27] But the Yadana pipeline project was the source of fierce criticism by human rights advocates for a number of reasons. Aside from the environmental issues, the SLORC had been accused of human rights violations, such as the use of forced labor to build roads, a railway, and other supporting infrastructure in the pipeline areas. The SLORC had also been credibly accused of forcefully relocating large segments of the civilian population in the area to make way for the pipeline and production operations that supplemented the offshore drilling. The troops that protected the pipeline construction used brutal tactics, including kidnapping and torture, to deal with sabotage or any subversive activities.

Of course, during these years, these sorts of human rights violations were not confined to the Burmese villages that were scattered along the route of the pipeline. Rather, human rights violations were pervasive throughout all of Burma. The Burmese government consistently relied on forced labor to build up its roads and weak infrastructure and it continued to suppress free speech and punish dissenters. No attention was paid to other basic rights, such as a fair trial and due process.

As foreign governments watched this display of military aggression, some took decisive action. In 1997, the United States banned future investment in the country, but it did not compel multinationals that had already invested to withdraw. The European Union removed Myanmar's preferential trade status, and in 2000 the United Kingdom's Foreign Office demanded that Premier Oil cease doing business in Burma. Other countries were not keen on imposing penalties, and the demand for further sanctions and economic isolation never achieved multilateral consensus.

In the midst of this evolving controversy companies were forced to decide whether to disinvest. U.S. foreign investment in Burma was sizable at the time, estimated at just over $6 billion. As the abuses worsened with no end in sight, many companies—such as Apple Computer, PepsiCo, Levi Strauss, and J. Crew—chose to leave. Other companies, including Deutsche Telekom, Siemens, ARCO, British Petroleum, and Acer chose to stay.[28] Both Total and Unocal (later acquired by Chevron) also chose to stay and to persevere with the Yadana project. By 2000, construction was complete, and natural gas began flowing through the pipelines into Burma and Thailand. Criticism subsided as NGOs and other rights groups turned their attention to other hot spots around the globe.

Both companies defended their decision to remain by vehemently denying any sanctioning or direct involvement in human rights abuses. But critics pointed out their indirect involvement by virtue of their participation in the joint venture with the MOGE, Burma's state-owned energy company. Both Total and Unocal benefited from those human rights abuses. They were the beneficiaries of the infrastructure, the roads and railway, built with forced labor. They benefited from the SLORC's heavy-handed pipeline security. Moreover, Total and Unocal provided state-of-the-art technology and know-how that enabled the Burmese military regime to generate much-needed capital and thereby sustain its power. And their presence in Burma helped the military government retain some residue of credibility.[29]

Unocal, however, was unmoved by these persuasive arguments and instead pursued a strategy of constructive engagement, believing that its presence would eventually bring about significant social change. According to Unocal's president, John Imle, there should be more investment in Myanmar, rather than less, since "that would strengthen American influence by speeding the transfer of U.S. business principles, fair labor practices, health and safety and environmental standards and technologies."[30] In its defense, the company also cited its policy of political neutrality. Unocal's goal in Burma was solely economic: to drill for oil and gas and make a reasonable return on its investment. In the process of realizing that goal, Unocal sought to transcend local politics.

How can we assess the decision of Unocal and Total to remain in Burma when so many companies chose to leave? We must keep in mind that Unocal and Total not only do business in Burma, but do so in a commercial alliance with the repressive Burmese government. Arguably, both companies had a clearer picture of the systematic human rights abuses taking place in Burma than IBM had in Germany in the early 1930s. How realistic and responsible is the strategy of constructive engagement? Could we have expected Burma's military junta to have changed its ways thanks to the influence of Western companies like Total and Unocal? Or will they be more likely to change due to the economic chaos and social deprivation created by widespread disinvestment?

While there may be some validity to the argument for constructive engagement, there is also room for skepticism. A strong case can be made that the investment of Total and Unocal could not be easily justified because both companies were reaping some of the benefits from the corrupt and unjust actions committed regularly by the SLORC for the sake of the Yadana project. It is immoral for any international agent to cooperate in unjust actions, either formally or materially (under certain conditions) and to benefit from those unjust actions.[31] By working hand in hand with the MOGE, which routinely authorized forced labor and violent relocation of people along the pipeline route, Unocal and Total facilitated its wrongdoing and contributed to the bad effects of its actions, even if they do not intend to do so. Instead of upholding and protecting human rights, they cooperated in the deprivation of human rights, such as the right to liberty or freedom from slavery, by lending both material and moral support to this regime. Second, as moral agents, companies like Unocal and Total have a duty to bear witness to injustice and are obliged to demand social and moral reforms, especially when they are proximate to this injustice. Their criticism of the SLORC, and demand for reform as part of "constructive engagement," lack credibility since their actions are inconsistent with their rhetoric. Both companies are negative role models instead of positive ones, and other corporations, which must decide about their own moral status in Burma, are more easily persuaded to follow their example and cooperate materially in the regime's wrongdoing.[32] Thus, for several reasons and despite any cultural variables, it is hard not to conclude that economic disengagement was the morally superior course of action.

Things have changed dramatically in Myanmar. The new president, Thein Sein, instituted democratic reforms in 2011, and the country is now an "open democracy." Aung San Suu Kyi has been released from house arrest and serves as president of the National League for Democracy. The country's leaders have relaxed their tight grip on the media, and Burmese reporters now write openly about controversial issues. As a result, Burma is no longer a pariah state in the eyes of the world. No one is sure why these changes have occurred but experts speculate that part of the reason is the country's dire economic straits, that resulted from the failed economic policies of the junta and the disinvestment of so many multinational corporations.[33]

Many companies that left Burma in the late 1990s have plans to return. Pepsi and Coke are already engaged in a new "cola war," vying for the biggest share of this untapped market. Both companies will move cautiously, however, as they export products before establishing local operations.[34] Also, companies that remained, like Total and Chevron (the owner of Unocal) are seeking to increase their investment. Burma continues to be a promising locale for international oil companies because of its rich holdings of offshore oil and natural gas reserves. Despite the prospects for a revived economy, it remains to be seen if the forces of progress and reform will continue to reshape this country.

The Condition-of-Business Principle

There is no conclusive evidence to affirm that Burma changed its ways thanks to the disinvestment of responsible corporations such as Pepsi and Levi Strauss. Nonetheless, a thin case can be made that this was a contributing factor to the country's growing economic chaos, and that chaos led to the dramatic reforms of the Thein Sein regime. Consequentialist reasoning, therefore, might be a promising avenue for the ethical analysis of disinvestment as an effective vehicle to induce social change. When there is severe injustice, companies should disinvest in order to bring about a greater aggregate social good.

However, a stronger case can be put forth for disinvestment than one based purely on utilitarian grounds. Consequentialism is ultimately indeterminate, since it is so difficult to definitively prove that multilateral disinvestment and trade sanctions will lead to a certain result. But, even if one cannot assure a good result, there are non-consequentialist reasons why transacting business with a country, based on mutual advantage, is morally unacceptable under certain conditions. What are those conditions and how do responsible multinational enterprises determine which regimes should be avoided in a world of ethical pluralism and cultural diversity?

As a guideline for the multinationals immersed in these situations, Donaldson proposes a condition of business principle that centers on the violation of human rights. The violation of rights causes great harm and third parties should not be complicit in bringing about this harm. Rights violations occur to some extent in every country. The United States, a country with a reasonably strong record of respecting human rights, was accused of violating the right to privacy by passing the Patriot Act after the terrorist attack on the World Trade Center on 11 September 2001. Hence, it is more realistic to argue that a country must be a *systematic violator of basic human rights* before it is subject to trade sanctions or other forms of economic disengagement. The basic human rights we have in mind were discussed in Chapter Four and include free expression, the right to life and health, the right to own property, and the right to be free from slavery and torture. Recall that these fundamental rights, which are rooted in our common humanity, were defended as necessary conditions of human flourishing. Although there is some room for a culturally informed interpretation of how to specify and properly limit some of these rights (like free speech), there comes a point where such limits become unreasonable if they virtually nullify the right in question. There is a big difference between limiting the right of free expression by forbidding pornography for minors (US), and forbidding any form of political dissent (China).

As we saw in the Burma case, the problem with a corporation doing business in a country with a corrupt government is that this transaction benefits or helps that corrupt government, which is not ethically permissible. The general moral principle at stake is that one must refrain from harming others but also not help another party (even indirectly) harm others. It is immoral, therefore, to assist a corrupt government in violating the rights of its citizens. The evil of such cooperation is compounded when the cooperating agent also benefits as a consequence of these activities that violate rights. There may be some circumstances where business transactions do not benefit rights violators but actually cause them some harm. If a Western news organization were able to penetrate into Burma and operate an underground newspaper critical of the military regime, the continuation of such an enterprise would be fully justified. Also, an exception must be made for the genuine possibility of a moral catastrophe that might ensue if a company stopped trade or terminated its investment. In virtually all cases of trade sanctions and disinvestment some innocent people will be harmed to some degree, but significant harm to an appreciable group of innocents should validate an exception. If a drug company like Merck were to depart from Burma and leave people without life-preserving medicines, its departure could lead to great suffering and even death. Under these conditions, the company should obviously remain in Burma. This assumes that Merck determines in good faith that no other domestic or foreign companies will fill the void left by its absence.

With these critical exceptions in mind, we offer this modified version of Donaldson's condition of business principle:

> *Ceteris paribus*, business transactions of company X with country Y are morally impermissible when Y is a systematic violator of fundamental human rights, unless those transactions actually discourage the violation of rights, harm country Y in consequence of its rights-violating activity, or the termination of these transactions would cause a moral catastrophe or its equivalent.[35]

The exceptions articulated in this principle may seem to open the door for many companies to avoid their responsibilities as they protest that their transactions fall under these exceptions. Hence, the exemptions from the condition of business principle must be carefully and conscientiously applied. The general moral norm is that it is immoral and unjust to transact business within corrupt regimes, which systematically violate the human rights of their innocent citizens. These transactions presuppose a mutual advantage between the multinational and the host country, and therefore a multinational's presence in a rights-violating country means that it is unjustifiably helping that country to benefit from its immoral activities.

How might this condition of business principle apply to the refusal of Unocal and Total to divest their holdings in Burma? First, it is evident that the exceptions do not apply. The activities of these companies help rather than harm the party abusing rights, that is, the Burmese government. Revenues from the Yadana project support the government economically and the ongoing commitment to this joint venture with the state-owned Myanmar Oil and Gas Enterprise implies a recognition of the regime's legitimacy. Aung San Suu Kyi affirmed this perception in several interviews. As the controversy lingered on, she pointed out that Total had become the "main support for the military government in Burma."[36] Unlike the withdrawal of a pharmaceutical company supplying life-preserving drugs, there is no reason to believe that the departure of these two companies would create any sort of moral or social catastrophe affecting scores of innocent people. Since the continuation of these business transactions in Burma cannot pass the condition of business principle, they should cease those transactions. In doing so, both companies might have contributed to the quicker demise of a corrupt and oppressive regime.[37]

A similar conclusion, in the case of IBM, also follows from this condition of business principle. While the picture may not have been clear in 1933, at the dawn of the Nazi regime, it should have come into focus by the mid-1930s, when IBM was increasing rather than decreasing its investment. As time progressed, it became increasingly obvious that the Third Reich was a blatantly racist regime and a systematic abuser of human rights. Also, the exceptions would not apply to most companies doing business there, including IBM and ITT. Conscientious companies, therefore, should have withdrawn rather than materially cooperate in advancing the reprehensible goals of this regime.

Management and Ethical Lessons from South Africa

South Africa has also been the scene of another prolonged conflict about disinvestment. When the National Party in South Africa, dominated by white Afrikaners (descendants of Dutch and German immigrants) took control of the country in 1948 it instituted a system of "Apartheid," an Afrikaner word that means "separateness." Apartheid was a tightly controlled, formalized system of racial segregation. Black political movements, such as the African National Congress, were suppressed. The laws inspired by apartheid called for "petty apartheid," that is, the physical segregation of blacks and whites. Accordingly, marriage and any sexual relations between whites and blacks were prohibited. All schools, restaurants, restrooms, dining halls, and public gathering places were segregated. Thanks to the Homelands Citizenship Act of 1970, all blacks were declared to be citizens of one of nine tribal homelands and were considered to be aliens in the White Republic of South Africa. Blacks, who represented 83 percent of the population, could only own land in their homelands area, known as the "native reserves," which comprised only 13 percent of South Africa's land surface. There were also laws aimed at "influx control," which stipulated that blacks could not visit a white urban area for more than 72 hours without a special permit. All blacks also needed special identification passes whenever they traveled in urban areas occupied by whites.[38]

Despite these restrictive apartheid laws, South Africa was an attractive venue for multinationals. The country was rich in natural resources such as gold, chrome, vanadium, and platinum. Over 50 percent of the world's discovered gold reserves were located in South Africa.[39] MNCs were also attracted by the African country's prosperous middle class. As a result, most of the leading United States and European firms had investments in South Africa. South Africa was third on the list of the United Kingdom's investment in foreign countries (following the United States and Australia). The investment of U.S. firms grew to $2 billion by 1979, with 55 of the Fortune 100 companies operating subsidiaries there.[40]

Although other foreign governments opposed apartheid on principle, criticism of this racist regime was surprisingly muted. The United States, for example, did not oppose or hinder foreign investment in South Africa. This indifference was largely a result of South Africa's dependable anti-Communist policies. Hence, for decades there was no coordinated international action against apartheid, and few countries chose to impose economic sanctions. The complex geopolitical situation at the time, compounded by Cold War fears of communism, stifled any multilateral consensus about how to deal with this rogue nation.

The apartheid laws did not bypass the workplace. Many blacks were gainfully employed by foreign firms, but the law banned blacks from holding skilled or managerial jobs if those jobs gave them any authority over whites. The law mandated racially discriminatory salaries. Black workers were generally confined to lower-level, unskilled jobs, and some occupations were reserved just for whites. Blacks were also excluded from management training programs.

By almost any moral standard, South Africa under apartheid "constituted an unethical social, economic, and political system."[41] The corrupt system ultimately created a serious dilemma for the U.S. and European multinationals, which were heavily invested in this African country. The system was inherently unethical and could not be fixed—the only political solution was apartheid's displacement with a non-discriminatory legal system. For a while, multinationals and their home governments ignored this reality. But in the late 1970s there was a heightened social consciousness about ethical matters, accompanied by a more acute moral awareness of the evils of apartheid. Student activists began protests at their universities demanding that they divest their portfolios of equities in companies doing business in South Africa. As a consequence, South African investments became a boardroom agenda item for most corporations, which had to explain themselves to a vocal minority of dissatisfied shareholders.

The debate about corporate involvement in South Africa centered on three broad options for multinationals doing business there. The first position was that any involvement in South Africa propped up the government and so the only responsible course of action was withdrawal and disinvestment. The second option was to remain and continue to provide the goods and services demanded by South African consumers. One of the rationalizations for remaining in South Africa was the need to provide some jobs for blacks who would find themselves unemployed, and at the mercy of less benevolent South African firms, if the multinationals suddenly pulled out. Opponents of disinvestment also took refuge in the popular principle of political neutrality.

The third option was proactive, or "constructive" engagement rather than the status quo or disinvestment. The Sullivan Principles, conceived by General Motors Board member and Baptist minister, Leon Sullivan, provide a blueprint for such constructive engagement. According to the Sullivan Principles, which were promulgated in 1977, companies could remain in South Africa under two conditions. First, they were required to disobey unjust apartheid laws that affected the workplace. In defiance of apartheid, multinational corporations had to be committed to equal and fair employment practices for all employees, equal pay for equal work for all employees, and an increase in the number of blacks in management and supervisory roles.[42] The second condition was that multinationals had to actively promote and advocate the dismantling of the unjust apartheid system. General Motors took the lead in following the Sullivan Principles and many other U.S. multinationals followed its example. An outside auditor was hired to ensure the compliance of each signatory to the principles. The South African government was anxious to avoid a mass exodus of multinationals, so it tolerated the civil disobedience of the signatories and ignored these violations of its apartheid laws.[43]

However, by 1987, it had become apparent to Sullivan that this approach wasn't working. Corporate civil disobedience, however commendable, had utterly failed to undermine the South African regime. "In spite of our efforts," Sullivan proclaimed, "the main pillars of apartheid remain, and blacks are still denied basic civil rights."[44] Many corporations had already reached this same conclusion and, under heavy pressure from some shareholders and other stakeholders, exited the country. In 1986, the United States Congress passed the Comprehensive Anti-Apartheid Act, which banned all future investment in South Africa and imposed trade sanctions. As a result, United States FDI in South Africa fell precipitously, from $2.6 billion in 1981 to $711 million in 1989. Nevertheless, some major U.S. and European companies chose to stay, including Johnson & Johnson, Royal Dutch Shell, Philips, and Unilever.

How do we assess the decision to stay or to opt for constructive engagement in light of the condition of business principle? There seems to be no plausible moral justification for remaining in South Africa and simply conducting business as usual. The case against remaining and continuing to follow apartheid laws in the workplace is unambiguous, since multinationals were acting unethically in obeying these discriminatory apartheid laws. They were explicitly violating the rights of their workers and contributing to an unjust system. These corporations cannot defend their actions by proclaiming the need to respect the host country's sovereignty and to obey its laws, since it is immoral to follow an unjust law. Law, defined by Thomas Aquinas as an "ordinance of reason for the common good of a community," must be regarded in any state as presumptively obligatory.[45] But that obligation is superseded if the law requires people to commit immoral and unjust acts. Unjust laws lack moral authority because that authority derives from the law's rational connection to some precept of morality that reflects the requirements of justice. Thus, laws that authorize such acts as rape, murder, or discrimination are a "corruption" of true law and lack any binding power.[46] Since the apartheid laws of South Africa's government, which disregard human rights and the common good for all members of the community under its authority, are unjust, they lack any normative force and should not be obeyed.

Secular philosophers like John Locke have come to the same conclusion about laws that violate, rather than protect, natural rights. According to Locke, there is a "tacit consent" by the governed to be subject to a sovereign's laws.[47] But for Locke, the contract is conditional, since "insofar as the civil authority does not protect natural rights, it ceases to be a legitimate authority."[48] In the case of South Africa, it is evident that the government has lost its authority because it does not protect the fundamental rights of all of its citizens.

What about multinationals that chose to stay and engage with the South African government by following the Sullivan Principles? These companies assumed the risk of willfully violating the apartheid laws mandating a segregated workplace, and instead they created a more egalitarian workplace environment. They are committed through their actions and public statements to working for reform and to the end of apartheid. Assuming that this approach was carried out conscientiously can it be defended as a viable ethical strategy?

This turns out to be a fairly complex question. Despite their laudable efforts to defy South African law by remaining in South Africa, these multinationals continued to prop up this unjust government through the hefty taxes paid on their revenues. They also continued to lend some credibility to the government, which could showcase the high level of foreign direct investment to the rest of the world. If these signatory multinationals were faithful to the Sullivan Principles, they would exert pressure on the government to amend its racist policies. It is difficult to demonstrate, however, that their rhetoric and action, no matter how sincere, would have led to any changes, and certainly by 1986 there had been no major changes in the government's policies. The claim that multinational activism would undermine apartheid through constructive engagement must be regarded with a healthy dose of skepticism. Thus, since we know with certitude that these firms materially sustained and lent credibility to the government, but we cannot conclude that constructive engagement actually harmed the regime, the weight of evidence suggests that the government was largely unaffected by corporate activism and continued to prosper from its rights-violating activities. It follows, according to the condition of business principle, that the only course of action was the termination of business transactions with South Africa.[49]

Finally, what lessons can multinationals learn from this South African experience? Perhaps the key lesson of this case, which is confirmed by IBM's experience in Germany, is the importance of defying a country's sovereignty when it imposes unjust laws on its people. Philosophers like Aquinas and Locke argue that our natural rights limit a nation's sovereignty and when the law asks us to violate those rights or cooperate in the violation of those rights, the only ethically responsible alternative is to choose civil disobedience. Of course, our natural rights imply universal duties and values, and one can question where universal values end and pluralism begins. As we have seen, philosophers offer different answers to that provocative question.

The second lesson is that, at least in some contexts, mass civil disobedience will not provoke a negative governmental response.

Corporations following the Sullivan Principles, that broke South African law, were able to do so with impunity. There were no negative consequences because these multinational firms were powerful enough to refuse to follow unethical practice.[50] Ultimately, this civil disobedience was ineffective and disinvestment was the only ethically reasonable alternative. How successful was this large-scale disinvestment in the 1980s in bringing about social and political change? Social welfare calculus cannot determine the impact of disinvestment on the final withering away of apartheid, since there were so many other factors at work. This inability to calculate the effects of one's decisions (even in retrospect) illustrates the weakness of utilitarian reasoning, which proposes that the right course of action is the alternative that will optimize the results. Given the difficulty of empirically testing the results of each option, it is far better to rely on a non-consequential normative principle, such as unconditional respect for natural rights.

To be sure, disinvestment and trade sanctions are never easy decisions and should not be taken lightly, because they disrupt the lives of innocent people. These are highly complex matters, with many factors at play, including assessing the tricky calculus of withdrawal's disparate effects. It can often appear that consequences will be optimized by a strategy of constructive engagement. But consequentialist rhetoric should not obscure the harsh ethical realities of doing business as usual in turbulent environments like Apartheid South Africa.

Conclusions

Corporate political activism by multinational corporations has a troubling legacy. United Fruit in Guatemala and ITT in Chile fought behind the scenes for regime change because their properties were threatened, but their policies undermined the right of people to determine their own political future. Union Minière unfairly supported a rebellious secession in the Congo that was incompatible with the country's common good. In the wake of these scandals companies embraced a non-interference policy, vowing to stay out of a host country's politics. This new ideology of political neutrality helped to allay fears about the abuse of corporate power. A sound non-interference policy, however, must be nuanced and reflect the fact that there is no apolitical way to do business in any country. Also, this principle can be taken too far if it implies an indifference to a corporation's social and ethical responsibilities. Companies cannot use neutrality as an excuse to ignore the impairment of human rights that is a direct effect, or a side effect, of their business transactions.

The second issue treated in this chapter was disinvestment. Under what conditions should companies refuse to do business in a country or liquidate their investment? Sometimes companies find themselves within a culture that tolerates, or even promotes, human rights abuses such as discrimination. There have also been flagrant examples of corrupt governments, such as the military dictatorship of Burma, which systematically violated the rights of its citizens. Rather than follow the example of most multinationals, which divested their holdings, Unocal and Total decided to remain and pursue an ethical strategy of constructive engagement. However, by choosing to remain in Burma, locked in a joint venture with an agency of the Burmese government, these companies buttressed this corrupt regime by providing desperately needed capital, tax revenue and credibility. Moral choices that lend support to a corrupt political system or culture are not ethically justifiable.

Following the lead of other ethicists, we proposed a condition-of-business principle, which stipulates that a multinational should not do business in a country when that country is a systematic violator of fundamental human rights, unless certain exceptions apply. This norm is premised on the general principle that moral agents, including corporations, cannot facilitate or cooperate with the objectively immoral actions of others. Such cooperation, especially in cases where human rights are being impeded, cannot serve an authentic common good. Above all, companies should not follow unjust laws in host countries, when those laws require the abuse of the rights of workers and other stakeholders. Unjust law has no normative force.

The proposed condition-of-business principle, however, is not the end of the debate about disinvestment, since there are many issues to be resolved about the scope and foundation of human rights. Where does universalism end and pluralism begin? And how can these universal rights and rational standards be reconciled with the popular notion of strong pluralism or "multiculturalism?" According to Raz, the world's different cultures are all worthy of respect.[51] This may be true, but when should companies defy cultural standards that endorse the denigration of human rights? The problem with multiculturalism or strong pluralism is that it becomes difficult to judge another culture or polity as morally inferior and an unfit partner for investment or trade.

Notes

1 "Business Leaders See Gain Continue," *New York Times*, January 2, 1935, 15.
2 See Emerson Pugh, *Building IBM: Shaping an Industry and its Technology* (Cambridge, MA: MIT Press, 1995).
3 The "Religion" column on the punch-card was to be marked as followed: 1 for Protestant, 2 for Catholic, and 3 for Jew. See Götz Aly and Karl Heinz Roth, *Die reslose Erfassung: Volkszählen, Identifizieren, Aussondern im Nationalsozialismus* (Berlin: Rotbuch Verlag, 1984), 28–30. See also Edwin Black, *IBM and the Holocaust* (Washington, D.C.: Dialog Press, 2001), 52–8.
4 "German Fugitives Tell of Atrocities at Hands of Nazis," *New York Times*, March 20, 1933, 1; and "Reich Post Ministry is Sifting Out Jews," *New York Times*, June 11, 1933, 1.
5 Kevin Maney, *The Maverick and his Machine* (Hoboken, NJ: John Wiley & Sons, 2003), 216.
6 "Watson Sends Hitler Notes of Gratitude," *New York Times*, July 6, 1937.
7 "10,000 Jews Flee Nazi Persecution," *New York Times*, April 15, 1933.
8 William Shirer, *The Rise and Fall of the Third Reich* (New York: Simon & Schuster, 1960), 203; 232–3. For a detailed timeline of events during the growth of Dehomag prior to World War Two, consult Shirer's reliable book, especially pages, 188–276.
9 Dan Koeppel, *Banana: The Fate of the Fruit that Changed the World* (New York: Penguin Group, 2008), 74–6.
10 Koeppel, *Banana*, 75.
11 Cole Blasier, *The Hovering Giant: U.S. Responses to Revolutionary Change in Latin America* (Pittsburgh, PA: University of Pittsburgh Press, 1976), 56.
12 Stephen Schlesinger and Stephen Kinzer, *Bitter Fruit: The Untold Story of the America Coup in Guatemala* (New York: Anchor Books, 1983), 65–77.
13 Thomas McCann, *An American Company: The Tragedy of United Fruit* (New York: Crown, 1976), 44.
14 Quoted in Schlesinger and Kinzer, *Bitter Fruit*, 199.
15 Daniel Litvin, *Empires of Profit* (New York: Texere, 2003), 159–69.
16 Litvin, *Empires of Profit*, 166–8.
17 Steven Wartick and Donnas Wood, *International Business and Society* (Oxford: Blackwell Publishers, 1998), 132–3.

18 "The International Telephone and Telegraph Company and Chile, 1970–1971," Committee on Foreign Relations, United States Senate by the Subcommittee on Multinational Corporations, June 21, 1973.
19 Central Intelligence Agency, "CIA Activities in Chile," released September 18, 2000; www.cia.gov/library/reports/generalreports-1/chile (accessed September 6, 2013).
20 The influential Harvard economist, John Kenneth Galbraith, had just published *The New Industrial State*, an admonition of excess corporate influence that called for the countervailing power of unions and government. See John Kenneth Galbraith, *The New Industrial State* (New York: Simon & Schuster, 1967).
21 See "The Good Company: A Survey of Social Responsibility," *The Economist*, January 22, 2005, 20–2.
22 See John Kline, "Political Activities by Transnational Corporations: Bright Lines versus Grey Boundaries," *Journal of Transnational Corporations*, 12 (1) (2003), 1–25.
23 Christopher Matthews and Samuel Rubenfeld, "NCR's Subsidiary in Syria Accused of Sanctions Lapse," *The Wall Street Journal*, August 13, 2012, B1, B5.
24 John Schermerhorn, "Terms of Global Business Engagement in Ethically Challenging Environments," *Business Ethics Quarterly*, (1999) 9 (3), 486–87. This article also presents the three options for divestment decisions discussed in this section.
25 Louise Kehoe, "Bold Fashion Statement: Levi Strauss's Decision Not to Invest in China," *Financial Times*, May 8, 1993, 9. However, five years later Levi Strauss reversed course and decided to expand its manufacturing operations in China and to start selling its apparel there. When interviewed about this stunning reversal, the company president at the time, Peter Jacobi, was asked about Levi Strauss' commitment to human rights issues. He expressed the company's continuing concern about human rights, but also said "Levi Strauss is not in the human rights business." See Mark Landler, "Reversing Course, Levi Strauss Will Expand its Output in China," *The New York Times*, April 9, 1998, D1.
26 John Rawls, *The Law of Peoples* (Cambridge, MA: Harvard University Press, 1999), 79. See also Steven Rockefeller's "Comment," in Charles Taylor, *Multiculturalism and the Politics of Recognition* (Princeton, NJ: Princeton University Press, 1992), 87–98.
27 "Myanmar: Trouble in the Pipeline," *The Economist*, January 18, 1997, 39.
28 Schermerhorn, "Terms of Global Business Engagement," 488–90.
29 Debora Spar makes some of these observations in her notes to "The Burma Pipeline," (Boston, MA: Harvard Business School Publications, 1998).
30 John Imle, "Keep Door Open in Myanmar," *Journal of Commerce*, February 28, 1997, 31.
31 The relevant moral principle is that a moral agent should not cooperate in the wrongdoing of another. If someone intentionally helps moral agent X carry out an objectively wrong choice, that person shares X's wrong

intention and deserves blame for helping X. But a distinction must be made between formal and material cooperation. While all forms of formal cooperation ("which concurs in the bad will of the other") are immoral, the issue of moral culpability is more complex when material cooperation is involved. To assess the moral acceptability of material cooperation one must consider the cooperator's actual actions (drilling for natural gas, building the pipeline, etc.), which must be good or indifferent in itself, and whether that action is proportionate to the *gravity* of the wrongdoing to which one's actions contributes and to the *proximity* of the contribution to the wrongdoing. Even if Unocal does not concur with these human rights abuses, the gravity and magnitude of these offenses and the company's proximity to them is beyond dispute; it also reaps the benefits of the evil actions in question. Thus, it is hard to see how this instance of material cooperation is not morally questionable. See Germain Grisez, *Difficult Moral Questions* (Quincy, IL: Franciscan Press, 1997), 871–85.

32 See Grisez, *Difficult Moral Questions*, 879–82.
33 "Special Report: Myanmar," *The Economist*, May 25, 2013, 3–4.
34 Patrick Barta, "Bringing PepsiCo Back to Myanmar," *The Wall Street Journal*, August 10, 2012, B1.
35 Thomas Donaldson, *The Ethics of International Business* (Oxford: Oxford University Press, 1989), 131–5. I am indebted to Donaldson's entire discussion of disinvestment in Chapter Eight of his book, 129–44.
36 M. Arnold, "Total Chief Rejects Calls to Quit Burma," *Financial Times*, May 18, 2005, 22.
37 For a different perspective on the case of Burma see Ian Holliday, "Doing Business with Rights Violating Regimes: Corporate Social Responsibility and Myanmar's Military Junta," *Journal of Business Ethics*, 61 (4) (2005), 329–42, and Judith White, "Globalization, Divestment, and Human Rights in Burma," *Journal of Corporate Citizenship*, 14 (1) (2004), 47–65.
38 E.J. Kahn, "Annals of International Trade: A Very Emotive Subject," *New Yorker*, May 14, 1979, 33–8.
39 Benjamin Kline, *Profit, Principle and Apartheid, 1948–1994* (New York: Edwin Mellen Press, 1997), 110.
40 Kahn, "Annals of International Trade," 37.
41 Richard DeGeorge, *Competing with Integrity in International Business*, (New York: Oxford University Press, 1993), 121.
42 Leon Sullivan, "Sullivan Principles," http://www.revleonsullivan.org/principled/principles.htm (accessed May 18, 2008).
43 DeGeorge, *Competing with Integrity in International Business,* 121–2.
44 Dennis Kneale, "Sullivan Urges Firms to Quit South Africa," *The Wall Street Journal*, June 4, 1987, A1.
45 St. Thomas Aquinas, *Summa Theologiae* (Summary of Theology) trans. Fathers of the English Dominican Province (New York: Benziger Bros., 1947–8), I–II, q. 90, a. 4.
46 Aquinas, *Summa Theologiae,* II–II, q. 57, a. 2, ad. 2. See also John Finnis' *Aquinas* (Oxford: Oxford University Press, 1998), 267–2. During the

height of the apartheid years, another pioneer in the fight for racial justice, Martin Luther King Jr., invoked this same natural law reasoning to justify his own civil disobedience of the South's unjust discrimination laws. According to King, segregation statutes are unjust because they give "the segregator a false sense of superiority and the segregated a false sense of inferiority." See Martin Luther King Jr., "Letter from a Birmingham Jail," *The Christian Century*, June 12, 1963.

47 John Locke, *Second Treatise of Government*, § 119.
48 Alasdair MacIntyre, *A Short History of Ethics* (New York: Penguin, 1985), 158.
49 Donaldson, *The Ethics of International Business*, 135–40. Some multinational companies like Johnson & Johnson claimed that their departure would leave people without needed medicine; if this is true, its decision to stay could be justified under the "moral catastrophe exception," so long as the company did not follow the country's unjust laws.
50 DeGeorge, *Competing with Integrity in International Business*, 123.
51 Joseph Raz, *Ethics in the Public Domain* (Oxford: Oxford University Press, 1995), 120.

9

Responsible Sourcing and Offshoring

Introduction

Every morning Kathie Lee Gifford engaged a national television audience with her personal warmth and infectious enthusiasm. But the popular talk show host could not believe the news she was hearing as she prepared to go on the air with her co-host, Regis Philbin. In a Congressional Hearing, Charles Kernaghan, Executive Director of the National Labor Committee Education Fund, had testified that Kathie Lee's line of clothing was being produced by 13- and 14-year-old children in large, decrepit factories in Honduras. The factories were referred to as "monstrous sweatshops," where workers were paid "slave wages." Reliable sources indicated that many of these children worked 75 hours per week for the minimum wage of $0.31 per hour. Ms. Gifford was accused of being a party to this gross mistreatment of children in these Honduran sweatshops.[1]

Kathie Lee Gifford's fashionable clothing line had been developed by the discount retailer, Wal-Mart. The giant chain recruited her for her name recognition, but it never told her anything about where and how the clothes carrying her name were to be made. Ms. Gifford received $5 million for promoting this line of clothing. As this Congressional testimony became headline news, Ms. Gifford was chastised in the media for days for her connections to these sweatshops. She contritely expressed her regrets about the endorsement, but also protested that she should not be held morally liable for the working conditions in the factories where this clothing was produced. "My first endorsement was for Kraft when I was 17, and I didn't think I had to go check out the cows," she told the reporters who had been dogging her for a statement.[2]

Publicity surrounding the Kathie Lee case brought to light the plight of sweatshop workers in poor countries like Honduras, Mexico, and Indonesia. Wal-Mart, which was directly responsible for producing the trendy Kathie Lee clothing line at this Honduran contractor, was not the only major multinational caught up in the escalating scandal. Companies like Nike, Reebok, IKEA, J. C. Penney, and many others were also involved in one way or another. This controversy over supplier working conditions has not gone away and still erupts into the headlines from time to time. The terrible Bangladesh fire in 2012, that killed 112 people, once again put the spotlight on this issue. That fire was followed by the collapse of a substandard building, also in Bangladesh, in the spring of 2013, which killed 1,127 garment workers. Both of these tragic incidents reflect how little progress has been made in ameliorating the working conditions of contractors in low-wage countries. Global corporations still have trouble policing their suppliers, and consumers seem to have few reservations about buying clothes made in countries like Bangladesh.

The problem is rooted in the economic reality that companies like Wal-Mart, Nike and Gap benefit appreciably from the lower costs of overseas manufacturing plants. They engage in a game of labor "arbitrage," moving from one country to another to find the lowest wages in order to keep their costs below the competition. This strategy may make good economic sense but it has elaborate moral implications that are often overlooked. It is a demanding task to keep labor costs exceedingly low while also safeguarding the fragile rights of the workers. To what extent can companies take advantage of the social and cultural differences between countries where they have their products made? Should they allow their contractors to hire workers who are only 13- or 14-years-old if that is the long-standing local custom? And in what areas (such as safety or environmental protection) should they strive for uniform corporate policies that transcend local cultural norms?

A more theoretical ethical issue at the focal point of this debate is the extent to which multinationals are responsible for the moral deficits of their suppliers. And what about the suppliers of those suppliers—where does accountability end in the global value chain? On what basis can multinationals interfere with their suppliers' operations, given that they are independent companies rather than wholly owned subsidiaries or even joint ventures? Do they have the moral authority to impose high labor standards on these companies? We will wrestle with these questions throughout this chapter, but first we examine the origin and explosive growth of outsourcing and offshoring, that has become so characteristic of this latest phase of globalization's history.

Offshoring and Outsourcing

The Nike corporation, well-known for its high performance athletic shoes, pioneered the idea of the virtual or "hollow" corporation. From its inception, the Oregon-based footwear company decided to outsource all but its core value-chain activities: design and marketing. The company focused solely on those critical functions, with marketing campaigns that relied heavily on celebrity endorsements. At the same time, it outsourced manufacturing and sales. Nike's CEO, Phil Knight, insisted that there would be no in-house production of Nike's athletic footwear. Knight's goal was to keep manufacturing costs low by outsourcing production in order to minimize overhead and labor costs. There was a growing consensus among strategists and consultants that the Nike approach was viable and that business activities should not be performed within the corporate hierarchy unless absolutely necessary.

To pursue its low-cost, outsourcing strategy, Nike first sought out independent contractors in South Korea and Taiwan, but then moved to lower-wage countries like China and Indonesia. Contractors in the latter countries could produce shoes for 50 percent less than shoes produced in Taiwan or South Korea.[3] During the 1980s in Indonesia, the Suharto regime had been accused of flagrant human rights abuses and the country was considered to be a "human rights sinkhole," where the rights of workers were virtually non-existent. Nike's Indonesian contractors paid exceedingly low wages so Nike was able to invest in its core activities and earn substantial rents on its brand. These contractors also relied heavily on underage children to do the work. But Nike paid a price for its unorthodox strategy. It quickly gained a reputation as an opportunistic and callous organization, willing to exploit cheap Asian labor to advance its strategic objectives. Worried about damage to the brand, Nike finally responded to its critics. In 1998, Nike committed itself to ending child labor and to allowing outside auditors to check the working conditions of its suppliers' factories. Employees now had to be 16-years-old to work in its contractors' plants, even in countries where it was commonplace for 14-year-olds to hold such jobs.[4] Little was done, however, about the meager wages paid by these contractors. Workers in Vietnam factories were making less than $2 a day, which is estimated to be well below the subsistence level for this country.

Despite the moderate ethical risk, many other Western companies jumped on the offshoring bandwagon in order to combat high labor costs in their home markets. Offshoring means moving work and jobs beyond the borders of a corporation's home country. It usually involves outsourcing, which means using outside contractors to do the work. China, Thailand, Mexico, and Indonesia were some of the many countries where these contractors could find adequately skilled labor for cheaper wages. In some cases corporations ran their own operations abroad rather than assume the risks and transaction costs associated with the use of independent contractors. Manufacturing investment in developing nations tripled in the 15 years from 1980 to 1995, to $56 billion.[5]

But other companies, like Nike, strongly preferred to rely on independent contractors. The problem with using these suppliers in countries like Indonesia and China is that it's difficult for a multinational to monitor and control the conditions of these factories. Even when conditions appear to be acceptable, there can be deplorable problems lurking behind the scene. The German company, Adidas, for example, found itself immersed in a troubling controversy over allegations that its soccer balls were being made by a Chinese contractor which had farmed out production to prisoners in rural labor camps.

Despite these ethical controversies, the offshoring and outsourcing trends intensified during the economic boom of the 1990s, as more companies sought to leverage global labor arbitrage. Multinationals are by nature oriented to recognize and take advantage of differences among countries where they compete or do business. As wage rates have risen in certain countries thanks to higher labor demand, companies have moved operations or sought out contractors elsewhere. Higher manufacturing wages in China have prompted many multinationals to move into Vietnam, Thailand, and India. Labor costs in China in 2013 were about $3 per hour but were still only $1 per hour in Sri Lanka and Indonesia. Some of this differential is offset by China's scale and well-developed supply chains, but not enough to keep manufacturers from fleeing to lower-wage countries. Due to China's higher labor costs, the U.S. based leather goods company, Coach, and clogs maker, Croc, have plans to shift a sizable amount of production to other countries within the next several years.[6]

Offshoring is unpopular in the West, however, because it has contributed to big job losses in high wage countries, especially for unskilled labor. When the United States entered into a recession in 2008 many expected U.S. multinationals like GE to invest more at home and help cushion the economic downturn, but this didn't happen.[7] Instead many of these cost conscious companies continued to increase foreign investment. Offshoring is the one element of globalization that workers in developed economies fear and loathe the most. In many countries, including the United States, people overwhelmingly blame offshoring as one of the prime sources of low economic development.[8]

But if offshoring is disdained in the West it is regarded by developing countries as a means of jumpstarting stationary and bleak economies. Sweatshops, described as "monstrous" by some NGOs, are regarded even by some heterodox liberal economists as the "essential first step toward modern prosperity in developing countries."[9] What is viewed as exploitation by people in developed economies, is regarded in low wage countries as "opportunity." Despite low labor standards and underage workers in Honduras, people have welcomed the sweatshops. According to one local labor leader, teenagers working at assembly plants are "a million times better off in here than out there on the street, because the maquila represents progress."[10] Critics of multinational corporations, however, have remained unconvinced. While it is true that multinationals like Nike and Coach put thousands to work and improve the conditions of the poor, the low priority given to the human rights issues raised by these production arrangements must be addressed more comprehensively.

Moral Responsibility in the Supply Chain

The moral accountability for all aspects of a multinational's manufacturing operations is beyond question. Companies are responsible for the wages they pay and for the working conditions at their foreign plants. But what about a corporation's responsibilities for the activities of its suppliers, which are legally independent and operate outside the official corporate hierarchy? When these issues about working conditions first surfaced, companies like Nike and Wal-Mart deflected responsibility by claiming that they could not realistically be held accountable for the actions of their many suppliers. "We don't make shoes," was the response of a Nike spokesperson who was queried about labor conditions in these Indonesian factories.[11] When asked about what was going on with its Indonesian suppliers, a Nike manager brusquely responded, "I don't know that I need to know."[12] In response to criticism over the Kathie Lee Gifford scandal, Wal-Mart complained that it lacked the ability to enforce global labor standards. "We have policies against child labor," a spokesperson said, but "we can't police every factory 24 hours a day."[13] Before media attention was focused on this issue, it was not common for corporations to screen suppliers for human rights violations because companies assumed that such violations were not their responsibility.[14]

The public and the media, however, did not accept these rationalizations and so, for the most part, companies have retreated from this weak line of defense. Some corporations have always assumed full responsibility for the activities of their multiple suppliers. In 1992, Levi Strauss & Co developed Global Sourcing Guidelines along with its Business Partner Terms of Engagement. The latter document laid out specific standards for suppliers and contractors abroad. The Terms of Engagement flowed from Levi Strauss' code of ethics that gave the firm an overarching set of principles to deal with moral problems. These "terms of engagement" required its contractors to provide safe and healthy working conditions, pay employees no less than prevailing local wages, limit the work week to no more than 60 hours, prohibit the use of child and prison labor, and allow for unannounced visits by the firm's auditors.[15]

Even if corporations adopt such high standards, monitoring contractors scattered throughout the world can be a costly burden and a demanding undertaking. After the embarrassing exposé about abuses in factories making its Kathie Lee clothing, Wal-Mart began to deploy auditors to inspect the factories of its contractors. Their task was to ensure compliance with Wal-Mart's revised code that forbad child labor and mandated certain working conditions in these factories. But these auditing systems have proven to be quite fallible and all too often miss serious problems and abuses. For example, a factory in China called Chun Si produced Kathy Lee handbags under the most dire and unsafe conditions. Workers at Chun Si earned $22 per month for 90-hour work weeks, were locked in the walled factory for all but an hour a day for meals, and had to pay $15 a month for their room and board. Chun Si was able to dupe the Wal-Mart auditors by setting up a phony factory.[16]

Most companies now rely on independent labor auditors, who are specialists at monitoring these factories and more savvy in identifying fraudulent situations. But the use of independent auditors has not completely solved the problem. Experts still believe that some factories in China break China's labor laws and ignore the standards required by their buyers. Random inspections by monitors catch some of these problems and suppliers are forced to fix them or lose their contracts. But many violations and human rights abuses still go undetected.

Companies like Wal-Mart, Eddie Bauer, and Gap are motivated to monitor and assume responsibility for supply chain activities in order to protect their brands and their corporate reputations. No company wants its branded products associated with sweatshop labor. Also, these abuses can undermine employee morale, especially if a company aspires to high ethical standards. Thus there are sound economic and organizational reasons to impose certain guidelines on its suppliers. There may be some concern for the need to respect local culture and avoid moral imperialism, but respect for different local cultures and for the political systems in which they are embedded cannot extend to the toleration of human rights abuses. What happened at Chun Si is a gross mistreatment of human persons that should not be accepted in any culture.

This perspective suggests that there are also ethical reasons, as well as economic ones, to reject the Nike defense and assume responsibility for supply chain activities within reasonable limits. Since this is not an employer–employee relationship, the basis of any obligation to the workers of one's independently operated suppliers must be approached differently. First, we assume that there are relevant universal rights that cannot be relativized based on culture. Second, we assume that the moral authority to act beyond corporate boundaries derives from a cooperative business relationship or partnership between buyer and seller, and the general obligation to prevent social injury by protecting against the deprivation of basic human rights.

We can profitably adapt Jeremy Bentham's argument to demonstrate the nature and scope of this obligation. Consistent with the new natural law (in this regard), Bentham argues for a twofold moral obligation to others: "A man's duty to his neighbor is accordingly partly negative and partly positive: to discharge the negative branch of it, is *probity*; to discharge the positive branch, *beneficence*."[17] Thus, we have a duty to avoid harming our neighbor (probity) and a duty to come to our neighbor's assistance when he or she is being harmed (beneficence). But under what circumstances does this duty of beneficence become morally relevant? According to D'Arcy and others, who have refined the Bentham argument, the duty for a moral agent to help another or intervene when there is wrongdoing applies only when several key conditions prevail. Under these conditions, a moral agent A is required to do X in order that Y does not happen to B. First, there is proximity, a closeness to the wrongdoing by virtue of a certain relationship or a knowledge of what is transpiring. Second, the need must be critical: there must be the danger of a significant loss, since there is no moral obligation to intervene for trivial matters. Third, there is the capability to act such that there is a strong probability that A's doing X will prevent Y. Fourth, A's doing X must be necessary to prevent Y, because X is the last resort for a remedy. Fifth, in most situations A is not obligated to assume a disproportionate risk to his own welfare in order to help B.[18] Under these conditions, a moral agent's failure to act in the face of wrongdoing constitutes a "wrongful omission."[19]

In the case of international corporations and their contractors, the duty of beneficence, which takes the form of intervention in order to protect rights from deprivation, seems almost axiomatic. First, there is adequate proximity, since multinationals are aware, or have the potential to be aware, of what's going on inside these factories. Social expectations and moral reasonableness demand that they be alert to critical need among key stakeholders such as contractors, especially where there is good reason to suspect poor workplace conditions in countries like Pakistan or Bangladesh. There is also a close commercial and contractual relationship between the international buyer and its foreign suppliers, which become important stakeholders. Although there are no formal ties of ownership, a global corporation such as Wal-Mart has entered into a partnership with its suppliers, which gives Wal-Mart the prerogative to investigate the presence of any rights violations or social injury occurring within their suppliers' factories. Second, the need is critical. Flagrant human rights abuses are sometimes at stake; unsafe working conditions, for example, mean that workers are in danger of severe injury or loss of life. The use of child labor means that children are not being able to exercise their right to a minimal education. Third, multinationals have the capability to take remedial action, by demanding that human rights abuses be stopped as a condition of future contracts, because they have substantial leverage over their suppliers. They surely have the authority to dictate quality and production standards, so it stands to reason that they can exercise the same authority by prescribing suitable working conditions. That capability might be compromised somewhat by the difficulty of monitoring so many foreign operations to ensure that human rights abuses are not occurring. But companies which make substantial profits thanks to these low wage suppliers are obliged to invest the necessary funds to maximize their monitoring capabilities. Fourth, given the impotence and disinterest of local governments in developing countries, multinationals are often the last resort for remedial action. Fifth, there is virtually no risk on their part, while the harm being prevented is substantial. Hence, their failure to act and protect workers from the deprivation of their rights conditions amounts to a wrongful omission.

However, the scope of this ethical obligation, to protect the rights of contractors' workers, must be confined to the direct suppliers of international companies. Asking a company like Wal-Mart to also take responsibility for the activities of its contractors' multiple suppliers imposes an unreasonable burden under ordinary circumstances. Wal-Mart has 100,000 global suppliers and contractors, and all of them have their own suppliers. It would be prohibitively expensive for Wal-Mart, or most organizations in this position, to monitor activities this far up in the supply chain. Beyond direct suppliers, responsibility is heavily mitigated by the lack of proximity and capability. Any responsibility for a corporation to deal with suppliers to its contractors must be considered on a purely *ad hoc* basis. If human rights abuses at one of those suppliers are particularly severe and a company is informed of such abuses, it would then be necessary to use whatever leverage it had with a contractor to demand an end to such abuses.

This conception of a broad but reasonable scope of corporate accountability for contractors' activities is reinforced by the valid expectations of the public. They assume that these international corporations have certain obligations to the workers of their contractors, since they realize immense economic benefits from having their goods manufactured in low-wage countries. The lower labor costs achieved with the help of these contractors contributes greatly to profitability and sustainable competitive advantage. But, as we saw in the previous chapter, no moral agent should benefit from the wrongdoing of another. I shouldn't profit from your robbing of a bank, and multinationals should not profit from oppressive working conditions or from the unfair wages paid to laborers by their contractors. To profit from the wrongdoing of contractors further aggravates the failure to protect against the deprivation of workers' rights. As a result, international corporations must insist on an end to the immoral conduct of a particular contractor or find another contractor which will be more ethically responsible.

Fair Wages, Working Conditions, and Child Labor

Now that we have elucidated the arguments supporting the responsibility of multinationals for the actions of their direct suppliers in the supply chain by virtue of their sufficiently proximate relationship and capability to act, we must consider how to define suitable conditions at these factories. How should wages be determined and what constitutes a "fair wage"? What are acceptable working conditions? And should child labor ever be tolerated? In general, what are the proper guidelines for the workplace standards of contractors?

We begin with a review of acceptable workplace conditions. Above all, the work environment must be safe and free of unreasonable hazards. Workers cannot be exposed to unreasonable health dangers, and therefore employers must take into account the potential impact of construction and production decisions on worker safety. As we argued in the preceding pages, life and health are intrinsic goods, sought after and valued for their own sake, and intentional acts contrary to human health are always wrong as well as unreasonably accepting side effects harmful to health. Constructing a factory with inferior electrical equipment, likely to cause a fire, is unfairly accepting the bad side effects to others' life and health that will follow if there is such a fire. Managers must ensure that the workplace environment is properly ordered to avoid such risks and foreseeable side effects by taking all reasonable safety precautions. In sum, a person's right to health and safety required of others in justice must not be deprived or jeopardized by employers and it must be protected by multinationals which source from those employers.[20]

In developing countries, where laws like the U.S.'s Occupational Health and Safety Act are either non-existent or unenforced, violations of safety rights are rampant. For example, in Mexico young workers were hired to "smear glue on the soles of sneakers" with their hands despite the warning that inhalation of this toxic substance causes "grave health damage."[21] Similarly, far too many companies in the Yonkang district of China have a terrible track record of worker safety. Yongkang, just south of Shanghai, is called the hardware capital of China: over 7,000 factories produce an endless stream of pots and pans, metal hinges, tools, fans, and hubcaps. But since most of the factories do not invest in safe machinery, with infrared devices that shut down when hands or limbs are extended past the "safety zone," Yongkang is also known as the "dismemberment capital" of China. So companies which source from this region and do not demand attention to safety issues share some of the blame for these conditions.[22]

There will always be risks in any workplace, and workers must be duly informed of those risks. But a safe environment implies an acceptable level of risk and a workplace area without recognized hazards that are likely to cause serious or fatal injury. Factories that routinely use machines like mechanical hammers and lathes without proper safety controls cannot be classified as a safe environment. The risk of dismemberment is disproportionately high and hence that risk is unacceptable. It follows that international companies that source from Yongkang's factories must protect the right to health and safety of workers by demanding that contractors use safe equipment with the proper controls as a condition of future contracts.

Decent working conditions include more than a safe physical environment. There must also be restrictions on the work week. Most companies impose the limit of a 60 hour work week for their contractors, which seems to be a fairly reasonable standard. Many factories in China now house workers who travel there from all parts of the country. At these factories there is a need for sufficient dormitory space and proper eating facilities. Unfortunately these standards are often not met. Apple's supplier policy, which calls for "safe and fair working conditions" throughout its supply chain, limits the work week to 60 hours. Yet China Labor Watch has reported work weeks that regularly exceed the 60 hour limit at Pegatron, a China-based supplier that makes products such as Apple's iPad Mini. Workers at Pegatron also complain of "packed cafeterias" and "tight living quarters."[23] These conditions require correction if Pegatron is to qualify as a morally suitable work environment. Finally, a decent work environment should recognize a worker's right to organize and form a labor union. These are rights recognized in the U.N Declaration (art. 23). National laws, however, sometimes forbid unions, and in these situations, international corporations probably need to allow their contractors to comply with the local law, or be accused of meddling in local politics. Disputably, this is one area where countries should be allowed moral free space.

What about the issue of wages? Recall that Levi Strauss' guidelines stipulated that workers be paid the "prevailing wage" in their locale, but there is some debate as to whether the market, or even the local law, sets a morally adequate standard for labor wages. Should multinationals simply ensure that contractors pay the legally mandated wage or the prevailing market wage in a country or region? Or should they always require that a fair wage be paid no matter what the market conditions are, and, if so, what is a fair wage? These different alternatives need some further elaboration.

One way to deal with the issue of wages is reliance on the free market principle, which allows wages to be determined by the local labor market, that is, by the forces of supply and demand. Wages are set at a level that individual workers are willing to accept and employers are willing to pay. Sometimes this can mean exceptionally low levels of remuneration. During the height of the Nike controversy the annual wages in Indonesia were a meager $241, and Indonesia was one of Nike's primary sources for its shoes.[24] In Bangladesh, an average garment worker, who works 10 hour days, has a take home pay of $70–80 per month.[25] This is well below the subsistence level for this worker and his or her family. Nevertheless, those who argue for this principle maintain that, as long as a multinational's contractors are paying market wages that are never lower than the minimum allowed by law they are not behaving unjustly. According to the law of supply and demand wages can never be too low or too high.[26]

This ethical posture on the wage issue might seem acceptable, since it depends on an unprejudiced and impersonal market that sets wages in a way that treats everyone alike. Also, the right to economic liberty appears to be intact, since workers are free to choose their occupation and their employer. But there is an asymmetrical relationship between international companies, which have the mobility to locate their factories anywhere in the world, and workers in low-wage countries, who are anxious for a job and have no alternatives. As a result, they are often willing to accept wages that are below the subsistence level. Implicit consent to a labor contract that pays low wages does not necessarily imply that the contract is a fair one. Markets are blind to social justice issues, and they allow multinationals to take unfair advantage of poor economies and the dismal situation of their workers. Even in the 1990s, a $241 annual wage in Indonesia, well below the subsistence level, is *too low* by any reasonable moral standard of fairness. Countries like Malaysia, Bangladesh, and Sri Lanka need multinationals and have little leverage or bargaining power to demand that workers be treated fairly.

A more equitable and simple solution seems to be called for, such as "equal pay for equal work," which stipulates that people ought to be paid the same for equal work no matter where they live. But this principle, however attractive, is unrealistic. Paying Mexicans the same as Americans for assembling cell phones makes little sense since the standard of living differs radically between these two countries. To insist on absolutely equal wages between two contexts with drastically different living standards is an unreasonable requirement even in light of the distributive equity demanded by social justice.[27]

A superior alternative, therefore, that avoids the defect of relying on volatile markets and the excess of "equal pay for equal work," is to insist upon a fair wage, or a living wage. Such a wage can be broadly defined as one that is adequate to support a worker and his or her family with the basic necessities of life. Quigley defines a living wage as one that will provide enough income to escape from poverty and become self-sufficient.[28] This fair wage is often referred to as the subsistence level wage, though the definition of "subsistence" is open to some interpretation. A compelling moral case can be put forth that employers owe something more to their workers than the market wage or the local minimum wage when that compensation is not commensurate with the work performed and the value added by the worker.

Everyone has a right to subsistence, but a corporation does not have a duty to aid those who are deprived of this right, when that deprivation has nothing to do with the carrying out of that corporation's business operations. A corporation's failure to provide food, clothing, and housing for the indigent in the host countries where it operates is not a rights violation on its part. On the other hand, if corporations pay below subsistence wages in their own factories, or tolerate such wages in the factories of their suppliers, they are derelict in their obligation to protect people from deprivation of the right to subsistence, since hiring and wage decisions fall within the scope of a company's operations. The right to just compensation proportionate to the worker's contribution is to be reasonably expected by any worker and reflects a corporation's respect for the equivalent humanity of others. But a meager and unjust wage for full time work prevents people from acquiring the material goods they need in order to survive. In these situations, the corporation is acting more like an agent of deprivation rather than a custodian of those human rights that are within its purview to protect.[29]

Catholic social doctrine, which has been advocating for worker rights for over a century, strongly supports this position, despite the Church's commitment to a free market economy. In the social encyclical *Laborem Exercens*, Pope John Paul II declared that every worker has the right to "just remuneration for work done."[30] Although previous popes such as Leo XIII and Pius XI also discussed fair worker compensation practices, this encyclical contains the strongest statement to be found in Catholic social teaching on a just wage.[31] According to John Paul II, payment of a fair wage is the primary means of ensuring a just relationship between workers and their employers. The just wage is also the most concrete and verifiable way of determining the justice of the economic system. While it is impossible to quantify a universal just wage, John Paul II provided a workable definition of a fair wage that is consistent with our point of view: "just remuneration for the work of an adult who is responsible for a family means remuneration which will suffice for establishing and properly maintaining a family and for providing security for its future."[32]

It is also evident that the philosophers of high liberalism, who put so much emphasis on the distributive dimensions of social justice, would be particularly aggrieved by these exceedingly low and unjust wages. As we have seen, high liberalism is more committed to social justice issues than to private economic liberty, which is not so much at stake in this debate. Recall that Rawls' prominent political theory focuses on justice as fairness. According to Rawls, the principles of justice are those which equal, rational, self-interested individuals would choose as the terms of a social contract for themselves and their descendants. One of those principles is called the *difference principle*: "justice requires that we seek to maximize the benefits of the least well-off."[33] This means that disparities in the distribution of wealth and other social goods would be tolerated *only* if they could be shown to benefit the "least advantaged," the lowest on the socio-economic scale.[34] A just society, therefore, is not necessarily an egalitarian one where all goods are distributed equally, but one in which inequalities must work to everyone's advantage, especially the most disadvantaged.

Rawls' theory could be endorsed as a sensible metric for assessing global distributive justice. From that lofty perspective, the institutional and corporate structures that permit the low wages we see in today's global economy are quite difficult to justify since they do not maximally benefit the poor. Advocates of a Rawls theory of justice would probably argue that these low wages are representative of capitalism's excess, a side effect of under-regulated markets that must be corrected by government intervention if necessary. We contend that international corporations, which are morally bound to help protect the right to subsistence when it is under their care, must pay fairer wages that would at least help to correct this inequitable distribution so it is more consistent with the requirements of social justice. Paying a fair wage is also consistent with an acknowledgment of the corporation's common good. Recall that the common good consists of efficient economic cooperation and fairness to all participants in this cooperative enterprise, including workers, who deserve a fair distribution of a corporation's benefits proportionate to what they contribute.

Finally, we must address the vexing issue of child labor, which was at the core of the Nike controversy. Anti-globalizers often seize upon this emotional issue as a basis for demanding a contraction of globalization because of its malicious effects on children and other vulnerable workers. As many companies have found out, child labor in the supply chain is another notable strategic risk that can quickly damage a company's brand and reputation.

Child labor, defined as labor performed by children under the age of 14, takes multiple shapes and forms. Some child labor, such as farm or house work, is ordinary and acceptable. But work performed outside the household or the farm is a more difficult matter, especially if it is hazardous and arduous. The International Labor Organization (ILO) of the United Nations estimates that one in six of the world's children between the ages of 5 and 17 work in some capacity outside the home with the highest proportions of these laborers in Asia and Africa.[35] Somewhere between 60 to 115 million children are working in India, most in agriculture.[36]

Child labor appears to be endemic to certain labor-intensive industries, like handwoven carpets, where children have proven themselves to be adept at weaving together this material quickly and efficiently. The Swedish furniture conglomerate, IKEA, which pursues a low cost producer strategy, has always sought out the lowest cost sources to purchase its goods. IKEA was identified in a Swedish documentary as a buyer of handwoven carpets made by children. But since this exposé IKEA has developed a comprehensive strategy for preventing child labor in its supply chain. There are industry-wide initiatives, such as Rugmark, that guarantee sourced rugs are not made by children, but IKEA chose to depend on its own monitoring process. IKEA and other companies have not felt fully confident in Rugmark's pledge that their mark is an assurance of no child labor.

One form of child labor that is particularly reprehensible is bonded child labor. In most of these situations, which are rampant in India, children are coerced into certain work places in order to repay a debt owed to the employer by the child's impoverished parents. Bonded child labor is entrenched in certain Indian subcultures with long traditions of ethnic and religious discrimination. This heritage makes the eradication of bonded labor quite demanding. Bonded child labor is also extensive. The Human Rights Watch claims that about 15 million Indian children fall into this category. A comprehensive study of children employed in India's silk industry shows that many of them still toil as "virtual slaves," because they are being held in some sort of bondage.[37] These children are unable to escape from arduous work that often leaves them illiterate and physically debilitated by the time they reach adulthood. They are bound to their employers in exchange for a family loan; they are unable to leave the work premises while in debt and earn such a small salary they may never be liberated from this virtual enslavement. India's child labor laws forbid bonded labor, but those laws are very poorly enforced. For reasons of inertia, caste bias, and rampant corruption, many government officials ignore the problem and even deny that it exists.[38] Global efforts to curtail bonded child labor have been futile thanks to the lack of cooperation from local government.

Who is to blame for all of this oppressive child labor? The list of those at fault in some way is a long one, beginning with the parents who allow their children to work before they finish school. Employers who hire them usually for very low wages are also to blame. Also on this list are governments which refuse to protect their children. India's Child Labor Act of 1986 only forbids the use of children in specifically defined hazardous industries; the handwoven carpet and other "craft" industries are exempt from this law. International corporations which source from these contractors using child labor cannot escape some indirect accountability for the problem. If child labor is part of a multinational's supply chain, it must assume some limited responsibility for that child labor, although the primary blame lies with negligent parents, governments, and their employers. Of course, the big culprit in child labor is poverty. Parents often send their children to work in "sweatshops" because they are destitute and need the income in order to survive. Moreover, the alternatives for children in low wage countries, such as street vending or scavenging, are much more dangerous than factory work.

According to the ILO, child labor is not economically justified. Based on their careful estimates, it would cost about $760 billion over a 20-year period to end child labor, but the benefits would be seven times as large. There would be significant gains in the quality and quantity of human capital, better health, and fewer lives lost due to a smaller number of accidents. Child labor prevents countries from investing in human capital, and this keeps many of their workers in low level, unskilled jobs. Also allowing child labor depresses wages for adults who have fewer options and lower pay. Thus, to some extent countries perpetuate poverty by tolerating child labor rather than trying to constrict it.[39]

If child labor is not economically justified, neither is it morally justified. Bonded labor of any sort is an infringement upon the basic human right of freedom and is never acceptable. Once again, we find a situation where the politics of recognition and diversity must yield to the reality of ethical universalism. But other forms of child labor, though perhaps not as exploitative, are also morally problematic, since they interfere with a child's right to an education. All children need at least a primary education in order to acquire enough knowledge and skills for better and more fulfilling jobs. International corporations have a duty to help protect the right to a minimal education, and this implies that they cannot allow child labor in their direct supply chains if that labor denies children the opportunity to receive a minimally adequate education.

But what should be done about child labor, given the severe problem of unintended consequences? Should conscientious multinationals simply terminate contracts with suppliers in India and Pakistan where child labor is so predominant? Terminating contracts often means that children end up back on the streets as they find themselves in worse jobs or scavenging for food. One option is to work with suppliers to ensure that, so long as there is no bonded labor, the children working in the factory work fewer hours so that they receive an education onsite. IKEA, for example, formed a partnership with UNICEF to fund education for 24,000 children in India's "carpet belt" who were not in school. How far companies should go is a matter of debate, but the complicating issue of unintended consequences cannot be neglected.

Perhaps the best moral approach to all of these problems—safe working conditions, child labor, fair wages—is the simplest: the Golden Rule. In the natural law framework, the golden rule is a key intermediate principle because it ensures that we look at moral dilemmas without partiality, so we are more apt to choose the solution that promotes integral human fulfillment. Multinationals must not tolerate policies that unfairly remunerate workers, risk worker's health and safety, or unjustly exploit children. To judge what is unfair a corporation cannot just look at prevailing practices or local law. Rather, after considering the relevant facts and cultural issues, managers should apply the Golden Rule and imagine themselves or their families in the places of each of those affected by their choices. Even despite the grinding poverty and low living standards of Malaysia, would they consider it just to be paid a below subsistence wage of $1 an hour?[40]

Factory Tragedies in Bangladesh

The media usually pay little attention to sweatshops and substandard working conditions since there are many other subjects that capture people's interest. But two garment factory disasters in Bangladesh put the spotlight back on the extremely poor working conditions that continue to plague low-wage countries. In November, 2012, 112 workers were killed when a moderate-sized garment factory went up in flames. When the fire alarm went off, workers were told that it was a false alarm and were ordered back to work. As the factory floor filled with black smoke, some workers were able to break windows and jump to safety, but most of them perished in the engulfing flames. There have been over 500 people killed in Bangladeshi fires since 2006, but this fire, in the Tazreen Fashions Ltd. factory, was the worst. The cause of this fire and several others appears to have been unsafe electrical wiring. The Bangladesh government sets low safety standards which are often abused by local factory owners. Many major Western brands were produced at the Tazreen factory, such as Wal-Mart's Faded Glory and Sean Combs' Enyce brands. Clothing for Sears Holding Corp was also made at this factory.[41]

The tragic Tazreen factory fire was followed by a factory collapse just outside the capital city of Dhaka in April, 2013 which killed 1,127 people. The sudden collapse of the eight-story Rana Plaza building, that housed a number of clothing factories, is one of the worst industrial disasters in history. Rana Plaza was built with shoddy materials, and the owner was arrested for constructing the building without safety permits. Managers repeatedly ignored signs of trouble. Workers were ordered back to work on the day of the building collapse despite an earlier evacuation after a huge crack was discovered in an outer wall. Shortly after factory workers re-entered the poorly constructed building, the edifice abruptly collapsed and they were crushed to death.

Both of these accidents, happening in such close succession, have put enormous pressure on the Bangladeshi government to establish and enforce more rigorous safety standards. The country's thriving $20 billion a year garment industry is one of the world's largest clothing exporters. Some of the chief U.S. and European retailers source their clothes from Bangladesh. Included in this group are U.S. companies like Wal-Mart, Sears, Gap, and J.C. Penney. Designer brands like Giorgio Armani and Ralph Lauren have also outsourced manufacturing to Bangladesh. Both Italy's Benetton and Spain's Mango used factories in the building that collapsed.[42]

Pressure on these retailers and fashion houses also intensified in the wake of the Tazreen factory fire and the building collapse in Dhaka. Labor activists insisted that a "race to the bottom," which still shapes the major segments of the garment industry, was at the root of the problem. As long as retailers relentlessly pursue the lowest manufacturing costs, their goods will be made in factories that lack adequate safety safeguards and worker protection. Apparel retailers, worried about another blow to their reputation by being linked with these tragedies, have few other low-cost options. Clothing factories in Myanmar, Pakistan, and Indonesia pose even greater safety risks. In September 2012, 300 workers died in two factory fires in Pakistan. The relentless drive to cut labor costs in all of these countries to satisfy retailers usually creates pressure to skimp on safety, and this means that there are probably more disasters on the horizon. With this in mind, activists called upon these retailers to finally invest in making factories better and safer.[43]

Many retailers like Wal-Mart and Levi Strauss shunned factories operated in buildings which were several stories high because they thought the risks were too great. The Italian company, Benetton, on the other hand, defended its use of these factories, observing that some of the multi-story buildings conform to the proper specifications and are "perfectly safe."[44] Such multi-level buildings in Bangladesh have been necessitated by the scarcity of open land and limited access to utilities. After the accident, J.C. Penney and Sears began phasing out the use of apparel factories located in these buildings. Other companies like Disney, the world's largest licenser, ordered an end to the production of any branded merchandise in Bangladesh. According to its public statements about the matter, Disney's decision seemed motivated primarily by anxiety over its brand as the company tries to recalibrate the balance between short-term profits and the durability of its reputation.[45]

In the aftermath of these tragedies in Bangladesh, apparel companies faced a stark choice. Should they follow the example of Disney and exit Bangladesh in order to protect their brands and reputations? A mass exodus of companies would be a blow to Bangladesh and its people who still need these jobs to escape from poverty. As a World Bank economist has pointed out, despite the low pay, "these are still better jobs than most other possibilities."[46] The other alternative is to stay and source from contractors operating in safe facilities. But how can companies be assured of safety in a corrupt country where so many people don't play by the rules? It's evident that apparel companies must do a better job of hiring monitors or auditors who will conduct full building inspections, including more extensive checking for structural soundness, electrical wiring, and fire escape routes. If there is a scarcity of such safe buildings, companies may need to invest in factory safety improvements as a condition for remaining in Bangladesh.

It is difficult to make a convincing case that companies have a moral obligation to remain in Bangladesh in order to help this country overcome its poverty. According to our framework, they do not have a *duty* to correct rights abuses by staying in a country to provide jobs and investing in its commercial infrastructure so that all its factories are safe.[47] However, if these companies are committed to a social agenda, an investment of resources in Bangladesh would be fitting and in their own enlightened self-interest, since it is apt to pay big dividends. On the other hand, if companies choose to stay, they must be committed to factory and building safety. All people have a right to safety or physical security, since safety directly preserves the intrinsically valuable goods of life and health. Hence international corporations have a duty to protect this right to physical security from deprivation by ensuring that their suppliers' factories are as safe as reasonably possible. They are indirectly to blame for deaths and injuries that result from a factory fire due to careless construction or shoddy electrical wiring if they did not take reasonable steps to ensure that this factory was a safe environment. This is especially true in a precarious political environment like Bangladesh where corruption and political chaos often means that there is a lack of adequate attention given to safety precautions.

It is obviously impossible to eliminate all risk from a factory or workplace, but the risk of poorly constructed multi-level Bangladeshi buildings is clearly unacceptable. For big corporations like Wal-Mart and Benetton the global supply chain is a tangled web which is difficult to monitor. Benetton has 700 suppliers dispersed around the world to make their various products. Moreover, apparel retailers have been duped by monitors in the past, which have falsely assured them that a contractor complies with safety requirements. Nevertheless, they must find a way to ascertain the safety of the facilities in which their suppliers operate to help protect the rights of those workers from being deprived by unscrupulous or careless contractors.

Wal-Mart, one of the biggest customers of Bangladeshi garment factories, approved a safety plan that tries to walk a middle road between an exit strategy and preemptive investment in safety improvements. The company is committed to remain in Bangladesh but has no plans to invest in safety enhancements. After the fire, Wal-Mart hired a reliable and reputable outside auditor, Bureau Veritas, to inspect all 257 factories where its goods are produced. Although the retailer will not pay for safety upgrades called for by the inspectors, it will expect the cost of those safety improvements to be reflected in the cost of goods it purchases. Wal-Mart is hoping that this expectation will send a clear signal that factories should never skimp or cut back when safety is at stake. Wal-Mart has also demanded that all of its factories put in place programs for fire safety training.[48]

Wal-Mart and Disney represent two different ethical responses to the Bangladesh tragedies. Some might plausibly argue that given its resources Wal-Mart could go further, but it has made a sincere commitment to safety rights and the physical well-being of the workers who make its products. Many European retailers have signed the Accord on Fire and Building Safety in Bangladesh which calls for all factories to be inspected within a year and boycotts imposed on those that fail inspection. All workers will get safety training and there will be a hotline to report any concerns. Some grants and low-interest loans will be provided to upgrade factories. Skeptics point out, however, that foreign firms have been promising for 20 years to do something about the dangerous working conditions in Bangladesh factories, so it remains to be seen if these newest efforts will effect any real and lasting changes.[49]

Conclusions

The pace of offshoring and outsourcing trends has increased over the last several decades as companies seek low cost venues to produce their products. This process is driven to some extent by the rise of discount retailers and their constant push to cut costs in the supply chain. But all segments of the apparel industry, including designer fashion houses, have been in the forefront of this trend. China, the world's largest clothing exporter, remains a popular location for companies looking for low wages, along with other emerging markets such as Bangladesh and Vietnam. But wages in China have been rising, and there are signs that China is losing its competitive edge as the exemplary low-cost manufacturing location.

Many well-known companies, like Nike and Wal-Mart, which were caught up in the initial wave of sweatshop scandals, disavowed any responsibility for activities in their supply chain. They tried to defuse criticism of sweatshop conditions at their suppliers' factories by contending that they should only be held accountable for the labor issues that occurred within their own corporate boundaries. But the media and the public rejected Nike's aloofness and demanded remedial action. Our ethical analysis has also demonstrated the disingenuousness of such arguments. Multinationals are responsible for certain activities of their direct suppliers, which manufacture their goods, by virtue of a close commercial relationship that creates adequate proximity. It is reasonable to expect international companies to be informed of the factory working conditions of their suppliers, and to be alert to critical problems, especially in emerging economies where reasonable labor standards are chronically compromised. International companies also have leverage over these suppliers, and hence they have the capability to prescribe acceptable working conditions as a condition of future contracts. Moreover, with indifferent and dysfunctional governments usually involved, these multinationals often represent the only recourse for justice. These factors such as proximity and capability impose a clear duty to protect the rights of workers in their supply chain. The scope of that obligation is somewhat limited, however, since it is unreasonable to assume that there should be any responsibility to protect the rights of those who work for the multiple suppliers of their direct contractors.

International corporations, therefore, must help ensure adequate factory working conditions. The work environment must be safe so that the workers' health and physical security is not subject to unreasonable risk. There must be decent working conditions, with limits on hours worked, vacations with pay, and the right to form a union if the workers determine this is in their best interest. Every worker is entitled to just compensation that will provide enough money to support herself and her family with the basic necessities of life. Most of these moral demands entail rights that must be honored by contractors and protected by international corporations that source from those contractors. In addition, international enterprises cannot tolerate any type of bonded labor or child labor that interferes with a child's right to a minimal education.

The Bangladesh tragedies indicate that there is much work to be done in improving the working conditions of developing countries. An unsafe work environment, driven by a push for lower costs, has led to a succession of deadly fires and a multi-story building collapse with a substantial loss of life. Companies may not have an obligation to stay in Bangladesh and invest in safety improvements, though such a strategy may be in their enlightened self-interest. But if they choose to remain they have a duty to protect against the deprivation of the right to safety and physical security by demanding that their suppliers are committed to high safety standards. In practical terms, this means finding a way to conduct effective audits and always pursuing negligent factory owners to fix any shortcomings.

Notes

1 Stephanie Strom, "From Sweetheart to Scapegoat: Looking behind the Kathie Lee Labels," *The New York Times*, June 27, 1996, D1, D5.
2 Strom, "From Sweetheart to Scapegoat," D1, D5.
3 Mark Clifford, "Pain in Pusan," *Far Eastern Economic Review*, November 5, 1992, 59.
4 John Cushman, "Nike Pledges to End Child Labor and Apply U.S. Rules Abroad," *The New York Times*, May 13, 1998, D1.
5 "Here, There, and Everywhere: Outsourcing and Offshoring," *The Economist*, January 19, 2013, 3–5.
6 Kathy Chu, "Not Made in China," *The Wall Street Journal*, May 1, 2013, B1–2.
7 Michael Mandel, "Multinationals – Are They Good for America?," *Business Week*, March 10, 2008, 41–3.
8 "Here, There, and Everywhere: Outsourcing and Offshoring," 5.
9 Allen Myerson, "In Principle, a Case for More Sweatshops," *The New York Times*, June 22, 1997, E5.
10 Larry Rohter, "To U.S. Critics, a Sweatshop: To Hondurans, a Better Life," *The New York Times*, July 18, 1996, A1, A14.
11 Quoted in Tim Larimer, "Sneaker Gulag: Are Asian Workers Really Exploited?," *Time International*, May 11, 2002, 30.
12 Adam Schwarz, "Running a Business," *Far Eastern Economic Review*, June 20, 1991, 16.
13 Quoted in Richard Spinello "Human Rights and World Markets," *Boston Business Journal*, August 2, 1996, 17.
14 The concept of responsibility is complex and has multi-faceted meanings. Kurt Bayertz distinguishes between the classical concept of retrospective [*retrospektiv*] responsibility and the more contemporary notion of prospective [*prospectiv*] responsibility. Our focus is primarily on the latter

meaning. These two concepts of responsibility are distinct but closely related. According to Bayertz "In the new [prospective] meaning of responsibility the focus is no longer on being held responsible for damages that have already occurred, but for the avoidance of damages in the future and for the preservation or creation of desirable conditions" (author's translation). See Kurt Bayertz, *Verantwortung: Prinzip oder Problem?* (Darmstadt: Wissenschaftliche Buchgesellschaft, 1995), 16.
15 Timothy Perkins, *et al.*, "Levi Strauss & Co. and China," in *Perspectives in Business Ethics* 2nd ed. Laura Hartman (New York: McGraw-Hill, 2002), 764–9.
16 Dexter Roberts and Aaron Bernstein, "A Life of Fines and Beating," *Business Week*, October 2, 2000, 122–8.
17 Jeremy Bentham, *Introduction to the Principles of Morals and Legislation* (Oxford: Oxford University Press, 1907), 312. See also Keith Baier, *The Moral Point of View* (Ithaca, NY: Cornell University Press, 1958).
18 Eric D'Arcy, *Human Acts: An Essay in their Moral Evaluation* (Oxford: Oxford University Press, 1963), 56–7. Also quite helpful is the discussion of these factors in John Simon, Charles Powers, and Jon Gunnemann, *The Ethical Investor* (New Haven, CN: Yale University Press, 1972), 22–6.
19 D'Arcy, *Human Acts*, 55.
20 Germain Grisez, *Living a Christian Life* (Quincy, IL: Franciscan Press, 1993), 532–3. See also John Finnis, *Natural Law and Natural Rights* (Oxford: Oxford University Press, 1980), 223–6.
21 Matt Moffett, "Underage Laborers Fill Mexican Factories, Stir U.S. Trade Debate," *The Wall Street Journal*, April 8, 1991, A1.
22 Joseph Kahn, "China's Workers Risk Limbs in Export Drive," *The New York Times*, April 7, 2003, A3.
23 Paul Mozur and Chao Deng, "Worker Group Alleges Abuses at Apple Supplier in China," *The Wall Street Journal*, July 29, 2013, B3.
24 World Bank, *World Development Indicators for 1999* (Washington, D.C: World Bank, 1999), 62–4.
25 Rubana Huq, "The Economics of a $6.75 Shirt," *The Wall Street Journal*, May 12, 2013, A15.
26 Henry Shue, "Transnational Transgressions," in *Just Business: New Introductory Essays in Business Ethics* ed. Tom Regan (New York: Random House, 1984), 271–9.
27 Shue, "Transnational Transgressions," 278.
28 William Quigley, *Enduring Poverty as We Know It: Guaranteeing a Right to a Job at a Living Wage* (Philadelphia, PA: Temple University Press, 2003).
29 See Edwin Hartman, "Donaldson on Rights and Corporate Obligations," in *Business Ethics: The State of the Art* ed. R. Edward Freeman (Oxford: Oxford University Press, 1991), 163–72.
30 Pope John Paul II, *Laborem Exercens* (Boston, MA: Pauline Books and Media, 1981), §19. Since the papacy of Leo XIII (1878–1903), it has

become customary for popes to address social and economic issues in their magisterial teachings. Pope Leo is credited with developing several core principles that shaped Catholic social thought for many decades: natural human rights grounded in the natural law, the principle of subsidiarity, and the integrity or "quasi-autonomy" of civil prudence. See Russell Hittinger, "Introduction to Modern Catholicism," in *The Teachings of Modern Roman Catholicism on Law Politics and Human Nature*, ed. J. Witte and F. Alexander (New York: Columbia University Press, 2007), 2–3.

31 Patricia Lamoureux, "Commentary on *Laborem Exercens*," in *Modern Catholic Social Teaching* ed. Ken Himes (Washington, D.C.: Georgetown University Press, 2005), 400.
32 John Paul II, *Laborem Exercens*, § 19.
33 John Rawls, *A Theory of Justice* (Cambridge, MA: Harvard University Press, 1971), 298.
34 Rawls, *A Theory of Justice,* 303. According to Rawls, "The intuitive idea is that the social order is not to establish and secure the more attractive prospects of those better off unless doing so is to the advantage of those less fortunate," 75. Although Rawls did not have in mind a global social order, his ideas about justice still apply to issues like wages, especially when the economy is so globalized and national economies so closely inter-connected.
35 "Sickness or Symptom," *The Economist*, February 7, 2004, 73.
36 See South Asia Regional Initiative, USAID India, "Combating Child Labor in India," 2005; available at: http://www/usaid.gov/in/aboutusaid/projects/childlabor.htm (accessed July 11, 2013).
37 Human Rights Watch, *The Small Hands of Slavery: Bonded Child Labor in India's Silk Industry* (New York: Human Rights Watch, 2003), 1–2; available at: http://hrw.org/reports/2003/India3.htm (accessed March 30, 2013).
38 Human Rights Watch, *The Small Hands of Slavery*, 11.
39 "Sickness or Symptom," 73. See also International Labor Organization, "Investing in Every Child: An Economic Study of the Costs and Benefits of Eliminating Child Labor," Working Paper, December 2003.
40 See Germain Grisez, *Difficult Moral Questions* (Quincy, IL: Franciscan Press, 1993), 463–6.
41 Syed Zain Al-Mahmood, Kathy Chu, and Tripti Lahiri, "After Fire, Pressure on Bangladesh," *The Wall Street Journal*, December 15, 2012, B1, B4.
42 Syed Zain Al-Mahmood, "Bangladesh Factory Toll Passes 800," *The Wall Street Journal*, May 9, 2013, A10.
43 Kathy Chu, "Tough Options for Apparel Retailers," *The Wall Street Journal*, May 8, 2013, B1.
44 Suzanne Kapner and Shelly Banjo, "Before Dhaka Collapse, Some Firms Fled Risk," *The Wall Street Journal*, May 3, 2013, A7.
45 Steven Greenhouse, "Some Retailers Rethink Roles in Bangladesh," *The New York Times*, May 2, 2013, A1, A4.

46 Gordon Fairclough, "Factory Paychecks Trump Danger, Long Days for Bangladesh Women," *The Wall Street Journal*, June 22, 2013, A 11.
47 For a different point of view, see Kevin Jackson, "Distributive Justice and the Corporate Duty to Aid," *Journal of Business Ethics*, 12 (1993): 547–51.
48 Shelly Banjo and Suzanne Kapner, "Wal-Mart Crafts Own Bangladesh Safety Plan," *The Wall Street Journal*, May 15, 2013, B1–B2.
49 "Clothing Firms in Bangladesh – Accord, Alliance or Disunity," *The Economist*, July 13, 2013, 57–8.

PART III
CONCLUSIONS

10

Epilogue

Arguably, the primary ethical test for the multinational corporation is resolving the dynamic tension between respect for universal ethical norms and sensitivity to the cultural and legal differences of their host countries. Cultural differences must be properly appreciated, and should not be suppressed out of some misguided ethnocentric impulse that leads to the imposition of one culture on another. At the same time, respect for cultural and legal diversity cannot serve as a pretext for moral transgressions. Many times, multinational corporations have fallen into the trap of giving too much credibility to local custom and law, even when that law lacks moral authority because it is unjust. The non-linear history of globalization is full of examples of corporations that excused questionable behavior by claiming that they were simply following the law of the land. We find this rationalization used by IBM in the 1930s to justify its surrender to Nazism, and decades later, we find it used by Microsoft to defend the content restrictions enforced on MSN websites in order to satisfy China's censorship laws.

To be sure, any multinational corporation's aspirations to moral integrity and social responsibility is immensely complicated by cultural diversity. When multinationals invest abroad they must contend with the "liability of foreignness" that is created by cultural, social, economic, and political differences. Cultural distance represents differences in religious beliefs, social norms and language. Sometimes those differences have ethical implications that are not fully understood, and this situation can be fraught with peril for the multinational enterprise. The seminal question for the multinational is whether to adapt to new cultural norms and moral standards in the host country, *or* introduce its own standards into a culture, even if this threatens a host economy's sovereignty. We have argued for a middle ground that respects cultural diversity and ethnic identity up to the point where that respect begins to accommodate injustice and the violation of universal human rights.

Along these lines, we demonstrated the problems with cultural ethical relativism which permits too much moral free space. "Foreignness" and cultural diversity is always tempered by the familiarity of our common humanity, our primary identity as human persons. That common identity is the ultimate ground of universal natural rights, which give normative recognition to human equality and dignity. While some philosophers, like Rawls, argue for a thin set of universal rights, the new natural law perspective endorses a much thicker set of rights, which proceed from intrinsically valuable human goods that constitute each person's human flourishing. These irreducible human goods entail an account of human nature which can only be provided by one who understands these goods practically, as reasons for choice and action.[1]

The rights that protect these intrinsic goods direct us to avoid acting in certain ways out of respect for the dignity and well-being of other persons. Fundamental human rights should direct corporate choices and prescribe acceptable corporate policies, but they should also limit the sovereignty of the state. The political authority of the state does not exempt its laws from being compatible with morality's requirements, which can be expressed in terms of natural rights. For the multinational corporation, upholding and protecting the rights of others fosters solidarity and overcomes market pressures that can convert economic liberty into opportunistic individualism. Although we have made the case in this book for a fairly thick set of rights, readers should carefully consider the alternatives proposed by Rawls and Walzer that give more weight to cultural particularity. Rights must be adequately specified and limited to take into account the comparable rights of others along with other aspects of the common good.

Rights entail three types of correlative duties, all of which must be performed if a right is to be properly upheld, but not all of which must be carried out by the same institutions and individuals.[2] In continuity with the work of other ethical thinkers, we have argued that multinationals have two duties with respect to these universal rights: they must not deprive people of their rights or cooperate in such deprivation, and they must protect these rights from being deprived when need for such protection arises in the course of their business operations. They do not have the obligation to correct human rights abuses or to aid the deprived. Thus, while there is an obligation to protect the human rights of its workers and even the rights of its contractors' workers within a developing country, there is no *duty* to help bring about distributive justice within that country. The philosophers of high liberalism (like Rawls) would probably argue for a broader corporate role that calls for more urgent attention to the distributive dimension of social justice. Corporations might voluntarily assume such a social agenda that incorporates a duty of assistance, but respecting and protecting fundamental human rights is the moral minimum for their conduct around the world.

In the main section of this book we applied this foundational rights-based framework to a number of different scenarios. We argued that complicity in the Chinese censorship system represented a situation where companies cannot conform to local norms and laws, since the fundamental right to free speech is universal and must be protected in any cultural context. Unfortunately, information intermediaries like Google and Yahoo have cooperated in violating this right to free speech in order to have a commercial presence in China. We saw that intellectual property rights, which can be justified on the non-economic grounds articulated in Locke's philosophy, sometimes conflict with the right to life-preserving medicine which safeguards the intrinsic goods of life and health. In these complex situations, where those who need patented pharmaceutical products are denied fair access, pharmaceutical companies have a duty to protect this right to health care and to life-preserving medicine by waiving their property rights. Locke's charity proviso recognized this need to help the poor by means of the mitigation of one's valid property rights in exigent circumstances. Multinationals also have a duty to protect the rights to health and physical welfare by not unfairly accepting bad side effects to others' health through a failure to take necessary and reasonable environmental precautions. When externalities do occur, it is the multinational's responsibility to clean up the mess and to pay compensation to victims, even if the cause is not their fault. Multinationals should avoid excessive political activism and never be in the business of regime change, which deprives members of a political community of their freedom and the right to choose their own government. There may be some countries where rights abuses are so systemic that the only prudent course of action is disinvestment. The government may be corrupt (Burma) or the whole cultural system may be corrupt (Apartheid South Africa). Pursuant to the condition of business principle, when rights abuses are systematic, the only responsible course of action is withdrawal (unless certain exceptions apply). Above all, self-respecting companies should renounce unjust laws, such as the laws that required the abuse of workers' rights in Apartheid South Africa. Finally, multinationals are responsible for certain activities of their direct suppliers and contractors by virtue of a co-operative business partnership that creates reasonable proximity and the capability to take effective action. Companies which source their products from low-wage countries like Bangladesh have a duty to ensure that workplace rights to physical security and just compensation are protected from deprivation in those factories that make their goods.

In all these cases, universal rights, adequately specified and accompanied by rational principles such as the Golden Rule, serve as a compass to guide multinationals against making unfair and unreasonable choices. The laws of every country should be expected to protect these rights, but a failure in the rule of law does not give multinationals warrant to cast these rights aside.

As we bring this book to a close we can see how its key themes cohere: free markets, ethical self-regulation, modified universalism, thick natural rights, and limited corporate duties correlative to those rights. Liberal capitalism depends upon broad property rights and free markets. In good capitalism, which is a blend of big firm and entrepreneurial capitalism, there is not only an incentive to innovate, but also to commercialize and globalize those innovations. Innovation and globalization promote economic growth which in turn is essential for escaping the throes of poverty. There are no anti-globalization success stories. Free markets are not just threatened by state capitalism but by excessive laws and regulations that often obstruct private initiative. One way to help restrain the state from responding to corporate predatory behavior with heavy-handed regulations is more sincere attention to the requirements of corporate responsibility.

Corporate self-regulation in ethical and social affairs is a far better alternative than intrusive regulations imposed by the state's visible hand. Ethical self-regulation founded on the right set of corporate values encourages a vision of foreign investments not as the exploitation of an incremental market but as an opportunity to further the company's mission. The practice of ethics, which is complicated in international areas by cultural and legal diversity, is enhanced by the embrace of a determinate, natural rights-based approach to morality, which overcomes the distortions immanent in the moral calculus popularized by utilitarian philosophers. This moderate universalism protects morality from a cynical nihilism or moral arbitrariness, which can sometimes promote the sort of rapacity that corrodes the credibility of global capitalism. Yet corporations should only be expected to uphold and protect these universal rights, but not be burdened with the duty to rectify the world's social problems.

It will always be difficult to concretely reconcile the principle of universalism with the reality of cultural pluralism. This challenge will be a constant source of tension for the multinational corporation. However, if multinationals prudently strive to maintain fundamental human rights while acknowledging the valid contributions of diverse cultural traditions, the integrity of globalization can be enhanced without defying the logic or legitimacy of a multicultural perspective.

Notes

1 See John Finnis, "Natural Law and Legal Reasoning," in *Natural Law Theory: Contemporary Essays* ed. Robert George (Oxford: Oxford University Press, 1992), 134–57.
2 Henry Shue, *Basic Rights: Subsistence, Affluence, and U.S. Foreign Policy* 2nd ed. (Princeton, NJ: Princeton University Press, 1996), 52.

Further Reading

Aquinas, St. T. (1947–8). *Summa Theologiae* (Summary of Theology) 3 volumes. Translated by the Fathers of the English Dominican Province. New York: Benziger Bros.

Barnet, R., and Muller, R. (1974). *Global Reach: The Power of Multinational Corporations.* New York: Simon and Schuster.

Baumol, W., Litan, R., and Schramm, C. (2007). *Good Capitalism, Bad Capitalism, and the Economics of Growth and Prosperity.* New Haven, CN: Yale University Press.

Becker, L. (1977). *Property Rights: Philosophic Foundations.* London: Routledge & Kegan Paul.

Bentham, J. (1907). *Introduction to the Principles of Morals and Legislation.* Oxford: Oxford University Press.

Bhagwati, J. (2004). *In Defense of Globalization.* Oxford: Oxford University Press.

——, and Panagariya, A. (2013). *Why Growth Matters.* New York: Perseus Books.

Boldrin, M., and Levine, D. (2008). *Against Intellectual Monopoly.* Cambridge: Cambridge University Press.

Borgmann, A. (1983). *Crossing the Postmodern Divide.* Chicago: University of Chicago Press.

Bourdieu, P. (1998). *Practical Reason: On the Theory of Action.* Stanford, CA: Stanford University Press.

Bowie, N. (1999). *Business Ethics: A Kantian Perspective.* Oxford: Blackwell.

Broadberry, S., and O'Rourke, K. (2010). *The Cambridge Economic History of Modern Europe.* Cambridge: Cambridge University Press.

Carson, T., and Moser, P., eds. (2001). *Moral Relativism: A Reader.* New York: Oxford University Press.

Caryl, C. (2013). *Strange Rebels*. New York: Basic Books.
Coase, R., and Wang, N. (2013). *How China Became Capitalist*. New York: Palgrave Macmillan.
Dam, K. (1994). The Economic Underpinnings of Patent Law, *Journal of Legal Studies*, 23, 247–71.
D'Arcy, E. (1963). *Human Acts: An Essay in their Moral Evaluation*. Oxford: Oxford University Press.
DeGeorge, R. (1993). *Competing with Integrity in International Business*. New York: Oxford University Press.
——. (2005). Intellectual Property and Pharmaceutical Drugs: An Ethical Analysis, *Business Ethics Quarterly*, 15, 549–76.
De Soto, H. (2000). *The Mystery of Capital*. New York: Basic Books.
Donaldson, T. (1989). *The Ethics of International Business*. New York: Oxford University Press.
——, and Dunfee, T. (1999). *Ties that Bind: A Social Contract Approach to Business Ethics*. Boston, MA: Harvard Business School Press.
Drahos, P., and Braithwaite, J. (2002). *Information Feudalism: Who Owns the Knowledge Economy*. New York: The New Press.
——, and Mayne, R. (2002). *Global Intellectual Property Rights*. New York: Palgrave Macmillan.
Economist, The. "Survey on Human Rights Law." December 5, 1998.
——. "A Bigger World: A Special Report on Globalization." September 20, 2008.
——. "Here, There, and Everywhere: Outsourcing and Offshoring." (Special Report) January 19, 2013.
——. "A Giant Cage: China and the Internet." April 6, 2013.
Ferguson, N. (2013). *The Great Degeneration*. New York: Penguin Press.
Finnis, J. (1980). *Natural Law and Natural Rights*. Oxford: Oxford University Press.
——. (1983). *Fundamentals of Ethics*. Washington, D.C.: Georgetown University Press.
Frankena, W. (1963). *Ethics*. Englewood Cliffs, NJ: Prentice-Hall.
Frederick, R., and Hoffman, W. M. (1995). Environmental Risk Problems and the Language of Ethics, *Business Ethics Quarterly*, 5, 699–711.
Freeman, E. (ed.) (1991). *Business Ethics: State of the Art*. Oxford: Oxford University Press.
Freeman, M. (2011). *Human Rights*. Cambridge: Polity Press.
Friedman, M. (1962). *Capitalism and Freedom*. Chicago, IL: University of Chicago Press.
——. (1970). The Social Responsibility of Business is to Increase its Profits. *New York Times Magazine*, September 13, 32–3, 122–6.
Ghemawat, P. (2001). Distance Still Matters: The Hard Reality of Global Expansion. *Harvard Business Review*, Sept–Oct, 138–52.
Goldsmith, J., and Wu, T. (2006). *Who Controls the Internet?* Oxford: Oxford University Press.
Grisez, G. (1993). *Living a Christian Life*. Quincy, IL: Franciscan Herald Press.

———. (1997). *Difficult Moral Questions*. Quincy, IL: Franciscan Press.
Hardin, G. (1968). The Tragedy of the Commons, *Science*, 162, 1243–8.
Hart, H. L. (1971). Bentham on Legal Rights. In *Oxford Essays in Jurisprudence: Second Series*, edited by A. Simpson, 211–39. Oxford: Oxford University Press.
———. (1983). *Essays in Jurisprudence and Philosophy*. Oxford: Oxford University Press.
Hayek, F. (2007). *The Road to Serfdom*. Chicago, IL: University of Chicago Press.
Hegel, G. W. F. (1952). *Philosophy of Right*. Translated by T. Knox. Oxford: Oxford University Press.
Heidegger, M. (1950). *Holzwege*. Frankfurt: Klostermann.
———. (1977). *The Question Concerning Technology*. Translated by William Lovitt. New York: Harper Colophon.
Horowitz, S. (2004). Restarting Globalization after World War II, *Comparative Political Studies*, 37, 127–51.
Human Rights Watch. (2003). *The Small Hands of Slavery: Bonded Child Labor in India's Silk Industry*. New York: Human Rights Watch.
Jackson, K. (1993). Distributive Justice and the Corporate Duty to Aid, *Journal of Business Ethics*, 12, 547–51.
James, H. (2012). *Krupp: A History of the Legendary German Firm*. Princeton, NJ: Princeton University Press.
John Paul II, Pope. (1981). *Laborem Exercens*. Boston, MA: Pauline Books and Media.
———. (1987). *Sollicitudo Rei Socialis*. Boston, MA: Pauline Books and Media.
Jones, G. (2005). *Multinationals and Global Capitalism*. Oxford: Oxford University Press.
Kao, G. (2011). *Grounding Human Rights in a Pluralist World*. Washington, D.C.: Georgetown University Press.
Kline, B. (1997). *Profit, Principle and Apartheid, 1948–1994*. New York: Edwin Mellen Press.
Kline, J. (2010). *Ethics for International Business* 2nd ed. New York: Routledge.
Koeppel, D. (2008). *Banana: The Fate of the Fruit that Changed the World*. New York: Penguin Group.
Ladd, J. (1973). *Ethical Relativism*. New York: Wadsworth.
Lessig, L. (1999). *Code and Other Laws of Cyberspace*. New York: Basic Books.
Litvin, D. (2003). *Empires of Profit*. New York: Texere.
Locke, J. (1988). *Two Treatises of Government*. Edited by Peter Laslett. Cambridge: Cambridge University Press.
Mackey, J., and Sisodia, R. (2013). *Conscious Capitalism*. Boston: Harvard Business Review Press.
MacKinnon, R. (2012). *Consent of the Networked*. New York: Basic Books.
Macpherson, C. B. (1962). *The Political Theory of Possessive Individualism*. Oxford: Oxford University Press.

Maddison, A. (2001). *The World Economy: A Millennial Perspective.* Paris: Development Center of the Organization for Economic Cooperation and Development.
Mayer, C. (2013). *Firm Commitment.* Oxford: Oxford University Press.
Merges, R. (2011). *Justifying Intellectual Property.* Cambridge, MA: Harvard University Press.
Midgley, M. (1981). *Heart and Mind.* New York: St. Martin's Press.
Moor, J. (2001). Just Consequentialism and Computing. In R. Spinello and H. Tavani, eds. *Readings in Cyberethics,* 98–104. Sudbury, MA: Jones & Bartlett.
Muchlinski, P. (1995). *Multinational Enterprises and the Law.* Oxford: Oxford University Press.
Nickel, J. (1987). *Making Sense of Human Rights: Philosophical Reflections on the Universal Declaration of Human Rights.* Berkeley, CA: University of California Press.
Paine, L. S. (2003). *Value Shift.* New York: McGraw-Hill.
Perkins, T. (2002). Levi Strauss & Co. and China. In *Perspectives in Business Ethics,* 2nd ed. Edited by Laura Hartman, pp. 764–9. New York: McGraw-Hill.
Rawls, J. (1971). *A Theory of Justice.* Cambridge, MA: Harvard University Press.
———. (1999). *The Law of Peoples.* Cambridge, MA: Harvard University Press.
Raz, J. (1995). *Ethics in the Public Domain.* Oxford: Oxford University Press.
Reinhardt, F. (1999). Bringing the Environment Down to Earth. *Harvard Business Review.* July–August: 149–57.
Richards, J. (2007). *Environmental Stewardship.* Grand Rapids, MI: Acton Institute.
Roberts, J. (2004). *The Modern Firm.* Oxford: Oxford University Press.
Sandel, M. (2009). *Justice.* New York: Farrar, Straus, and Giroux.
Schermerhorn, J. (1999). Terms of Global Business Engagement in Ethically Challenging Environments. *Business Ethics Quarterly,* 9, 486–7.
Schlesinger, S., and Kinzer, S. (1983). *Bitter Fruit: The Untold Story of the American Coup in Guatemala.* New York: Anchor Books.
Schmidt, E., and Cohen, J. (2013). *The New Digital Age.* New York: Knopf.
Shirer, W. (1960). *The Rise and Fall of the Third Reich: A History of Nazi Germany.* New York: Simon & Schuster.
Shue, H. (1996). *Basic Rights: Subsistence, Affluence, and U.S. Foreign Policy* 2nd ed. Princeton, NJ: Princeton University Press.
Sigmund, P. (1977). *The Overthrow of Allende and the Politics of Chile.* Pittsburgh, PA: University of Pittsburgh Press.
Sirico, R., Rev. (2012). *Defending the Free Market.* Washington, D.C.: Regnery.
Smith, A. (1976). *An Inquiry into the Nature and Causes of the Wealth of Nations.* Oxford: Oxford University Press.
Spar, D. (1998). The Spotlight Effect and the Bottom Line. *Foreign Affairs,* 77, 7–12.

Spinello, R., and Bottis, M. (2009). *A Defense of Intellectual Property Rights.* Cheltenham: Edward Elgar.
Strauss, L. (1950). *Natural Right and History.* Chicago, IL: University of Chicago Press.
Talbot, W. (2005). *Which Rights Should Be Universal?* New York: Oxford University Press.
Taylor, C. (1992). *The Ethics of Authenticity.* Cambridge, MA: Harvard University Press.
——. (1992). *Multiculturalism and the Politics of Recognition: An Essay by Charles Taylor.* Princeton, NJ: Princeton University Press.
Thompson, C. China's Google Problem. *New York Times Magazine,* April 23, 2006, 51–62.
Tomasi, J. (2012). *Free Market Fairness.* Princeton, NJ: Princeton University Press.
United Nations Charter. (2008). The Universal Declaration of Human Rights. In *Moral Philosophy for Managers.* 5th ed. edited by Richard Spinello, 293–7. New York: McGraw-Hill.
Vincent, R. J. (1998). *Human Rights and International Relations.* New York: Cambridge University Press.
Waldron, J. (1988). *The Right to Private Property.* Oxford: Oxford University Press.
Walzer, M. (1994). *Thick and Thin: Moral Argument at Home and Abroad.* Notre Dame: University of Notre Dame Press.
Wartick, S., and Wood, D. (1998). *International Business and Society.* Oxford: Blackwell Publishers.
Werhane, P., and Gorman, M. (2005). Intellectual Property Rights, Moral Imagination, and Access to Life-Enhancing Drugs. *Business Ethics Quarterly* 15, 604–15.
White, J. (2004). Globalization, Divestment, and Human Rights in Burma. *Journal of Corporate Citizenship,* 14, 47–65.
Wilkins, M. (1974). *The Maturing of Multinational Enterprise: American Business Abroad from 1914 to 1970.* Cambridge, MA: Harvard University Press.
Winner, L. (1978). *Autonomous Technology: Technics Out-of-Control as a Theme in Political Thought.* Cambridge, MA: MIT Press.
Wolf, M. (2004). *Why Globalization Works.* New Haven, CN: Yale University Press.
Zaheer, S. (1995). Overcoming the Liability of Foreignness. *Academy of Management Journal,* 38, 341–63.
Zimmerman, M. (1986). Implications of Heidegger's Thought for Deep Ecology. *Modern Schoolman,* 44, 19–43.

Index

Africa 14, 19–20, 148–9, 256; *see also* South Africa
AIDS 149, 153, 163–7, 169, 171–3
Alien Tort Claims Act (ATCA) 83, 201
Allende, S. 216
Android 128, 131
anti-Semitism 133, 210
Apartheid 231–5, 274
Apple, Inc. 41, 252
Aquinas, St. T. 177n.62, 233
Aramco 59
Arbenz, J. 16, 212–14, 217
Aristotle 55, 75n.2
AZT 164

Baidu 121, 128–31
banana industry 16, 19, 212–13
Bangladesh xii, 20, 242, 249, 253, 259–63, 265, 274
Bayer, 9, 150, 157
Belo Monte 193
Benedict, R. 65
beneficence principle 248–9
Benetton 261–2
Bentham, J. 248
Berle, A. 20

Berners-Lee, T. 18
Big Pharma *see* pharmaceutical industry
big-firm capitalism 41–2, 274
bonded child labor 257–8
Botswana 59–60, 164
Brazil 11, 21, 43, 144, 149, 155, 162, 189, 193
bribery 80–2
Brin, S. 127, 131
British Petroleum (BP) 49, 179, 181, 196
Burma 83, 222–6, 228–9, 236, 274
Burroughs-Wellcome 164

capitalism 28–30, 35–45, 50, 274
Carson, R. 183
Castillo, C. 213
categorical imperative 86–7, 107
censorship 117–19
Central America 19, 212, 214
Central Intelligence Agency (CIA) 216
charity proviso 170–1, 177n.61, 273; *see also* Locke
child labor 256–9, 264
Chile 16, 21, 23, 215–17

282 INDEX

China 14–15, 17–18, 21, 51, 57–8, 115–17, 119–35, 184, 221, 244, 247, 251, 264, 271–3
Chongqing 126
Cipla 149, 157, 165
Cisco 116, 124–7, 142
claim right 90
Coca-Cola 104, 226
communism 30, 34, 50, 57
condition-of-business principle 226–9
Confucian philosophy 71, 137–8, 141
Congo 214–15, 217, 235
consequentialism *see* utilitarianism
constructive engagement 220, 224–5
Corn Law (of Britain) 7
Crixivan 164, 166–7
Czech Republic 85, 152

DeBeers 60
deep ecology 194–5
Dehomag 208–9
Derrida, J. 63
Diamond v. Chakrabarty 154
difference principle 255
disinvestment 219–22, 235–6, 274
Disney 261, 263
Doha Declaration 166, 173
Donaldson, T. 72–3, 94–5, 227–8
DuPont 182, 187, 190–1, 202–3

Eastern Europe 13, 17
economic liberty 30–1, 35–6, 50
Ecuador 20, 180–2, 203
Egypt 116, 119
entrepreneurial capitalism 41–2, 274
environmental degradation 182–6
Ethiopia 163
ethnocentrism 62, 67, 74, 271
European Union 205
expropriation, definition of 26n.23
externalities, negative 46, 49, 199, 273
Exxon Mobile 179, 197

Facebook 61, 116, 123, 125
fair wages xii, 250, 252–6, 274

Falun Gong 120, 122, 129
Finnis, J. 94, 98
firewall 122, 125
Food and Drug Administration (FDA) 153, 164
Foot, P. 70–1
Foreign Corrupt Practices Act (FCPA) 81–2, 106
foreign direct investment (FDI) 7, 9–12, 15, 21–2, 57
France 3, 14, 125, 152
free market 29–38
free speech rights 61, 85, 92, 135–40
Friedman, M. 104–5, 218

Gap 242, 247
Gazprom 44–5
General Electric 15, 41, 45
Genzyme 38, 152
Germany 3, 11–12, 18, 68, 207–11, 234
Ghandi, I. 14
Gifford, K.L. 241–2, 246
global warming 184–7
Golden Rule 101–3, 259, 274
Golden Shield 122, 143
Google 48, 60–61, 115–16, 127–31, 138, 141–2
great firewall of China 119–22, 143
Guatemala 212–14, 235

Hamied, Y. 165
Hart, H.L. 94
Hayek, F. 33–5
Hegel, G. W. F. 6, 32, 68
Heidegger, M. 192, 294n.31
Heidinger, W. 207–8
Heinz Corporation 191
Herder, J. 62
history of globalization 3–23
Hitler, A. 3, 14, 208–11
Hohfeld, W.H. 90
Hollerith, H. 207–8
Honduras 241–2, 245
Hong Kong 131
human goods (basic) 97–104, 107
human rights xiii, 87–103, 107, 272–3

INDEX

Human Rights Watch 129, 257
Huntington, S. 136
hypernorms 72, 74, 79

IBM 15, 17, 42, 207–11, 215, 219, 229, 234, 271
IKEA 242, 256–7, 259
Imle, J. 224–5
India 14, 19, 23, 61, 80, 150, 155, 157, 163, 189, 245, 256–9
Indonesia 242–6, 253
information feudalism 161–2
Intel 41–2
intellectual property rights 157–63, 273
International Labor Organization 256, 258
International Panel on Climate Change (IPCC) 185–6, 188
International Paper Company 57–8
International Telephone and Telegraph (ITT) 12, 16, 215–17, 219, 229
Internet 18, 60–1, 73, 118–20, 124
Iran 115, 119
Islamic culture 61, 89, 137–9
invisible hand 33, 47; *see also* capitalism

Japan 16, 18, 41, 43, 67, 69, 81, 84
J.C. Penney 260–1
John Paul II, Pope 17, 195, 255

Kant, I. 32, 86–8, 107
Kelsen, H. 90–1
Kiobel v. Royal Dutch Petroleum 109n.13, 201
Krupp 3–6, 8
Kyi, A. 223, 226, 229
Kyoto protocol 188–90, 201

labor theory of property 159–61
Laborem Exercens 255
Latin America 15, 19, 40, 162
legal positivism 90–1
Lenovo 19, 44
Leopold, A. 183
Lessig, L. 118–19

Lever Brothers 9
Levi Strauss & Co. 60, 221, 238n.25, 246, 252, 261
liability of foreignness 57, 73, 274
Locke, J. 31–6, 159–61, 169–70, 174, 233, 273
Lockheed 81
Lumumba, P. 214–15
Lyotard, J.F. 63

Malaysia 84, 253, 259
Maritain, J. 109n.23
market failures 45–50
Marx, K. 30
McKinley Act 9
Merck 12, 149, 151, 164–6
Mercosur 19
Mexico 5, 13, 63, 163, 182, 184, 217, 242, 244
Microsoft 42, 48, 115–17, 128, 138, 271
Midgley, M. 69
moral isolationism 69
moral rights *see* human rights
multiculturalism 64, 68, 236
multinational, definition of, 25n.6
Mynamar *see* Burma

Napoleon 7
National Institute for Health (NIH) 168–9
natural law 64, 97–103, 222
Nazi regime 3–4, 68, 91, 133, 207–11, 215, 219, 229, 271
Nestle 10
Nickel, J. 93–4, 97
Nigeria 49, 59, 83, 195–201, 203, 218
Nike 242–6, 253, 264
Nokia 115–16
non-governmental organizations (NGO) 21, 165, 172, 245
non-involvement principle 218–19
Novartis 150, 157
Nuremberg laws 211
Nuremberg trials 4, 7

offshoring 243–5, 263
Ogoniland 59, 197–9, 201
oil spills 180–2, 195–201
oligarchic capitalism 40, 43
Oruma 197
outsourcing 243–5, 263, 274
ozone depletion 184, 187

Pakistan 261
patents x, 82, 150, 153–63, 167–73
Pfizer 149–51
pharmaceutical industry 148–62, 172–4
Philip Morris 85–6
pluralism, moral xi, 67, 72, 138–9, 234
Poland 13, 17
post-modernism 24, 63, 70–1
property rights 29–35, 274; *see also* intellectual property rights
public goods 47

Rana Plaza 260
Ranbaxy 150
Rawls, J. 35–6, 91–3, 102, 107, 136, 161, 221, 255–6, 272
relativism, cultural 55–7, 64, 136, 272
relativism, moral 56–7, 62, 64–73, 272
Reno v. ACLU 119
Ricardo, D. 8
rights *see* human rights
Roche Holding Co. 150
Royal Dutch Shell 13, 20, 49, 83, 179, 195–203, 218
Russia 5, 10–11, 14, 44, 51
Russian revolution 11

safety *see* workplace safety
Sanofi-Aventis 150, 152
Saro-Wiwa, K. 197, 200–1
Saudi Arabia 59, 116
Schlesinger, A. 55–6
Sears Holding Corp. 260–1
Shirer, W. 210
Shue, H. 95–6
Siemens 9, 20, 82, 115
Singapore 43–4
Singer Sewing Co. 10, 22, 82, 115
Skype 116
Smith, A. x, 8, 33–5
Smoot-Hawley 12
solidarity 24, 79
South Africa 10, 149, 163–7, 230–5
South Korea 23, 43, 243
Standard Oil 13
state-guided capitalism 39–40, 274; *see also* capitalism
Steinway & Sons 12
Sullivan principles 232–5
sustainability xii, 190–1, 194
Switzerland 150, 156
Syria 219

Taiwan 23, 243
Tao, S. 134–5
Tata Group 19, 28
Taylor, C. 50
Tazreen Fashions 260
technicity 192, 194
Texaco 180–2, 203
Thailand 222, 245
Tibet 122, 129, 134
Total 222–6, 236
Toys 'R' Us 58–9
TRIPS xi–xii, 82, 104, 149, 156–7, 162, 166, 173
Turkey 15
Twitter 116, 123, 125, 144

Union Carbide 20
Union Minière 214–15, 217, 235
United Fruit 16, 81, 212–14, 217, 236
United Kingdom 4, 7, 9–10, 13–14, 155
United States Constitution 88, 158
Universal Declaration on Human Rights (UDHR) 88, 96, 107, 140, 144, 222, 252

Unocal 83, 222–6, 236
utilitarianism 84–5, 131, 144, 220–1, 227, 235, 275

Vehbi Koc 15
Vietnam 244–5, 263
visible hand 29, 275

Wal-Mart 20, 41, 45, 82, 241–2, 246–7, 249–50, 260, 264
Walzer, M. 93, 96, 272
Watson, T. 207–11
White, L. 195
Williams, B. 71
Wilson tariff 9
Winner, L. 118
workplace safety 250–2, 259–64

World Health Organization (WHO) 164–5
World Trade Organization (WTO) 18, 156, 173
World War I 4, 7, 10–12
World War II 3–4, 13–14, 22

Xiaoping, D. 17
Xinjland 123

Yadana project 223–5, 229
Yahoo 73, 115, 128–9, 132–5, 142, 273
Yang, J. 132, 135
Yongkang 251
YouTube 61, 115, 123, 128

Zheganz Geely 19, 28
ZTE 124

UNIVERSITY OF ST. THOMAS LIBRARIES

DATE DUE

PRINTED IN U.S.A.

**WITHDRAWN
UST
Libraries**

Global Capitalism, Culture, and Ethics

This book aims to deepen the student's understanding of the complex ethical challenges that businesses face in an increasingly globalized world. As the world moves towards greater interdependence, it has been demonstrated that globalization is linked to economic growth. This raises a critical question: as a key player in fostering economic growth, how does the multinational corporation function as a moral agent?

Global Capitalism, Culture, and Ethics offers a sophisticated analysis of theoretical ethical issues such as universalism versus pluralism; the connection between law and morality; the validity of a corporate social agenda; and the general parameters of moral responsibilities for multinational corporations. With these foundational issues addressed, the book proceeds to analyze a number of specific controversies such as the proper scope of political activism, disinvestment, environmental sustainability, and responsible sourcing from low wage countries. The analysis of globalization is not confined to a treatment of the moral obligations of multinational corporations, but also reviews the history of global capitalism, the interdependence between governments and multinational corporations, and the beneficial and harmful effects of globalization on social welfare.

Weaving together themes from economics, history, philosophy, and law, this book allows the reader to appreciate globalization from multiple perspectives. Its theoretical cogency and uncompromising clarity make it a rewarding read for students interested in issues of ethics and globalization.

Richard A. Spinello is an Associate Research Professor at Boston College, USA, where he teaches courses on ethics, social issues in management, and corporate strategy. He has written nine books on ethics, and has published in journals such as Business Ethics Quarterly and Ethics and Information Technology.